VOLKSWAGEN GOLF GTI

Other Titles in the Crowood AutoClassics Series

VOLKSWAGEN GOLF GTI

JAMES RICHARDSON

THE CROWOOD PRESS

First published in 2008 by
The Crowood Press Ltd
Ramsbury, Marlborough
Wiltshire SN8 2HR

www.crowood.com

British Library Cataloguing-in-Publication Data
A catalogue record for this book is available from the British Library.

ISBN 978 1 84797 048 0

Acknowledgements
The evolution of this book from concept to completion has been made
considerably easier thanks to the assistance in various ways of Neil Birkitt
(Editor, *VW Driver*), Matt Harrison (Retrowagen VW memorabilia) and
Brian Screaton (avid collector of all VW printed matter).

Typeset and designed by D & N Publishing
Lambourn Woodlands, Hungerford, Berkshire.

Printed and bound in Malaysia by Times Offset (M) Sdn Bhd.

Contents

Introduction

The inevitable danger when writing about a car still in production, albeit in a guise considerably different to that of its early ancestors, is that between the date of the completion of the text and the time when the book first appears on the bookseller's shelves, there will have been further innovations. During the in-print lifetime of the edition, still more changes will undoubtedly occur. The result might appear to be an out-of-date and incomplete story. What's more, it's a situation that isn't going to change, as manufacturers recognize that, whereas not long ago it was perfectly practical to run a body shape for the best part of a decade, in order to stay in the driving seat nowadays, as soon as one generation is launched, the next has to be in the planning stages. The only solution for an author has to

From much sought after run-out model for the Mk1 Golf GTI to the stunning Mk5 version introduced for the same purpose – the image tells the story of the book – five equally fascinating generations. (Photograph Courtesy of Volkswagen AG)

be to name a particular cut-off point and stick with it. In the case of Volkswagen's fabulous Golf GTI, and its equally scintillating derivatives, a solution presented itself in the form of five past generations, from the now much coveted Mk1 GTI and particularly the stylish Campaign run-out model through to and including the quarter-of-a-century later Pirelli final fling model and a neat cut-off at the end of 2008.

Hence this book powers through the story of the launch of the original and now much coveted hot hatch, its then earth-shatteringly homely but stunningly modern design, and the dynamic updates of extra gears, and more power for the right foot pertaining to its later years. From the limited edition Campaign model first generation GTI, the next step was straight into the territory of possibly the best of the pack to date in the form of the brand new Mk2, a car duly boosted as the years passed by with slick and speedy 16-valve technology. However, this wasn't the end of the Mk2 story, for not only was there the ultra-exclusive Rallye Golf, a supercharged Adonis in metal with the hottest of grunts to match, but also the equally stunning GTI G60, a powerful potentate that sadly never made it officially as far as right-hand-drive form. Then it's a much needed sprint with the Mk3 GTI, covering the initial disappointment of the loss of a 16-valve engine, equal discontent at softer suspension, plus a weight-watchers' protest, as the third generation model had piled on the pounds. Intriguingly, there's the anomaly of the VR6 to consider too, and whether it was GTI territory, hot-hatch technology, or a pandering to luxury class motoring. So to the Mk4, and again the question when is a GTI not a GTI, to which the answer has to be when it's not a 1.8T! Only the anniversary model could upstage such a still frequently talked about vehicle; or was the electrically stunning, body-kitted R32 better still? Once upon a time almost the exclusive preserve of the tractor-driving fraternity, alongside the Mk4 the new diesel engines have to be studied as a possible threat to petrol supremacy, while asking the question whether

Three magic letters – GTI – make the story of this book. The well-known GT refers to Gran Turismo, *while 'I' conceivably stands for* iniezione, *the Italian for injection. The GTI badge depicted is on a Mk5 Golf.*

an oil-burner can ever be considered as a sporting model. And finally, upwards and onwards to the Mk5 and the dynamic revival of a separate red-line identity for the GTI; a visual powerhouse if ever there was one. Another anniversary model, the Edition 30, took real power at least one step further, while the Pirelli really racked and wrapped the story up, but for some fans the new version of the R32 didn't come up to expectations. Why wasn't it an R36 and what was the purpose of dressing it up in shiny brightwork? Then there was the start of the GT phenomenon, combining electric performance with green-approving fuel economy. As a result, had the GTI finally lost its vice-like grip on the world?

Not to worry, of course, if some of the terminology above means little or nothing, for that's the delight of this book, the pages of which multiply into the complete story. But if it is to be a veritable encyclopaedia of all things from 'G' to 'I', aspects other than power-packing generations have to be covered. Tracking the highs and lows of the all-important American market, from fast-breeding Rabbit to near extinction and why putting the boot in was an essential ingredient of the story, is important reading. No GTI volume would be comprehensive without a creditable look at the birth of the Golf too, and the reasons why this simple

Five generations of Golf GTI have driven off into the sunset, mostly having benefitted from a cavalcade of accolades during their relatively short production lifetimes. Five vehicles that won't be forgotten as the years pass by, and if, as some maintain, there has been a weaker link in the chain of success, who knows, perhaps the storyteller revives a reputation!
(Photograph Courtesy of Volkswagen AG)

Beetle replacement was ideal fodder for GTI innovation.

And the aim of all this? First and foremost an informative and enjoyable read for those with a Golf GTI, or two, in the garage and, for the rest, to engender an interest bordering on a passion for the marque, ensuring that on the day a further volume comes out at some point in the future, there's an eager readership ready and waiting.

James Richardson, 2008

A note on Horsepower

Metric measures are inevitably synonymous with a product of the German nation. Reference to some of the earliest material produced for the home market indicates that performance was reckoned in metric horsepower or *Pferdestärke* – ps. Accordingly, this measure is used throughout, thus avoiding confusion between British and American bhp, for example; 1ps equates to 0.986bhp DIN (James Watt), hardly an earth-shattering difference!

1 Birth of the Golf

Without question, the death of Heinz Nord-hoff, post-World War II Volkswagen's first Director General, on Good Friday, 12 April 1968 was the catalyst for change at Volkswagen. His labours of the last twenty years had slowly but surely focused upon a most unusual policy, one of perfecting a single model by a process of continual improvement. Few operations, let alone any other major manufacturer, had even considered such a philosophy. Nordhoff saw no credibility in pandering to the whims of stylists, or others as they introduced ever more powerful cars playing the go-faster game; his goals were ever-increasing production and profitability bred through a reputation for quality, reliability and longevity. It is just conceivable that in a different age, and without the all-conquering Beetle at his disposal, a car such as the Golf might have emerged from his inner sanctum. However, that a hot-hatch version such as the GTI would even have been considered, let alone produced, is unthinkable.

Volkswagen's Initial Success Story

Although for many years it has been fashionable to at best play down and quite often belittle Nordhoff's achievements, his twenty-year stint as Volkswagen's Director General saw production of the legendary Beetle grow from 19,244 cars in the year he took over at Wolfsburg to more than one million in a twelve-month period, that achievement coming in 1965 at a time when close on eight million such cars had been sold on the home market or exported to Volkswagen's much proclaimed 136 countries.

But the Beetle was by no means Nordhoff's only achievement. He had also personally overseen the introduction of a revolutionary concept in small commercial vehicles, the renowned Transporter. From its introduction in 1950, more than 1.8 million examples had been sold before a brand new model replaced the heavily modified original in the summer of 1967. A larger saloon, the VW 1500, had joined the Volkswagen family in 1961, at a time when Wolfsburg could finally hope to match production with ever-increasing demand for the Beetle. Apart from offering a medium-size saloon to which those who had grown out of the Beetle could aspire, for the first time Volkswagen was also able to present an ever-versatile variant as part of its range. A further and even bigger car, the 411, planned as a two- and four-door saloon, and a two-door variant, was only six months away from production at the time of Nordhoff's death. While unable to justify the distraction of a soft-top Beetle at Wolfsburg, Nordhoff had been quick to recognize Ferdinand Porsche's original pre-war intentions and to acquiesce to the requests of independent bodies to create just such a vehicle. The handcrafted and much sought-after four-seater Beetle Cabriolet, introduced in 1949 and produced by Karmann of Osnabrück, led indirectly to the creation of Volkswagen's delightful coupé and Cabriolet, forever known as the Karmann Ghia. Styled by Ghia of Turin, lovingly assembled by Karmann and marketed by Volkswagen, this Beetle in disguise, for the Karmann Ghia was no sports car, did nothing to distract from Nordhoff's main intentions for Volkswagen, while adding an extra dimension to the line-up on offer.

Throughout most of his lengthy time in office Nordhoff had generated healthy profits, with Volkswagen quickly coming to be seen as the shining star of a revitalized and rapidly developing post-war Germany. Satellite operations had been established in South America, South Africa and Australia, and the Beetle had become an icon of the modern world.

Throughout this period, and contrary to what was rumoured later, Nordhoff's design and development department had been far from idle. Amongst their work, many a Beetle replacement was proffered, only for each and every one to be rejected by Nordhoff as below par when compared to the original.

Changes Afoot

For a time, it had been assumed that when Nordhoff retired, an event he wished to postpone as long as possible beyond his sixty-fifth birthday in January 1964, he would be succeeded by his chosen protégé, the one-time head of Volkswagen in America, Carl Hahn. However, this was not to be. Recession in Germany and beyond in late 1966 and throughout most of 1967 saw Volkswagen's fortunes temporarily fade like those of so many others. At last the economic miracle seemed to be over. Disappointed by government policy with regard to the motor industry, Nordhoff spoke out, openly criticizing

As the Golf moved from concept to reality, Volkswagen soldiered on with the Beetle. The image from the cover of an American market brochure dating from 1974 depicts the Super Beetle, otherwise known as the 1303S.

already defensive politicians. Their revenge, spearheaded by the finance minister of the day, Franz Josef Strauss, was swift and, as far as Nordhoff was concerned, terrible. Volkswagen, and by implication Nordhoff, was bombarded with condemnation; the knife was out for the then thirty-year-old Beetle design. Too few ideas had emerged from Wolfsburg; too many cars of a single type had been produced. As for Nordhoff, he was no longer to be his own master. Plans to choose his successor for him were to be drawn up without his involvement, while the date of his retirement would be decided on his behalf. Despite his assertions in January 1968 that the Beetle's star was still shining as brightly as ever and that there was still so much to do to it, menacing clouds threatened for both Nordhoff and his creation.

Four Costly Years of Delay

Although the scene had been set, Nordhoff's departure from Volkswagen didn't work out quite as anticipated. Dogged by recurrent ill health for much of 1967, he appeared to rally in the early months of 1968. His anointed successor, Kurt Lotz, a man without a background in the automobile industry, had been selected, the worst of the recession was over, Beetle sales were growing once more and the car had even been sufficiently revamped to warrant the marketing people heralding it as 'The New Beetle'. Sadly, though, Nordhoff exerted himself once too often. He collapsed in March and was rushed to Wolfsburg's hospital, where he died during the course of the following month.

Lotz's immediate decree on the death of his predecessor, and in due deference to the wishes of those politicians who had manoeuvred him into the top job, was that a successor to the Beetle would be sought. After all, he complained, hadn't Volkswagen been 'immovable' for long enough? The company would surely not make the same mistake Ford had when it perpetuated the existence of the Model T.

Concept vehicles were ready and waiting to be developed; the question was whether Lotz

had the skill and understanding to channel Volkswagen in the right direction. Although it took time, the inevitable decline in profitability, combined with the launch of a disastrous and costly new model, eventually convinced the Volkswagen Board that Lotz was not the man to change Volkswagen, or even to maintain the status quo.

In 1969 Volkswagen purchased NSU, the precedent already having been set for such an acquisition in 1965 when Nordhoff bought Auto Union GMbH in Ingolstadt. Based in Neckarsulum in southern Germany, NSU was a small company, but for Lotz it did possess the decided advantage of having a car virtually ready to launch. Designed in-house by Klaus Luthe, the K70, a 1605cc, water-cooled, front-wheel-drive saloon of similar proportions to the largest Volkswagen, the 411, had already been shown at the Frankfurt Motor Show, where it had received considerable praise from motoring journalists and general pundits alike. Lotz's decision was to spend a fortune on the K70, making it in the process suitable for mass production, rather than the 45,000 units anticipated by NSU. Such was the level of investment that it amounted to more than NSU's entire development budget for the car. Still not satisfied, Lotz hurried through a brand new plant at Salzgitter to be built exclusively for the K70's production.

Launched in the autumn of 1970, the K70 was available with two versions of the 1605cc single ohc engine, one developing 75ps, the other 90ps. Made ready for the US market, the K70 never actually went on sale in that country, while in Europe it could at best be described as an also-ran. Regardless of the inspiration it had aroused in press circles, its bland three-box shape did little to rouse interest, despite Lotz's best endeavours. So desperate was he to prove to the world that decisive action had been taken to sound the death knell of air-cooled supremacy that he trimmed margins to an absolute minimum, accepting the paltry sum of just 33DM profit per K70 sold, incidentally jeopardizing sales of the similarly priced 411 in the process. Heavy fuel consumption intrinsically linked to a dreadful coefficient of aerodynamic drag (Cd) factor of 0.51 (even the pre-war design of the Beetle offered a more respectable 0.44) further soured the intentions of would-be buyers. Finally, when the K70 also betrayed signs of premature rusting, something unprecedented in Volkswagen circles, the car's fate was more or less sealed.

Volkswagen's flirtation with water-cooling and front-wheel drive could easily have been brief – its share of home-market sales had dropped to just 24.3 per cent by the time Lotz was relieved of his duties in the autumn of 1971. A mere 211,000 or so K70s would be built before the next man at Volkswagen's helm finally axed it.

Crucial to Lotz's replacement were two factors, both of which were linked to the K70, albeit some would say indirectly. The first was the issue of profitability, for in his first year Lotz had returned a profit of 330 million DM for Volkswagen, but this was to slip to 190 million the following year, and then to spiral rapidly downwards to an all-time low of just 12 million DM in his final year. A K70 sold with only 33DM available for Volkswagen didn't help; neither did a factory built to manufacture this car, but which stood idle for much of the time. Worse still was that Lotz had failed dismally to press ahead successfully with his quest to find a replacement for the Beetle. A new model was very little nearer than it had been at the time of Nordhoff's death. The K70 characterizes Lotz's time at Volkswagen and it was this intrinsically poor model policy that determined his departure after just four years in the job.

The New Generation of Water-Cooled Cars

Rudolph Leiding, the next person into the hot seat after Lotz, has yet to be fully recognized as the man who successfully created the new generation of water-cooled Volkswagens, that distinction generally going to his successor, Toni Schmücker. The huge investments required to transform the by-then troubled giant inherited from Lotz, coupled to an unforeseen world oil crisis, rampant inflation and attendant recession, would prove to be Leiding's downfall. In his final year in office, Leiding recorded Volkswagen's first-ever loss; a staggering deficit too, totalling some 555 million DM. However, when Leiding resigned in January 1975, allegedly on health grounds, the difficult decisions had been made and the new cars brought to production. Theoretically, all Schmücker had to do was sit back and wait.

Some contemporary journalists did recognize that in Leiding there was a very different animal to Lotz. D.O. Cozzi, writing in *Car and Driver*, put it thus: 'The page has finally been irrevocably turned on 1937 by VW's Chairman ... Rudolf Leiding. He has created a new thought process and resulting product line in a company once too firmly wedded to the past ...VW, once the most successful of the mavericks, is back in the fold.'

Unlike Lotz, Leiding had a solid grounding not only in the automobile industry but also with Volkswagen. Joining in the early days of Nordhoff's tenure of office, in 1958 his unstinting hard work was rewarded when he became head of the Kassal operation. From there, he was entrusted with Auto Union (Audi) following its acquisition by Volkswagen in the 1960s, before being despatched to Brazil with the brief to return sales to the dominant position that the satellite company there had enjoyed for many years. With that task accomplished, Leiding moved back to Audi, on this occasion to resolve the issue of unit costs, and it was from there that he became Volkswagen's third post-war Director General. Such success is invariably not achieved without a degree of ruthlessness, and Leiding's reputation in this direction was legendary. Within weeks of Leiding's arrival at Wolfsburg, Lotz's four-year dallying had been countered. Costly, dead-end projects were halted and the final decision to break away from air-cooling was taken.

Although blatantly untrue, it has often been written that Nordhoff stuck so rigidly to the

Das kleine Golf ABC.

Ein Grundlehrgang in Golf.

Before the Golf was available in the showrooms, Volkswagen published a wealth of material to promote the new car. This brochure dates from April 1974.

Beetle and its larger brethren that he wouldn't countenance development work on any form of replacement. At least a couple of projects current at the time of his death continued to develop through much of the Lotz era, one being a front-wheel-drive car with an air-cooled flat-four engine positioned at the opposite end of the vehicle to where most would have expected to see it. More sophisticated was a different development order, *Entwicklungsauftrag*, or EA number, of 1966 origins. This particular example was to be progressed by Porsche, something far from unusual in that the two operations had worked together in one form or another for many years. Undoubtedly a progressive design, this vehicle featured a 4-cylinder engine, mounted more or less on its side, and, most unusually for what was planned as a family-budget-priced vehicle, was located under the rear seats. The complexity of such an arrangement not only made its progression towards production slow, but also came hand-in-glove with a number of problems that included both interior noise and service accessibility. Development costs were undoubtedly escalating, while issues such as unacceptable smells in the cab area were no nearer to resolution. Lotz had also failed to pay sufficient attention to planned exhaust emission legislation in the USA, something any self-respecting engineer could easily have prophesied would be difficult, if not completely impossible, for an air-cooled successor to the Beetle to meet. Faced with this barrage of issues, it should have come as no surprise when Leiding decided to terminate the project forthwith.

Ludwig Krauss, a key figure in the Audi operation, afforded author Jerry Sloniger the luxury of an interview during the compilation of his 1980 book, *The VW Story*, in which the matter of the mid-engined car arose. Krauss had advised his old boss to abandon the car, despite the idea being supported by Ferry Porsche and Ferdinand Piëch. Apart from the already appreciated references to both 'smell and noise right underneath the passengers', Krauss added a further difficulty to the list, this coming in the form of 'construction height'. Once axed, Leiding revealed to Krauss that the project had already cost 250 million DM and that, if it had been allowed to go further, would have added a supplementary bill of between 350 and 400 million DM, a sum Krauss described as 'a lot of money then'.

With the mid-engine concept abandoned, Leiding turned towards development order 337, a project referred to as long ago as 1969, but one which, in true Lotz style, had been left to the last minute when pressure was already mounting to move it forward. The concept behind EA337 came from the pen of Giorgetto Giugiaro, and in many ways he would achieve for Wolfsburg what Sir Alec Issigonis had accomplished for BMC in 1959 with the Mini, a car that by the 1970s had already developed from its original position of trend-setter to iconic status. There were differences, of course, most notably that unlike Issigonis at BMC, Giugiaro was not on Volkswagen's permanent payroll, creating the opportunity for Wolfsburg to change as much or as little of EA337's make-up as it wished, without fear of having to work with a recalcitrant, or petulant, individual as a result. Unlike the less than successful A35 that preceded the Mini, EA337 had to contend with and move Volkswagen on from the Beetle and its many millions of contented owners. That the small car made the grade, and created the genre for many successors, the combined production total of three of which finally amounted to more than the Beetle's in 2002, is of even greater significance when it is considered that very little that might be considered noteworthy was changed from the Giugiaro's original concept.

EA337 was not, in fact, Giugiaro's first concept for Volkswagen, as in May 1970 he had presented a design to Wolfsburg for a larger vehicle, the VW 1600, or 411 class. This was the Volkswagen that Leiding would offer to the world in general as the Passat and to the USA as the Dasher, albeit in a much different and more cost-effective way than the designer had originally envisaged.

All the evidence appears to confirm the rumour that, just as with the larger car design, Giugiaro was given a completely free hand with EA337. Supposedly, what he wasn't allowed on this occasion was time. From the original front, side and back elevations, the next stage was a meticulously scaled drawing. There then followed a full-size model from which the stylists could work. The end result was a vehicle that Giugiaro himself described as unique in its two-box shape, bearing little, if any, resemblance to a variant, but instead appearing both stylish and practical. The initial two-box shape was characterized by a substantial C-pillar behind the rearmost side window, a feature that would follow through with each successive design of Golf, and one that incidentally lent

---

G for Giugiaro; G for Golf

Born in 1938, at a time when Volkswagen's story was starting to gather pace under its Nazi rulers and his home country was under the control of Mussolini's fascists, Giorgetto Giugiaro was the latest addition to a family of artistic descent. His grandfather was a well-regarded fresco artist, his work extending to many a luxurious villa and ornate church. His mother, a talented seamstress, taught her son the intricacies of creating a masterpiece in dress design from a simple line drawing. By the age of fourteen, Giugiaro had moved to Turin to unfurl the delights of both art and technical drawing. Project work included automotive design, his exhibition work being spotted by one of Fiat's leading designers of the day. Almost inevitably, this led to the start of Giugiaro's working career as a member of Fiat's Special Cars Styling Department. From there he moved to specialist coachbuilders Bertone, where his designs led to the creation of the Ferrari 250GT and, more particularly, the Alfa Giulia GT, in the process propelling him to the forefront of international attention and acclaim. After a brief spell at Ghia, a name already associated with Volkswagen through Karmann's coupé, in February 1967 Giugiaro established his own design studio, Ital Styling. His genius might be measured by the fact that at this point he was less than thirty years old; nor will it come as a surprise that critical approval followed where he led, first with the birth of the Alfasud for Alfa Romeo in 1971 and then with the Lotus Esprit the following year.

Of the Golf, Giugiaro wrote that his 'unique two-box shape was stylish and practical, but it looked nothing like a station wagon'. The maestro was enthused by Volkswagen's willingness to give him a free hand, and although the inevitable suppressive rules and regulations symptomatic of America then and Europe today meant that some modifications had to be made to the design, Giugiaro was happy to confirm many years later that he would have changed very little: 'I think that the dimensions and proportions are perfect. ... The Golf reflects my philosophy of simple forms and clean lines, which is the basis for all creations.' (From the preface to James Ruppert, *VW Golf: The Complete Story*, The Crowood Press 1996)

itself particularly well to the sporting GTI in three-door form of any generation. The front-end styling might best have been described as both truncated and angular, the latter particularly diametrically opposed to the practice of old-school designers, but eminently suitable for a modern look in the 1970s.

While Giugiaro must have been aware that Volkswagen had already experimented with the notion of an opening rear window, he can justifiably claim to have designed the world's first hatchback in the EA337 concept. The flimsy arrangement on which Giugiaro based his idea was little more than a pane of glass surrounded by a delicate frame, very much in the style of an opening rear side window. It was certainly not robust enough to withstand frequent use over a number of years, so Giugiaro extended the metalwork enveloping the glass to embrace a great deal more of the rear of the car. In so doing, not only did he create a feature sufficiently robust to stay the course, but

also an attribute that contributed positively to the structural nature of the rear of the vehicle. Perfected by the time the car went into production, only the base model depended upon a simple strap to keep the top-hinged hatch open, all other options benefiting from a gas strut. Other manufacturers, recognizing the potential sales advantages of such a characteristic, were quick off the mark to emulate Volkswagen, this in itself being praise for the innovative nature of Giugiaro's design.

Although EA337 shared the size of its wheelbase with that of the Beetle at 2,400mm (94.5in), the car overall was in the region of 200mm (8in) shorter, yet it afforded considerably more space both in terms of passenger area and luggage accommodation. The early Golf's dimensions were 3,705mm (145.9in) length, 1,610mm (63.4in) width/1,630mm (64.1in) GTI, and 1,410mm (55.5in) height/1,390mm (54.7in) GTI; the Beetle in comparison stood at 4,060 × 1,550 × 1,500mm (159.8 × 61 × 59in).

Very few early Golfs have survived the rigours of time due to the inadequacy of Volkswagen's anti-rust protection. This example, photographed in 2007, has either been fully restored or led a very sheltered life in a heated garage for many years. The remaining images in this chapter come courtesy of Volkswagen's archive publicity and depict cars that might include elements not relevant to the British market.

While the space factor can be partly explained by the Golf's greater width, the ingenuity of the design lay in the compact nature of the transverse front engine and transmission carefully positioned slightly ahead of the front-wheel centre line and the abandoning of the traditional three-box design. Not only did this dispense with the need for an intrusive and inherently bulky transmission tunnel that automatically restricted the amount of available space in the vehicle, but also, thanks to the unique hatchback, created a usefully adaptable amount of luggage room in the boot, or interior when the backrests of the rear seats were folded down, which easily surpassed the three-box saloon's carrying capacity. Greater gain was there still, for thanks to EA337 being one of the first concepts to benefit from new computer stressing techniques, the design could be tempered to save a significant amount of weight. As all the strain of the drive, front suspension, and in reality a large percentage of the braking stresses too, could be held within a compact but strong box centred around the front bulkhead, inner wings and engine mounts, this meant that the rest of the car could be made deliberately lighter than would normally have been the case. Taking into account the necessary precautions required for rigidity under impact, EA337 had an unladen weight of less than 771kg (1,700lb).

At first sight somewhat staid, or at best conventional, EA337's suspension hardly seemed fitting for such a dynamically modern design of car. At the front, MacPherson struts were hardly earth-shattering news. However, a defining combination of modern bush materials and offset coil springs overcame the original objection to the MacPherson arrangement by offering a low-speed ride that could no longer be described as jerky. The addition of negative steering geometry, as first seen on the Audi 80 and Passat, granted an element of self-correcting stability if braking when one side of the car was on a slippery surface, or in cases of a front tyre puncture. At the rear, the starting point was undoubtedly the already established principle for a front-wheel-drive car of a pair of trailing arms, coupled to an anti-roll bar, offering a measure of rear-roll stiffness, while cutting down the anticipated under-steer of any vehicle made up in such a way. The hidden ingenuity in the design came by locating the anti-roll bar more solidly to the trailing arms in an arrangement that consisted of these elements plus angled spring and damper units. The result was that stresses on the arms capable of twisting them out of line were more or less eliminated, while the rear roll stiffness could be more accurately tuned through a cleverly designed cross-beam, strong in bending and yet not too stiff in torsion. Being both light in nature and cheap to construct, it nevertheless played the stresses off one against the other within the U-frame, leading to both a lighter body and above all to a degree of handling much envied elsewhere.

With regard to the proposed engines, Leiding put a stop to one of the two options immediately on deciding that in EA337 there was the ideal Beetle replacement. As with his one-off K70 power unit, Lotz had failed to recognize that across the group there was plenty of scope to utilize an existing power unit, the logical choice under the general development order of 827 being the 70ps engine, which had been a brand new design for the Audi 80, and was destined to make its debut in a Volkswagen model with the Passat. Although modern in its design, the technology behind the engine was hardly revolutionary. Nevertheless, this toothed belt-driven, single ohc layout, plus a cast-iron block and light alloy cylinder head, 1471cc engine was ideal for the EA337, despite Giugiaro's design specifying a transverse engine mounting. The other models referred to were planned and executed with a longitudinal engine position in mind. All that was required was a reworking of the exhaust system, a redesign of the engine mounts leading to a 20-degree rearward tilt and an all-new transmission. With a bore of 80mm and a stroke of 76.5mm, 70ps was achieved at 5,800rpm. Inlet and exhaust valves were on the same side, making it theoretically less efficient than a cross-flow engine, but allowing a more convenient transverse installation. As the other Golf engine, to be discussed in greater detail very shortly, was somewhat pedestrian in its performance, it's worth noting that Golfs fitted with the larger power unit were no sluggards; indeed far from it. With a top speed of 160km/h (99mph), and 0–60mph (96.5km/h) achieved in a very respectable 11.9sec, this was more than adequate to stand up to the toughest opposition from other manufacturers in terms of both top speed and acceleration through the gears.

Before the pedantic point out that their workshop manual lists a 1588cc engine for 1975, or the 1976 model year, it is worth pointing out that times were moving fast and Volkswagen progressed from one to another engine within the space of a very short time. In the high summer of 1977 it was all change again, as for the 1978 model year a second, or rather new 1500 displaced the 1600. This time the 1457cc engine again developed 70ps, but the bore at 73.4mm and stroke at 79.5mm was different to that of the earlier version.

The second engine might have been claimed as all new, although when it is realized that it was intended for use in more than one model, and that its other home was the planned baby of the Audi range, the 50, all becomes clear. The Audi 50, a project well-known to Leiding, who had been boss there not long before, was to be more or less purloined by Volkswagen and named the Polo. This move was arguably the result of near hyperinflation in the mid 1970s, a situation that made the Golf a more expensive vehicle than first envisaged and conceivably no longer the planned direct replacement for the Beetle in terms of budget motoring. As for the engine, Leiding was right to use what resources he had at his fingertips, for without Volkswagen there had been little chance of Audi moving onwards and upwards. With a displacement of 1093cc, the cross-flow engine produced a maximum of 50ps at 6,000rpm, was capable of taking the Golf from 0–100km/h (0–62mph) in 16.7sec

and produced a top speed of 140km (87mph). This engine, capable of returning in the region of 7.86ltr/100km (37mpg) if driven realistically, was destined to power the entry-level car throughout the lifespan of the first-generation Golf.

To elaborate the thinking, or at least the latter-day interpretation of Leiding's policy and his engineers' ingenuity, an official press document written more than a decade after the event relayed the engine story thus:

> The second period in the history of VW technology begins with front-wheel drive and an engine entirely unlike any of its predecessors. The EA827 was a neatly laid-out 4-cylinder version with a grey cast-iron cylinder block and aluminium head. The vertically arranged valves were actuated by a single overhead camshaft and bucket tappets. … Both in appearance and character, the new engine represented a total breakaway from the 'Beetle philosophy'. Short-stroke design and unimpressive performance data were thrown overboard. Despite higher piston speeds, the 827 still revved very freely; indeed, the top-of-the-range version set new standards in the medium-size car category.

Brakes were in the form of solid discs at the front on the larger engine model and drums at the rear, while what should really be described as the base specification came with drums all round.

It might come as something of a surprise to discover that Giugiaro wasn't required to make any body changes; however, Leiding could save both time and money by using Volkswagen's in-house designer, Herbert Schäfer. The net result was a car with a more upright windscreen, while the overhang at the front was increased by some 70mm (2.75in), the bonnet being both lengthened and made flatter to achieve this purpose. This had the result of making the vehicle appear more abruptly squared off and noticeably less soft than the original Giugiaro concept, but was crucial if EA337 was to comply with the rigours of extensive American legislation. At the front

Der Golf EA337 Gains a Name

In what is best described as Volkswagen's air-cooled era, a period stretching back to the dark days of Nazi rule, names were of little significance. Admittedly, Hitler decreed that the Beetle should be called the KdF-Wagen, or Strength-through-Joy car, but the motive was political and such an appendage was rarely used outside Nazi circles. After the war, the Beetle was simply the Volkswagen, literally the People's Car, as its designer, Ferdinand Porsche, had intended. In 1950, the Transporter was launched without a name, while the Karmann Ghia coupé and convertible were simply known by the names of the coachbuilder responsible for their construction and the design studio similarly involved with the look of the vehicle. The advent of a larger Volkswagen in the autumn of 1961, the VW 1500, complicated matters a little and the practice developed of referring to the Beetle as the Type 1, the Transporter as the Type 2 and the new notchback and variant as the Type 3. The appearance of the Type 4, or 411, only confirmed the reliance on numbers, even though by this stage the Beetle was known the world over by its nickname rather than by its official designation.

The first water-cooled model, the bought-in K70, came with its *nom de plume* intact, with the result that the first genuinely Volkswagen-developed water-cooled car was named the Passat, a reference to the prevailing warm winds off the Canary Islands. Just a few months before EA337 was launched, the sporty Scirocco made its debut, the vehicle adopting the name of the hot, burning wind that blows off the North African coast. Although rumour has it that EA337 was to be christened 'the Blizzard', it duly saw the light of day as the Golf – the German spelling for gulf, as in Gulf Stream, which although not exactly a wind, is at least a flowing current. Motoring journalists went some way to educate readerships used to air-cooled Volkswagens being synonymous with numbers. *Car and Driver*'s scribe put it better than most, advising readers that the new car was to be called, ' "Golf" in Europe (pronounced as in "of Mexico", not as in Nicklaus)'. Indeed, had the smallest member of the new range of Volkswagens, which was launched in 1975, been named the Jetta, Vento, Bora or Corrado, as future cars would be, all would have been well. Instead, it was called the Polo: a name with just one meaning, a game involving people sat on horseback.

When the Golf GTI appeared with its quirky golf-ball gear stick, speculation approached fever pitch. Was the Golf named after a game, or a current, and in the end did it really matter? Leiding's regime, which had named the car, was long gone and the vehicle was an outstanding success whatever the meaning of its identification tag. At least it hadn't ended up adopting the American deviation of Rabbit; allegedly a fast, agile creature, but to many a rather dim-witted mammal content to hop into the dazzling lights of another manufacturer's products.

The Mk1 Golf as it was launched in 1974. This example is an LS model, a designation that indicated a higher trim level, two giveaways being the chrome trim line round the grille and chromed bumpers. (Photograph courtesy of Volkswagen AG)

and rear of the vehicle, Schäfer was requested to look at the light housings, both of which appeared costly to produce en masse. At the front, rectangular-shaped lamps were replaced by readily available circular ones, while at the rear the clusters were simply reduced in size. To the aesthetic perfectionist, such as Giugiaro, neither amendment benefited the car, but to would-be purchasers the changes were of no importance.

Launching the Beetle's Successor

With such a big story up its sleeves, Volkswagen's press and public relations department was eager to reveal initial details as soon as possible. There were other reasons too, for not only was this a time of recurrent fuel crises, with the consequent knock-on effects for all car manufacturers, but after many, many years in the ascendancy, the faithful Beetle was finally starting to fail its masters. By the end of the year of the Golf's launch, 1974, production demands would have dropped from the more than comparatively healthy 1,206,018 vehicles of 1973 to just 791,053 cars, taking the Beetle back to

1960 levels. Leiding was only too aware of the potentially critical state of Volkswagen's finances too. Development costs had been enormous, the years of Lotz's mismanagement having seen to that.

Exactly when Golf production began at Wolfsburg depends on which of the official Volkswagen histories are read. The most recently published suggests that the Golf entered the schedules in January 1974. Earlier versions imply that the Golf was presented to the press in May and June, with production beginning in earnest in August. This at least ties in with the oft-quoted end to Beetle production at Wolfsburg at 11.19am on 1 July, the decision having been taken to transfer Beetle manufacture to Volkswagen's Emden plant. However, it might be worth reporting the rumours that the first Golfs became available for retail sale in June, at least for the home market. British dealers would have to wait until October, while the all-important American market could not be catered for until the following year. Ranging from the 1093cc three-door basic Golf, sometimes known as the 'N', the same engine was offered in a car with more

This publicity shot shows the early Golf in basic trim form, as evidenced by silver-painted metal bumpers and the lack of trim around the grille and windscreen. (Photograph courtesy of Volkswagen AG)

luxurious trim, the 'L'. The S and LS were powered by the larger 1471cc engine, while the latter again featured a higher level of trim.

A press document produced to celebrate the sixty-millionth Volkswagen, a car that left the factory on 1 November 1991, fifteen years after the launch of the Golf, serves to illustrate the by-then corporate policy, or interpretation, of the range-defining Golf at its birth:

> Twelve months on [in 1974], Volkswagen made waves in unveiling the elegant Scirocco coupé built by Karmann, and today's most popular model, the Golf with transverse engine, went into production in Wolfsburg. It was an immediate success, forging ahead at a level rare in automobile history. … The company required only 27 months to produce 1,000,000 Golf models. The anniversary car left the assembly line on 27 October 1976. … The contrast between the first Volkswagen and its latter-day successor, the Golf, could hardly be greater. A comparison of their design principles reveals that the Golf takes humans' space and transportation requirements as its starting point, whereas the Beetle is a product of a 'chassis-orientated' design era.

The Golf models so far outlined were Leiding's intended range. He would have expected to tweak and modify the models each year in line with other manufacturers, even if the improvements related to minor issues such as new or additional paint options, or an upgraded style of upholstery. Likewise, as Leiding was a thoroughly competent Director General, no doubt he would already have made a note to look to Volkswagen's future with a new car some years down the line. What Leiding hadn't contemplated initially was the added dimension of a hot version of the hatchback, just as no other manufacturer had at the time. His job had been to return to the days of Nordhoff's prosperity, but with a new line-up of models designed for the 1970s. That he had selected the ideal concept to develop into a sports model could only be regarded as entirely fortuitous for Volkswagen and particularly so for Leiding's successor.

The interior of the early Golf depicts its awkward and angular-looking dashboard and basic instrumentation, at least when compared to the products of up and coming Japanese brands. (Photograph courtesy of Volkswagen AG)

2 One: The World's First Hot Hatch

Setting the Scene

That Volkswagen's Golf was inspiringly different from anything that had emerged previously in the world of motor manufacturing became increasingly apparent to the world. The next stage in the story, the clandestine development and revolutionary nature of the Golf GTI, the world's first genuine hot hatch, was truly amazing.

At the time of the GTI's evolution, enthusiasts were captivated by such sporty marvels as the diminutive Fiat Abarth, the one-size-up Renault Gordini and the NSU Prinz TT. With

The Mk1, the founding father of the GTI legend and the car that other manufacturers were determined to copy, is depicted here in the guise it assumed for the last year of the model's production. Behind it is the iconic Mk2 GTI, a worthy successor if ever there was one. Both vehicles belong to Volkswagen UK and were photographed shortly before the arrival of a summer thunderstorm, adding a further dimension to the stormy mood created by the Diamond Silver hot hatch.

The Golf GTI. Nine seconds to get to know it.

We were convinced that there must be a few smart men and women around who are looking for a thoroughly thoroughbred, elegant car. But one which does not require them to do without the solid advantages that owning a Volkswagen brings with it.

It was for these people that we developed the Golf GTI—a performance to crown the brilliance of our brilliant Golf series. With 110 mph to be exact.

The Golf GTI is easy to get to know. Nine ticks of the second hand on your watch pass as you are pressed back into the sportily comfortable seats and the speedometer needle rises from 0 to 60. Fifty it reaches in a bare 6.1 seconds.

These are figures which signify a maximum of active safety when overtaking. And they are also likely to make their mark at circuit races and rallyes in the near future. Since the engine concept has what it takes to make a flying start into motor racing.

But for all that the Golf GTI is no high-strung nervous steed, since we are well aware that you

will be driving it under normal traffic conditions and not on a race track. It has nerves of steel that enable it to take the stress of normal motoring without a murmur. And to keep you just as happy, we have made its equipment not sportily Spartan but sportingly lavish.

Volkswagen's first-generation Golf brochure covers were visually inept, using a single colour, a few words and nothing more. Inside, things got better as this double spread from the first UK market GTI literature serves to indicate.

a leap and a bound in terms of size, others were entranced by the rasp of the BMW 2002, Alfa Romeo's Giulia, and the Fiat 124ST. However, without exception these cars were traditional three-box saloons. Quite simply, the Golf GTI broke the mould and within a short time of its inception at Volkswagen, other manufacturers had little option but to blaze similar trails in its wake.

For Volkswagen, the development of a dynamically hot version of their staple product was unprecedented; it was a sure sign that a new age had finally arrived. Stepping back in time to the Beetle's heyday, on the British market as an example, the Mini launched in 1959 had rapidly spawned a sporting Cooper version, which, although only developing 55bhp, nevertheless offered a 62 per cent increase in performance

over that of the 0–60mph in 26.5sec of the straightforward Austin Seven or Morris Mini Minor. The then Director General at Volkswagen would never have countenanced the notion of anything other than a single 30ps and, from August 1960, a 34ps engine.

When Volkswagen added the medium-family-sized VW 1500 to its range in the autumn of 1961, Cabriolet and variant versions were contemplated to supplement the so-called notchback and variant, while an elegant coupé courtesy of Karmann and Ghia used the same running gear, but there was no hint of a sporting version. Ford in Britain was only months behind Volkswagen when it launched its similarly sized medium-family saloon, the ubiquitous Cortina. Initially only available with a 1200cc engine, a 1500 version was quickly added to the range, while it wasn't long before Cortina bodyshells were being sent to the Lotus works, where they were fitted out with twin-camshaft engines, racing suspension, plus light alloy doors, bonnets and boot lids.

Such was the success of derivatives on the main theme for many manufacturers that a sporting version of the next generation of smaller family cars was taken as read. Not so, though, for Volkswagen, for although Director General Nordhoff had died in the spring of 1968, his successor didn't immediately think it appropriate either to beef up the Beetle, or, for that matter, to add a zippier version of the much larger K70 to the price list.

Come the Leiding era and the replacement of the elegant but sadly aging Karmann Ghia with the Scirocco, it might have been assumed that as both the old and new cars benefited from the seductive charms of a sporting body, at least in the case of the latter it would possess the power to match. To the disappointment of some, Nordhoff's Karmann Ghia had always qualified as the original sheep in wolf's clothing and, to be brutally honest, the Scirocco at its launch was very little better. Designed by Giugiaro just like its cousin the Golf, the sportily clad and purposeful body of the Scirocco, specifically designed to be launched just a few months before Volkswagen's new mainstream model, could muster no more than a respectable but hardly earth-shaking maximum of 85bhp from its 1.5-litre engine. To compound matters, also on offer was the straightforward, albeit brand-new, engine of 1.1-litre capacity destined for the base rankings of the Golf.

Leiding's thrust throughout his relatively brief tenure of office was overwhelmingly one of putting Germany's now sadly sleeping giant back on track. Deviation from that goal simply wasn't affordable, despite the cluster of engineers, such as Herbert Schuster and Friedrich Goes, who were also great racing enthusiasts and who could have both openly and easily set wheels in motion for an official sporting version of the Golf.

Out-of-Hours Project

As a result of Leiding's sound but restrictive policy, and very much in the spirit of an after-hours experiment in the school chemistry laboratory, the first ideas for a high-performance version of the key member of Volkswagen's post Beetle, post-air-cooled family range were concocted by what might best be described as an eager but small band of engineers who had spent their daytime hours working on the prototype EA337. In part inspired by a youthful Alfons Löwenburg, a boffin delighting in performance and a member of the Testing Department, a small group of four or five, including both Schuster and Goes, gathered discreetly if not actually secretly, away from the eyes of inquisitive managers and also away from the prying tentacles of the always over-enthusiastic, but sometimes dangerously unfocused, sales department. Thus the notion of a 'Sports Golf' was very much an evening and weekend venture.

Exactly who was the mastermind behind the project from this point onwards seems unclear, but in the spirit of attributing the creation of the Beetle to Porsche and the design of the Golf to Giugiaro, one other name to that of Löwenberg undoubtedly deserves a mention – Dr Friedrich Goes. It has been alleged that Goes had an excellent knowledge of all aspects of Volkswagen's and Audi's parts make-up, ranging from complete Audi-badged engines, to wide wheels (at least in comparison to the skinny affairs fitted to the standard Golf) and Recaro sports seats, although this last-mentioned item in the end didn't find its way into the 'Sports Golf'.

First Game

Work started as early as 1973, but it was only after the official launch of the Golf in N, L and LS guise that the project really gathered momentum. What had been apparent from the start was that the Golf's compact dimensions combined with its basically sporting chassis made it an ideal vehicle on which to apply the principles of the GTI. The Audi 50/Polo would have been too small, the Passat too large. The Golf could be fast, it was unquestionably comfortable and compliant, plus its handling was excellent. Having involved Dr Reckhorn of the body-testing department by asking if it was viable to develop reinforcements that would stiffen the Golf's chassis, and therefore take maximum advantage of a revised package of sport suspension then undergoing development, news seeped to senior management, including Anton Konrad, the head of Press and Public Relations. As yet another avid racer, he proved useful, being most vocal in support of the project.

While far from ecstatic about the sporting project, tentative approval was given for work to progress on the now so-called 'Sports Golf'. The scenario was a difficult one. On the one hand, the dangerous downward spiral in sales had to be addressed, which was undoubtedly best achieved through mass demand rather than through the creation of further niche markets. On the other hand, Volkswagen's reputation might be enhanced at least, if not totally rebuilt, by entering the field of motor sport and reaping the potentially enormous benefits of winning in such a field. Conversely, the aftermath of the recent energy crisis encouraged negative sentiments in management circles and it was assumed that the general public felt the same way.

Amongst those higher echelons of Volkswagen's corridors of power, most dubious of all were the very people that in future years would be keen to exploit the brand fully. The single biggest problem for those with sales and marketing expertise was that the 'Sports Golf' had no clear place; amazing as it might seem nowadays, three decades and more ago there was no obvious market sector for such a model. Astonishingly, no other manufacturer at this time had a track record of success or otherwise with such a venture.

As an almost inevitable result, it was with more than a degree of reluctance that the sales and marketing people agreed to back the new car. Their scepticism regarding its place and potential success was relieved somewhat by the solemn undertaking that no more than 5,000 examples of the hot Golf would be built. Such a strategy was obvious to all but the most effectively blinkered, as such a relatively low number would ensure that the dealerships across Europe would not be saturated, or lumbered, with an unknown and untested product, while the criteria to qualify for Group 1 Production Touring Car Racing was immediately met (the rules stated that 5,000 cars had to pass through the showrooms). Inevitably, the rumour was quick to emerge across large swaths of the continent that the 'Sports Golf', at least under the name it would be given later, was indeed nothing more than a mere homologation special.

The month was May 1975, less than a year into full-blown Golf production, and part-way through the first year of Toni Schmücker's tenure of office, a time when losses were still a reality and when Golf production would only amount to less than one-third of that of the Beetle when that car was at its peak. However, despite the reluctance of many, once the decision had been taken the pressure was undoubtedly on to release the new sporty model as quickly as possible. The scale of the development team expanded rapidly, the original four or five quickly becoming one hundred, if not more.

A convincingly well-prepared prototype was put on display at the Frankfurt Motor Show in September 1975, while feverish activity ensured that the car could go on sale the following June in Germany and other key left-hand-drive markets.

Development Story

At the time that the official nod was given to add a 'Sports Golf' to the line-up of Volkswagen's new core model, albeit on a limited-edition basis, work on the prototypes had progressed significantly, with them later proving to have been somewhere in the region of 80 per cent complete.

A mere six such cars had been built before the hot Golf became an official project; very much against the burgeoning trend of the decade, only a further fifteen durability cars would be built for rigorous testing before the 'Sports Golf' was launched. 'Sports Golfs' were duly despatched to the freezing conditions of the far north and Scandinavia, plus the searing hot and incredibly dry deserts of North Africa. Satisfied with the results on both counts, a number of the test cars were remorselessly thrashed on the autobahns of West Germany, again without the unwelcome discovery of any major fault, although at least one test vehicle was subjected to an unprecedented 49,900km (31,000 miles) of high-speed motoring. Throughout, the aim was clear, despite the threatened restriction to a run of just 5,000 cars, and that was the creation of a new market segment, something Volkswagen achieved with remarkable ease and success, as it would soon become abundantly apparent. According to the literature of the time:

> For all that, the Golf GTI is no high-strung nervous steed, since we are well aware that you will be driving it under normal traffic conditions and not on a race track. It has nerves of steel that enable it to take the stress of normal motoring without a murmur. And to keep you just as happy, we have made its equipment not sportily spartan but sportingly lavish.

100ps and Rising

As far as the fire behind the 'Sports Golf' went, the original plan had been to borrow the engine from the Audi 80GT; the Audi sporting engine was essentially a stretched version of the larger of the two units already allocated to the Golf. Put simply, this involved lengthening the stroke of the 1.5-litre engine by 3mm to 79.5mm, creating in the process an almost square unit and granting it a capacity of 1588cc. A considerable amount of work had

been accomplished to ensure that the engine breathed more easily and with a dual-choke Solex carburettor the effect was an engine that produced 100ps at 6,000rpm. While this certainly qualified the car to become a sports model, there was a general feeling that more had to be achieved to make the car a true success. According to the August 1976 Golf GTI brochure, 'The Golf GTI is easy to get to know. Nine ticks of the second hand on your watch pass as you are pressed back into the comfortably sporty seats and the speedometer needle rises from 0–60. Fifty it reaches in a bare 6.1sec.'

The logical move was to make use of the work already carried out to ensure that American versions of the Golf, the Audi 80 and the Passat (respectively known as the Rabbit, the Fox and the Dasher) were compatible with California's strict regulations on emissions. As in the days of air-cooled supremacy, this meant mechanical fuel injection, in this instance the new Bosch K-Jetronic arrangement. Much simpler than previous systems, fuel was maintained at a constant pressure by an electric pump, while the flow was managed through a large flap valve acting as an airflow meter. The greater the volume of air passing this valve to a fuel-metering valve, the more it was opened and the greater the amount of fuel that was permitted into the injection rail. Although there were additional valves to monitor both cold and hot starts, plus warming-up, the constant, or 'kontinuous' (hence the 'K' before Jetronic), system was both straightforward and robust in its nature.

The net result of employing fuel injection in the 'Sports Golf' was to boost performance by an additional 10ps to what for the day was an outstanding 110ps at 6,100rpm. Having stated above that to avoid confusion output will always be expressed in ps terms, the launch model GTI is sufficiently important to warrant terminology that covers all markets. Thus the output in DIN bhp terms was 110 at 6,100rpm and when expressed as SAE bhp, 105 at 6,100rpm. According to the brochure,

The Golf GTI, 110 horses and not much feed … The main difference is that this 1.6-litre engine produces a full 110 DIN bhp, while its thirst for fuel stays well within bounds: 35.2 miles per gallon of premium fuel. A performance like this for so little fuel is something quite exceptional. And this exceptional something has a name: the K-Jetronic – a novel type of injection system which provides exactly the right amount of fuel for the intake ports whatever the rev range.

There were numerous targets and challenges to be met at either the twin carburettor stage, or at the point when fuel injection was added to the specification. Improved breathing was achieved through the fitting of larger diameter inlet valves and Heron-type combustion chambers recessed into the piston crowns, these replacing the originals, which were of a bathtub shape. New inlet and exhaust manifolds ensured improved gas flow, while also allowing space for the installation of the injection pump. An extra pulley was inserted into the run of the camshaft-drive toothed belt. The ideal combination of smooth, yet understatedly exhilarating performance, inevitably demanded that an ignition cut-out, or rev limiter, became part of the package, kicking in at 6,900rpm. Anticipated usage suggested an oil cooler would be beneficial and a console-mounted oil temperature gauge was duly specified to accompany this.

While the Deluxe, or larger engined, version of the standard Golf could hardly be described as a sluggard, the 'Sports Golf' offered 57 per cent more power and a torque factor of 140Nm at 5,000rpm, which in turn was a big improvement over that of the next closest model in the range. The innate smoothness of the engine, combined with its abundance of torque, gave the owner of the car a feeling of driving a much larger engined vehicle than was the case. Thanks to the injection system that was behind this feeling, the 'Sports Golf' could not be regarded as the archetypal big car gas-guzzler. Even when driven with spirit, it was perfectly feasible to achieve 9.4ltr/100km

(30mpg), while Volkswagen's own figures for constant speeds of either 80 or 96.5km/h (50 or 60mph) indicated a highly unrealistic but nevertheless truly amazing 5.6 and 6.8ltr/100km (50.4 and 41.5mpg), respectively.

Although the size of the clutch was increased, the 'Sports Golf' wasn't endowed with a five-speed gearbox, instead relying on the same four-speed arrangement, with the same ratios, as the rest of the range. However, the final drive ratio was amended from 3.9:1 to 3.7:1. This arrangement would last until 1979, at which point, some have alleged, Volkswagen had reserved sufficient money in its once depleted coffers to develop a five-speed box.

Specification Matters

Volkswagen's performance records indicated that the traditional 0–60mph benchmark figure was achieved in 9.0sec, although *Autocar* on its initial test declared a figure of 9.8sec. The top speed of 182km/h (113mph), again taken from Volkswagen's own figures, was suitably impressive in the mid to late 1970s. With such a pedigree it was imperative that the 'Sports Golf' could be brought to halt with an appropriate braking arrangement. As a result, 239mm ventilated front discs coupled to a larger 200mm power vacuum servo unit replaced the solid front disc brakes of the higher-powered standard Golf range. The marketing spin on this story ran as follows in many of the earlier brochures: 'The safety that goes with this kind of performance is provided by a low-slung chassis with a wide track, carefully balanced springing and shock absorbers. Both axles are given additional stabilizers. The disc brakes are internally ventilated and a brake pressure regulator makes for the equitable distribution of braking power.'

Perhaps surprisingly, the relatively small 180 × 30mm drum brakes on the rear wheels were left more or less untouched, the only addition being a pressure regulator that would stop them locking up when the car was unladen. This stubborn, or possibly cost-cutting, retention of drums led inevitably to one of the very few criticisms levelled at the new car.

The number of owners who would have been happy if the 'Sports Golf' had been shod with the relatively skinny tyres allocated to the Deluxe elements of the ordinary Golf range might well have been counted on one hand. In the skinny stakes, the Golf and Golf L ran on 4½J rims coupled to 145 SR-13 tyres, while the LS tripped along with 5J rims clad with 155 SR-13. However, the 'Sports Golf' was duly endowed with 5½J rims and shod with 175/70 HR-13 tyres.

The spring ratings were increased, with the standard dampers, or shock absorbers, being replaced by specially rated Bilstein units. Roll stiffness was increased through the addition of a 17mm larger diameter anti-roll bar at the front of the car, and at the rear via a small supplementary bar mounted within the transverse torsion beam. The front track was increased from the normal Golf's 1,390mm (54.7in) to 1,405mm (55.3in).

Wrongly as it turned out, the engineers decided initially not to tamper with the standard ride height applicable to the remaining

---

Golf GTI Mk1 1600, 1976 to 1979

Engine

Type	Transversely mounted 4-cylinder in-line		(0.6in) compared to other Mk1 Golfs
Bore and stroke	79.5mm × 80mm	Steering	Maintenance-free self-adjusting rack and pinion
Capacity	1588cc	Tyres	175/70 HR-13
Valves	2 valves per cylinder – 38mm inlet, 13mm exhaust	Wheels	5.5J × 13 (initially twelve-spoke alloys – then steel for UK market until 1980)
Compression ratio	9.5:1		
Fuel injection	Bosch K-Jetronic		
Max. power	110ps at 6,100rpm	**Brakes**	
Max. torque	101lb ft at 5,000rpm	Type	Diagonally divided dual circuit with brake servo and brake pressure regulator
Fuel capacity	45ltr (9.9gal)		
		Size	Front 239mm (9.4in) diameter discs, internally ventilated
Transmission			Rear 180mm (7.1in) diameter self-adjusting drums
	Front-wheel drive		
Gearbox	Four-speed manual		
Clutch	Single dry plate	**Dimensions**	
Ratios	1st 3.45	Track	
	8km/h (5.0 mph)/1,000rpm	Front	1,405mm (55.3in)
	2nd 1.94	Rear	1,372mm (54.0in)
	14.3km/h (8.9mph)/1,000rpm	Wheelbase	2,400mm (94.5in)
	3rd 1.37	Overall length	3,705mm (145.9in)
	20.1km/h(12.6mph)/1,000rpm	Overall width	1,628mm (64.1in)
	4th 0.97	Overall height	1,390mm (54.7in)
	27.8km/h (17.3mph)/1,000rpm	Unladen weight	810kg (1,786lb)
Final drive	3.7 to 1		
		Performance	
Suspension and Steering		Top speed	177km/h (110mph)
Front	MacPherson struts, coil springs, anti-roll bar		0–80km/h (0–50mph) 6.1sec
Rear	Torsion beam, trailing arms, coil springs, anti-roll bar Suspension lowered by 15mm		0–100km/h (0–62mph) 9.0sec

vehicles in the range, being of the belief that the centre of gravity was not only already sufficiently low to make handling ideal, but also that, if a reduction in available wheel travel occurred, there would be a perceptible loss in terms of ride comfort. However, as sales of the GTI started to multiply, Volkswagen succumbed to popular demand and lowered the car by 20mm (0.78in), at a stroke improving the looks of the car, if not necessarily the handling.

The Elegance of the Sportsman

The sportsman in the Golf GTI is outwardly quite discreet. No need to go in for effects. The enlarged front spoiler, the widened mudguards and the wide 70 tyres do not exactly go out of their way to draw attention … [add] a whole set of styling characteristics to emphasize its sporty nature with discreet mat., 65t-black – the wide strips on the side, the rear window frame and the bumpers, in particular.

Regarding the general looks of the 'Sports Golf', the backroom stylists carried out sufficient tweaks to distinguish the new model from the rest of the pack, but in true Volkswagen style

nothing too adventurous or garish was contemplated. Externally, reference has just been made to lowering, although not from the very start of production. At the front the car sported a discreet, although larger than normal, 'chin' spoiler, the result of which, it was claimed, was to assist with high-speed stability through reducing front-end lift by some 30kg (65lb) at a nominal 160km/h (100mph). That the back of the car lacked an equivalent device was no cost-saving scheme. The 'Sports Golf' didn't need a rear spoiler, even though the visually sporty Scirocco most certainly did if it was to be propelled in anything approaching a straight line. Sadly, there was no attempt to upgrade the utilitarian-looking girder-style bumpers, complete with plastic end caps, which were eminently more suitable to household guttering. To make matters worse, at least in the context of this particular item, Volkswagen's not totally unexpected thoughts on a sporty colour centred on black, which when applied to the bumper had the effect of creating a cost-cutting, no-frills base model look. Fortunately, that's not to say that black didn't work well elsewhere, whether it related to the prominent trim between the car's wheel

Note how in this press image the early Mk1 GTI sported steel wheels. (Photograph courtesy of Volkswagen AG)

arches, the door handles, or in the form of a vinyl surround to the hatch window. Of importance were the plastic wheel-arch surrounds, which beefed up the width of the vehicle, instantly making it more attractive to those whose sporty driving pretensions were in reality centred on the looks and status of owning a fast car.

For his part, Giugiaro disliked the wheel extensions with a vengeance, but at least he had the good grace to accept that it was unrealistic to expect that the body of the sporting version of a mass-production model would be customized in metal. On the downside, early models were fitted with nothing more adventurous than basic design steel wheels, while the chrome effect GTI badging on the front grille and lower part of the tailgate, although visible to all but the most blurred naked eye, was more than a little too discreet for many. Curiously, the typeface of the GTI badge as depicted at the model's launch at the Frankfurt Show, although similarly discreet, was different to the style that enthusiasts came to know and regard with respect.

On an entirely practical note, the 'Sports Golf' specification included a rear window wash/wipe system, something only available on the options list for other models of Golf at the time, as well as a twin-tone horn, halogen headlights and an air blade on the driver's side windscreen wiper.

Best of all, however, was a tiny touch that cost Volkswagen virtually nothing to produce. Base model Golfs lacked any form of trim line around the front grille. Not so the LS, though, which carried a neat chrome effect moulding in this area. For the GTI, the trim remained in place but was painted red, a colour synonymous with hot, racy and even passionate performance. This feature would survive throughout the years of Mk1 and 2 production, disappear over the lifetime of the next two generations, only to resurface to great acclaim with the birth of the Mk5 GTI. Red-line looks, the vital symbol of red-line performance, did more than anything else to set the appearance of the GTI apart from its lesser brethren.

Dress-Coat

Almost by accident and in one instance entirely to the detriment of the car's most distinctive trim feature, in the early days the Golf GTI was only available in three colours. From an assortment of early Golf colours, most of which would have been entirely familiar to a 1970s Beetle owner, ranging from Rally Yellow, Marino Yellow, Ocean Blue, Lofoten Green and Atlas White to Viper Green and Diamond Silver

A three-quarters rear shot of an early GTI finished in Mars Red; a shade far from exclusive to the GTI, but nevertheless eminently suitable to boost the hot-hatch image.

metallic, by the time the 'Sports Golf' was launched the palette ranged from Black, Mars Red and the aforementioned Diamond Silver to Riyad Yellow, Miami Blue, Bali Green, Polar White, plus two additional metallic offerings – Bronze and Bahama Blue. Volkswagen decided that the GTI would only be available in a selected colour range and offered a racy red, sleek silver and sportingly menacing black: 'Elegant Black is not the only colour for the Golf GTI. We have selected two impressive colours for you to choose from: either Diamond Silver metallic. Or Mars Red.'

While in later years a GTI could be purchased in just about every colour under the sun, those early-day key choices have stuck with the GTI image throughout. Perhaps the name has changed, with Diamond Silver currently being expressed as Reflex Silver for example, but the principle hasn't changed over the decades.

Interior Decor

> And you will see that we have not skimped inside either. There is tartan cloth upholstery on the sporty seats. A three-spoke steering wheel. A rev-counter and an oil temperature gauge. There is a sportily-styled shift-lever handle: a golf-ball – this time in black. And black velours [sic] carpeting.

The argument runs that initially it was supposed that the majority of GTI sales would come from young enthusiast drivers and that as a result the interior would be trimmed in a fairly basic manner. However, it soon became evident that the 'Sports' concept had great appeal to older and undoubtedly more affluent buyers, who would be less likely to forgo the creature comforts they had worked hard to afford. As a result, the emphasis switched fairly rapidly towards high-quality fitments.

Having grasped the criteria required to design a popular interior amenable to all tastes, the option chosen for the 'Sports Golf' created divided opinion from the outset, a feeling that remains today. By far the most striking

attribute was the upholstery covering the sporty and reasonably well-bolstered seats. Garish cried one author, eye-catching another might have added. A basic Golf of the 1970s was fitted with seats upholstered in a simple black and white houndstooth pattern of material, while more upmarket members of the clan featured either wide pattern cord velour, or even luxury plain velour for owners of the GLS model. While clearly something had to be done to distinguish the 'Sports Model' from

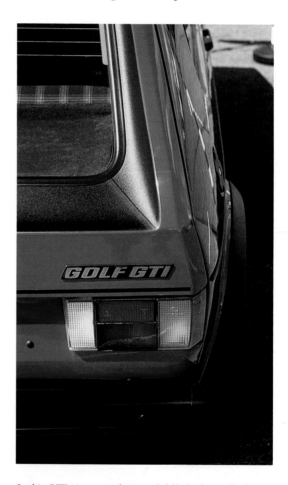

In this GTI picture are the extended black plastic wheel arches, black vinyl rear window surround, a glimpse of the rather loud tartan seat upholstery and the magic GTI letters. Common to all Golfs of this early period are the small rear light clusters leaving a large area of painted metal between the lenses and the licence plate and girder-style bumpers with plastic end-caps.

the rest of the pack, this could easily have been achieved through the inclusion of excellent Recaro-style seats, coupled to separate headrests. Instead, Volkswagen went one stage further and the jury is still undoubtedly out when it comes to the bold, indeed loud, black and red cloth attributed to the Mars Red car and the almost as dazzling black and silver material allocated to the other colours of car. Whether the seat covers might best be described as being of a tartan design is not entirely clear. Those of Scottish descent would undoubtedly prefer the term 'check' to be used. This German usurper has not been attributable to any particular clan, but for most, including Volkswagen's copywriters, tartan remains both appropriately descriptive and admirably apt. Sadly, experience taught owners that the fabric was nowhere near as robust

as it might have appeared, wearing through at an alarming rate in the hands of all but the most careful custodians.

Equally quirky, and in this instance frivolously serving no practical purpose, was the inclusion of a golf-ball-style gear knob, although it did help to fuel the fallacy that the Golf had been named after a game rather than the Gulf Stream. For the most part, though, the 'Sport Golf's' interior was uncompromising black, a deliberate decision taken so that the car's interior to an extent at least complemented its exterior. Black carpets were rightfully luxurious, black door cards were entirely suitable, and although a black vinyl headlining was slightly oppressive, it was apparently wholly acceptable to journalists and would-be owners alike.

However, when it came to a black dashboard instrument panel there were those who had

A view through the window of the early GTI, noting that all such cars were left-hand-drive models even when supplied to countries such as Britain. Highlighted by the sunlight are both the three-spoke sport steering wheel and what Volkswagen officially described as the GTI's large check upholstery. This was available as a black and red print in conjunction with Mars Red paintwork, and in black plus silver with the other colours of cars then available.

second thoughts. From the in-vogue brushed aluminium instrument panel of the Deluxe Golf models, the GTI appeared to join with the base model in that it was clad merely in black plastic. Perhaps there was compensation to be had in the form of the special three-spoke steering wheel, which comprised aluminium spokes, a black plastic rim and, as a fitting centrepiece, a carefully recessed horn button bearing a much simplified version of the Wolfsburg crest. However, for some unknown reason Volkswagen forgot to include a glovebox lid to the GTI's interior specification, which unravelled any good created out of an upmarket steering wheel.

Inevitably, the GTI joined other deluxe models in that its specification included a slimline centre console; however, where it outshone the rest was with the instruments it housed. For starters, the observant would have noticed that the speedometer provided a higher reading than the other models. As the clock had been displaced from its dashboard home in favour of a prominent rev-counter, just as it had been in other so-called luxurious Golf models, a location was found for it within the centre console. However, unique to the 'Sports Golf' was the inclusion of an oil temperature gauge, which related to the fitting of the oil cooler, already referred to earlier in the chapter.

What's in a Name? From 'Sports Golf' to GTI

Although the hot Golf had been known throughout its various stages of development as the 'Sports Golf' it was decided that such an appendage was inappropriate. Nothing could have been more embarrassing than a car with a name that didn't live up to its expectations. In abandoning the 'Sports' designation Volkswagen inadvertently created a name of far greater significance, one that outshone the word Sports many times over and one that other manufacturers were eager to emulate.

Volkswagen must still bitterly regret that it lacked the foresight to patent the coupling of those three letters G, T and I. Of course, those whose primary responsibility it was to market the new hot hatch, the very people who normally wouldn't miss a trick leading either to a growth in overall sales, or the establishment of a distinctive brand, hadn't appreciated the potential; indeed, it was only the buying public's vote, demonstrated by an enthusiastically persistent desire to be an owner of a GTI, that triggered volume manufacture of what had once been strictly a one-off, never to be repeated production run.

GTI then it was. The two letters GT, or the *Gran Turismo* of Italian descent, tend to be recognized the world over as a symbol of sporty prowess, despite the many unintentional attempts to devalue the concept by attaching such an appendage to the more sedate models of a manufacturer's range in the invariably forlorn hope that an otherwise dull, if not distinctly boring, car might suddenly receive a welcome boost in sales. Sadly, even in the 1970s the letters GT had been somewhat devalued, although at least the message was instantly recognizable. The remaining digit, however, was altogether a different matter and even now the selection of 'I' remains something of a mystery. For starters, the German word for injection is *einspritzung*, suggesting that GTE should have been preferable to GTI. However, as the almost newly wedded sister company of Audi had a version of the 80 model that had been dubbed the GTE, it may have been to fellow German manufacturer BMW that Volkswagen turned for inspiration. Now probably long forgotten, at the time that company produced a Bosch fuel-injected coupé, designating it the CSi. However, another theory is undoubtedly worthy of consideration. In continuation of the *Gran Turismo* theme, perhaps the 'I' stood for *iniezione*, the Italian rather than German word for injection.

Whatever the truth of the matter, those who have avidly followed the Volkswagen marque since its infancy will appreciate that the hot Golf was always intended to be a GTI, rather than a GTi. Many will also know that journalists over the decades, and even Volkswagen itself fell into the trap of using a lower case letter when writing about the car. Take, for example, the plain orange-coloured cover of a British version of the brochure devoted to the car that bears the word Golf, closely followed by 'GTi'. Curiously, this transgression of 1976 vintage doesn't extend to the interior pages!

The very nature of the GTI lends the car to at least an element of personalization. As sales of the Mk1 GTI in Britain in left-hand-drive guise were somewhat limited, most surviving examples of the breed tend to date from 1980 and onwards, so are cars that in original guise would all have had the larger and more protective plastic-covered bumpers. As the story here is of the GTI's history as delivered to customers from Wolfsburg and the dealers' showrooms, the more extreme examples of the custom cult have not been included.

Only the clear indicator lenses are noticeably out of step with originality.

An attractive Mk1 GTI with alloys that suit the look of the car.

Somewhat unusually, the owner of this Mk1 GTI has sought to replace the original black trim strip on the side of the car with a chrome-effect version. Other shiny additions come in the form of the petrol cap filler and the door handle.

Non-standard alloys and clear indicator lenses don't detract from this Lhasa Green GTI.

Rapid Acceleration in GTI Sales

Once the 'Sports Golf', or in reality the GTI, was on the market, sales blossomed out of all proportion to the numbers that those of a depressingly pessimistic disposition had predicted. The general public took the GTI to its heart just as it had done with lesser Golf models. Essentially starved of high-performance cars during the oil crisis from which the motoring world had only recently emerged, there was a realization that with the GTI, not only was it fuel-efficient when compared with the likes of either a sporty Mercedes or BMW, but also it

This GTI features both shiny side trim and a similarly finished strip at the base of the hatch.

was perfectly capable of standing up to the pace of far more expensive vehicles. The motoring press took to the new model with great enthusiasm, as the extracts from the following contemporary reports indicate. *Motor*, through journalist Phillip Turner, gave the GTI a glowing testimony, at least in terms of its handling:

> It cruised happily on the autobahn at a steady 180km/h indicated (nearly 112mph) without feeling in any way stressed, but really came into its own over the country roads, for it felt very stable over roads noted for their camber and their poor surface…. The gear change, in spite of a longish movement, was good, and second gear proved very useful on those twisting roads, for one could whip down into it then hurtle past a car or lorry in front and be back on one's own side of the road again in a very short length of straight. The steering is surprisingly light for a front-wheel drive car, and is precise with adequate feel. The brakes gave the impression there was plenty in reserve even after using them hard on the swervy downhill bits. The ride, too, had not had its comfort destroyed by the firmer suspension.

For *Autosport*'s John Bolster the problem was finding anything to criticize! Describing the car as 'outstanding', the author of the report had to say 'straight away' that he was 'enormously impressed'. A whole catalogue of superlatives followed, giving the distinct impression that a thesaurus sat at his side as the text was compiled. The engine, for example, was:

> so vibration-less that it would be hard to guess, at any speed, how many cylinders it has. The acceleration is so completely smooth from 1,000rpm. …The acceleration is very vivid indeed and I would guess that the claimed figures could be surpassed without difficulty … The precision and rapidity of the gearbox adds to the performance … The ventilated discs are a great improvement and there is no fading in mountainous country. … The new GTI Volkswagens are such outstanding cars that for once I am at a loss to find anything serious to criticize. They combine performance with

refinement, extremely quick cornering with side-wind stability, and speed with safety. I can't say fairer than that.

The *Autocar* report was similarly full of praise. From a starting point of a comparison with the top of the range Golf 1600LS, the magazine quotes from its own report covering this vehicle of earlier months. 'When the moment comes to push the throttle down the car responds in the most exhilarating fashion with a bound of instant skirt' – high praise indeed for a 'standard' hatch. To top the LS, *Autocar* proceeded to relay how it followed that 'the GTI is a very special animal indeed'. Sadly, the test car they were given wasn't the best, with even Volkswagen's press department of the day admitting that the vehicle was 'slightly down on power'. Nevertheless, the author of the report anticipated that a 'good Golf GTI would have no trouble holding 115 given a good downhill run-in and calm conditions'. Of more genuine significance was the judgement that, 'at a true 100mph … the rev counter was indicating only 5,600rpm with still a long way to go to peak power. This was the GTI's happiest speed – it was unaffected by wind and slight gradients on motorways and would hold it on rather less than three-quarter throttle opening'. Without delving into the minutiae of further praise, the conclusion is certainly worthy of repetition more or less in full:

> The GTI is a significant and important performance leader for the top end of the Golf range. It signifies the interest that is generated in Germany for performance machinery, now that the fuel crisis has dwindled in people's memories. Priced at over £3,700 in this country, the GTI is more expensive than its obvious competitor, the Ford RS2000. Our test example was also slightly slower, but it would be difficult to separate them on the road. The Golf scores in exuberance and urgency. It is an infectiously enthusiastic little car in which to hurtle around the countryside, and it has the advantage of a hatchback over the

RS2000. Even would-be Roger Clarks have to carry dogs, children and the odd washing machine around sometime.

Right-Hand Drive

As this book concentrates primarily, but by no means exclusively, on the British market, the GTI's non-appearance in right-hand-drive guise at launch, while understandable, is nevertheless of significance. Would-be owners, desirous of a right-hand-drive model, were to be confounded for some considerable time. Available to special order only, in itself frustratingly restrictive, the left-hand-drive GTI was first introduced to British customers in the autumn of 1976, the exact month varying between September and October dependent on which account of events is to be believed. Relatively costly at £3,956, and inevitably less compatible with British roads than the rest of the Golf range due to the position of the steering wheel, more than a passing interest was still quickly generated, in part inspired by reports emulating from Germany indicating just how startlingly good the GTI was.

For those with sufficient cash burning holes in their pockets and unable to countenance left-hand drive, a small number of specialist firms, GTI Engineering being one such example,

were happy to convert cars to right-hand drive, and in the main did so to a particularly high and professional standard.

Sales of right-hand-drive GTIs commenced at the end of July 1979, much to the relief of the network of Volkswagen dealers. Roaring inflation ensured a price tag of £5,010, or an increase of nearly 27 per cent compared to the sum requested when the left-hand-drive model was first issued in Britain. During the comparatively brief period before the arrival of a five-speed gearbox at the end of the calendar year, 1,183 GTIs were sold. Over a similar period after that introduction, 1,064 GTIs were sold, implying that the upgrade had very little influence when it came to the decision-making process to buy or not to purchase the GTI. Regrettably for all concerned, static sales figures were nothing to do with would-be customers, but rather a reflection of Volkswagen's inability to supply, a situation that became increasingly desperate as demand multiplied.

For potential British owners, basic Golfs were promoted under the heading of three million owners not being wrong, while 'L' specification models came with 'economy engines' and 'luxury trim'. Stepping up a level or two, the 'GLS' became the 'Golf with everything', while most importantly here, the GTI's greatest asset was neatly summarized with the

This later model Mk1 GTI shows how the larger rear light clusters almost bonded with the licence plate, creating a tidy look akin to Giugiaro's original styling concept. This car also carries the standard 5.5J × 13 sport alloys of the time.

A particularly fine example of a late model Mk1 GTI finished in Diamond Silver and on show in the Concours at the largest GTI gathering in the UK.

cleverest of headings. 'The Golf GTI. Nine seconds to get to know it.'

Volkswagen's impeccably high promotional standards of yesteryear did not extend to the British version of the early brochures produced to promote the right-hand-drive GTI amidst the rest of the range. The principal image was of a not too carefully reversed picture of a left-hand-drive GTI, as evidenced by the GTI script appearing on the wrong side of the grille on the GTI's front, while the text referred to 'handsome alloy wheels', although the photograph shows quite clearly nothing more than simple steel affairs.

Of intense irritation to the family man who wished to drive a GTI, unlike its continental counterparts the car for the British market was only offered as a three-door; a fate that was also to await American owners when they too were finally offered the sporting version of the Golf.

The Launch Model GTI Evaluated

With the benefit of many years' hindsight and knowledge of what was to emerge over the next three decades, it is remarkably easy to criticize the Golf GTI as launched on a number of grounds. Some points have already been referenced, while others have not yet been recorded. This appraisal of the launch model GTI affords an opportunity to collect each and every potential dissatisfaction together.

Steel wheels and budget-style girder bumpers top the bill with regard to the GTI's external appearance, although the limited number of paint options should be cited as a secondary gripe. Possible runners–up might also include the lack of sporty twin headlights and an issue that was only to emerge as the car aged and not one that was exclusive to the GTI, namely the dreaded 'tin-worm'.

Top of the list as far as contemporary reviews went was the retention of woefully inadequate drum brakes on the rear wheels, although to modern eyes the specification of a four-speed gearbox at a time when a fifth gear

---

Mk1 Golf GTI Paint Options, Circa 1976

Paint options for the Mk1 GTI have already been touched upon, but here's a cautionary note for budding experts. From a straightforward start of universal Black, Mars Red and Diamond Silver, by the end of the 1970s a degree of complexity had developed. In the UK, even with the advent of a right-hand-drive GTI, there was no change, but in Germany Alpine White and Inari Silver – a metallic silver with a hint of green – had been added to the list of options. For simplicity's sake, the paint options mentioned here will always refer to the UK market and relate to a specific year.

As a footnote to Mk1 GTI colours, it is worth noting that for the 1983 model year, Volkswagen in the UK offered four colours. Black and Mars Red were two options, while Alpine White had joined the ranks in third position. However, apparently at the expense of Diamond Silver, Lhasa metallic was added to the list. Lhasa was a silvery green-blue shade and looked particularly attractive on the Campaign, or run-out, model.

ABOVE: All Mk1 GTIs sported the VW roundel on the grille at the front of the car. Contemporary literature indicates that some emblems were finished in black and others in a 'chrome' look. All cars carried the magic letters GTI.

ABOVE: All Mk1 GTIs carried an identifying badge incorporating the brand name and model type on the lower right of the hatchback tailgate.

ABOVE: The tailgate badge is shown in context here on a later Mk1 GTI. Note the larger rear light cluster lenses.

ABOVE: An attractive, if hardly sporty looking, alloy fitted to some of the later Mk1 GTIs. Described in contemporary literature merely as 5J × 13 light alloy sport wheels, they were available as factory-fitted optional equipment for all models.

ABOVE: Although not exclusive to the GTI, the distinctive black petrol cap suited the general trim style of the car.

was becoming relatively commonplace would run a close second.

Garish upholstery, the dull base model-like finish of the dashboard, plus the general air of cost-cutting and shoddy workmanship typified the interior, but there was another issue. Inconsistencies of fit and finish were apparent, leading to a muted cacophony of rattles, squeaks and clunks. In addition, British customers could complain about the lack of a right-hand-drive version of the GTI and the impracticalities of being offered and expected to cope with the inevitable problems associated with a left hooker in a right-hand-drive country.

When the Mk1 GTI gave way to its successor at the end of 1983 virtually all the issues raised above had been addressed, the most noticeable omission being that of drum brakes once more. How this occurred is undoubtedly of interest to any enthusiast of the marque.

Volkswagen of the 1970s was no longer the year-in, year-out heavy profit-making organization it had once been. Recall Leiding's final year in office as an example, and the heavy losses dangling dangerously over his head. If his successor, Tony Schmücker, was to prosper, care had to be taken to keep unnecessary costs at arm's length. For a vehicle of which it was assumed, indeed agreed, that only 5,000 examples were to be built, it was hardly necessary to pile on the Deutschmarks. However, as Volkswagen bounced back into the black and the GTI proved to be no five-minute wonder, and crucially with demand per month building to such a level that it way outstripped the total planned production, money could be slowly but surely pumped into the model that was creating a whole new genre in the motoring world.

That the irritations experienced with the early GTI were resolved is apparent in the model's sales figures. As a guide to the success story behind the GTI, 10,366 such cars were produced in 1976, a figure which had tripled to 31,746 in 1977 and more than doubled again, to 72,394 vehicles in 1981.

The 1979 Model Year – Better Bumpers

The GTI shared the first visual change to its appearance with all the other Golf models in the range. For the 1979 model year, out went the less than attractive girder bumpers, to be replaced by altogether more appealing and modern-looking wrap-around plastic units. Such was the area of the car protected by the new bumpers that with the GTI at least they linked directly with the matt black plastic extensions fitted to the wheel arches, looking every bit that this had been the intention from day one. Bumpers offering this level of coverage inevitably implied less danger and more protection when parking, or more realistically when someone else was manoeuvring into a relatively tight space either to the side, front or behind the GTI.

The Alloy Story

Alloys came and went according to which way the wind was blowing in Wolfsburg, of that there's no doubt. Different markets were granted varying specifications in terms of standard equipment, making one single statement in this respect inapplicable. For example, around the time of the GTI's first upgrade, for the British market at least, alloys of the Audi 80 and or Passat-style started to appear as standard, while for most European countries such luxuries remained optional at extra cost.

Driving Out the Rust Bug

Apart from that certain lack of appeal afforded by a left-hand-drive GTI in a right-hand-drive country leading to depressed sales, there remains another reason why very few GTIs are to be found on the Concours circuit – before the 1980 model year Volkswagen's rust treatment was sadly lacking. Gone were the days of a separate chassis and easily replaceable bolt-on wings, both characteristics of Volkswagen's first great triumph, the Beetle. Fortunately, with effect from the summer of 1979, measures, including wax injection, were introduced to help to keep rust at bay and such was Volkswagen's confidence that the company was prepared to offer a six-year anti-rust warranty.

Again, as with the introduction of modified bumpers, the measures taken to combat rust were not an exclusive preserve of the GTI, as evidenced by the plentiful examples of late Mk1 models still in existence. Unfortunately, the protection measures ran into problems and to Volkswagen's infinite embarrassment the company had to mask over the message, which in German read: '*nieu: 6 jaar garantie tegen roest*', with the message, '6-year body protection warranty. Within the terms of Trade Description legislation the description of the 6-year body protection warranty given in this brochure is inaccurate. Please see your local Volkswagen dealer for precise details.' Once any technical difficulties had been ironed out, however, the revised message certainly inspired a confidence in line with days of old, and above that of many another manufacturer:

> Volkswagen was the first company to offer a six-year warranty to cover bodywork corrosion. ... A manufacturer who gives this kind of warranty is quite sure of the longevity and quality of his product. Special rust proofing of internal body sections and panels protects against internal corrosion. This treatment applied at the time of manufacture guards against through rusting from the inside. Should this occur, rectification will be made free of charge. Naturally, during the bodywork warranty period the car must be cared for in compliance with the operating instructions and the bodywork must be checked every two years by an Authorized Dealer. With this warranty you may be totally confident that the bodywork of your car is fully protected against any defect in manufacture.

From Four to Five

The golden rule concerning not just the GTI but all models and makes of car was and remains that a four-speed box coupled to a high-revving engine is neither a recipe for optimum acceleration, nor relaxed cruising. Although Volkswagen's own literature dating from August 1979 indicates a five-speed gearbox was a part of the 1980 model year's make-up, most are agreed that it was around Christmas time 1979, or from January 1980, dependent upon which report is consulted, that the GTI finally benefited from a five-speed close-ratio gearbox, so much more in keeping with the image of the sports model (first 3.45:1, second 2.118:1, third 1.444:1, fourth 1.129:1, fifth 0.912:1).

Compared to the previous 27.8km/h (17.3mph)/1,000rpm for the four-speed, fifth gave 31.4km/h (19.5mph). Second proved to be lower than before, while the necessary change to third occurring at 88.5km/h (55mph) resulted in some suggesting a marginally slower 0–60mph time of 9.2sec and others timing themselves at a mere 8.5sec. Volkswagen's own figures however claim that the five-speed GTI powered its way to 96.5km/h (60mph) in just 8.8sec. Whatever the truth of the matter, 0–113km/h (0–70mph)

remained unchanged at a very respectable 12sec. Volkswagen claimed a new top speed of 180km/h (112mph), compared to 177km/h (110mph) previously, but some of those in the driving seat alleged a further boost to either 182km/h (113mph), or even 183km/h (114mph). Despite the odd bicker relating to the accuracy of figures, the extra gear ensured that engine revs were kept down at high cruising speeds.

Curiously, Volkswagen's own literature, or at least that produced for the British market, made little play of the general and sporting significances of a five-speed box. After all, the ratios had been particularly well chosen, with one gear taking up at exactly the point where the previous one had left off. The nub of the message in the main text cannot be faulted, but to underplay it so much seems a little odd. 'A performance with economy made possible by the novel K-Jetronic fuel injection and a five-speed gearbox'; and that was it, no more, no less! Amazingly, it was left to the potential GTI purchaser to scour the technical specification page to discover the reality of the change from earlier years.

The 1981 Model Year

For the 1981 model year, although only really coming into place in the final months of 1980, the GTI's facia, along with those of other models, was extensively revised, bringing to an end the era of visually haphazard design, incredibly angular presentation and, for the hot hatch particularly, the danger that it might be mistaken for the base model, thanks to the use of matt black rather than brushed aluminium.

That the new design was more integrated was immediately apparent, despite a continuing reliance on an angular binnacle, albeit more softly rectangular than previously. Formerly housed in separate recessed circular bezels, the main instruments were now integrated behind a general panel of clear plastic, while other control buttons, switches and warning lamps were positioned more adroitly. Most notably the clock became digital, while ten warning lights in two banks of five looked particularly neat between the speedometer and rev counter. The design of the centre console was amended slightly, so that three smaller instruments could be positioned there, rather than the two of the previous design. Ventilation and air-circulation were also improved thanks to the addition of intakes immediately above the centre console, while storage facilities, and particularly so for the front seat passenger, were considerably improved. For the GTI, if not the lesser models in the range, the steering wheel changed to an attractive four-spoke, four push-button design and included a substantial central pad (carefully emblazoned with those magical initials GTI), which was intended to give far better protection than previously should an accident occur. Curiously, Volkswagen's brochure for the British market makes reference to the old 'alloy spoke steering wheel', but as the GTI's dashboard isn't featured in the illustrations this apparent textual error wouldn't have been obvious.

Sadly, all was not instantly improved and in a thankfully short-lived but decidedly retrograde step, a brash, brassy and bold red trim line clung to the peripheries of the facia in a failed attempt to mirror the distinctive and sporty hallmark trim line around the car's mock radiator grille.

For many, Volkswagen's decision to banish forever the strident and poor-wearing tartan upholstery was warmly welcomed. The new material was a much more elegant, modern and typically understated cloth, a material deemed to be entirely more appropriate for a sportily stylish car like the GTI. Available in black and red, or black and silver, the new upholstery was matched to the GTI's paint-work, just as it had been previously, with the red option being linked to Mars Red, while the silver alternative was the choice for both the Diamond Silver and Black cars.

Externally, and no doubt to designer Giugiaro's delight, larger, or perhaps more accurately, longer rear light clusters, much more in keeping with his original concept sketches, replaced the small and relatively unattractive units of old. Gone as a result were the large expanses of painted metal either side of the registration plate, a feature that to a perfectionist like Giugiaro had always looked out of place.

A-pillar fairings, or windscreen pillar deflectors, borrowed from Volkswagen's first attempt at energy conservation, the Golf Formel E, offered further aerodynamic assistance, while adding to the sporty black look of the car in an area that had previously been the same as the other models in the range. Inevitably, the description of these aids was angled towards economy in the context of the Formel E, but is still worthy of repeating here: 'More aerodynamic. As wind-resistance is a major factor of a vehicle's fuel consumption, aerodynamic front pillar covers and a deep front spoiler … ensure that further savings can be made.'

Volkswagen's copywriters must have been instructed to allocate space to the latest design of alloys, as in the generic Golf brochure dated January 1981, where the text was strictly limited on each page due to the generous amount of room given over to photographs, specific reference was made to the 'handsome' nine-spoke wheels fitted to the GTI.

With the changes that came into effect during the 1981 model year, the Mk1 GTI had moved forward considerably from the original car presented at Frankfurt in September 1975. Volkswagen was proudest of the Car of the Year review published by *What Car?* in April 1981, even going to the lengths of preparing a special reprint to highlight the accolades offered by the magazine. The preamble written by a well-qualified copywriter read thus:

> During the last 12 months *What Car?* tested many types of car. In their 'Cars of the Year Review' they divided them into nine sections – rating them for value, comfort, road behaviour and servicing. The winners were picked in each section to suit that type of buyer's requirements. Volkswagen Golf won two out of the nine sections: the Golf GTI was voted best sporting car and overall car of the year …

The text in *What Car?* that clinched it for Volkswagen also demonstrates why after a model year of great activity, the quest to keep the Mk1 GTI in pole position was not over, even though it would be some eighteen months before the most significant development of all made its debut:

It must say something for the sophistication of Volkswagen's much loved Golf GTI that it has for the second successive year fended off challenges from both Ford and Alfa Romeo to retain our best sporting car title. For no one has yet managed to approach the silky smoothness of VW's potent injected four, the refinement of the transmission (now five speed) or the sheer efficiency of the whole package. The Golf's imitators are getting close, however: the Escort has better steering, the Alfa marginally better handling and both have much better brakes, but neither is as sensible or as practical as the GTI. This is the secret of the VW's success: it provides the best of both worlds by being tremendous fun as a driver's car yet losing none of the standard Golf's vice-free everyday behaviour.

Without doubt, the Escort XR3 in particular was a threat. *Motor* had lined up one of Henry's marvels against the GTI in November 1980 and could conclude that:

as a practical means of transport the Escort has a lot going for it. Significantly cheaper than the Golf, it offers more perceived value. It is more attractively finished and looks terrific – few mass-production cars have ever attracted as much favourable interest from passers-by as our XR3 test car … It also happens to be an unusually fast car, that should be cheaper to run than the Golf. With these qualities it will probably sell like hot cakes.

Fortunately, the fight wasn't quite over for the Golf, for *Motor* had to admit that 'this success will not … be at the expense of the GTI'. And the reason behind that apparently blatantly obvious remark followed: 'For the enthusiast who appreciates and demands dynamic sophistication from a car, the GTI is altogether the superior driving machine. It not only goes and handles that little bit better but also –

and this is the acid test – it does it all with that much more finesse, efficiency and comfort.'

More Clout – French Style

As a preamble to the next big development as far as the GTI was concerned, it's worth making reference at this point to one of Volkswagen UK's internal memos dating from 1981. The subject matter was the GTI 16S and the suggestion was that this special, prepared under the wing of Volkswagen France, should be given careful consideration as an option for the British market. There was one major drawback and that related to a price tag of some £8,000, inevitably making the car considerably more expensive than the standard GTI, indeed to a tune of some 50 per cent. Nevertheless, it was proposed that a predicted sales total of some 200 units was completely realistic, providing the special was marketed as just that; an exclusive high-performance car, deliberately limited in production numbers. Regrettably, no action was taken.

The GTI 16S was born out of the need to stay well ahead of the competition in France, where the GTI accounted for 50 per cent of total Golf sales and had been the recognized market leader. However, over the five years of GTI production, other manufacturers had been far from idle. The Escort XR3 from Ford, and the homespun Renault 5 Gordini, to name but two examples, might well be described as realistic threats. Wolfsburg's closely guarded secret work in the direction of turbocharging had run into apparently terminal difficulties. While 150bhp and upwards was much more than just a vague notion, a combination of wallet-draining fuel consumption and unacceptably high under-bonnet temperatures, the latter a result of both inlet and exhaust valves being placed at the back of the engine, made the application of turbocharging nonviable.

Volkswagen in France turned to the German tuning firm of Oettinger and its Okrasa 16-valve aftermarket kit designed specifically for the Golf GTI. Calculated to bolt straight onto the 1600cc engine, the kit revised the compression range to 10.5:1 and saw power output increase to 136ps at 6,500rpm. Likewise, torque moved from the standard 110lb ft at 5,000rpm to 116lb ft at 5,500rpm. A top speed of at least 196km/h (122mph) was commonplace, while the all-important 0–60mph time was clipped back to 7.4sec.

Once the notion of selling the ready-mixed Okrasa package through dealers became reality, it was declared necessary that such a modified car had to undergo extensive testing in order that the full VW dealer warranty could be applied. To everyone's delight, the 16S passed with flying colours, thus gaining a full VW dealer warranty, while Wolfsburg was delighted that once 400 such cars had been made it could homologate the 16-valve engine for Group 4 competition.

The arrangement between Oettinger and Volkswagen was that the latter would supply complete GTIs to the former, who in turn would modify the engine and return the parts no longer required, which included, for example, both cylinder heads and pistons.

Without entering into the full technical specification, the GTI 16S was made even more attractive to serious 'collectors', thanks to the addition of a Hella twin-headlamp grille and a BBS body kit. This comprised a full-width air dam, extended wheel arches and sills, while 6J × 14in alloys were 'standard'. Additional instruments adorned the interior and a 16S, or *soupapes* (valves) decal decorated the steering wheel. The GTI 16S was available in white or metallic black.

Bigger Engine – 1982 and 1983

The 1982 model year saw only minor tweaks to the GTI, as month by month, slowly but surely, the opposition crept closer to their target of dislodging the crown from Volkswagen's flagship Golf. Note was taken of the French method of dealing with the pretensions of rival manufacturers, while the impending threat of not one but two hotspot rivals from the Ford stable, in the form of the XR3i and the even more spectacular RS1600i, implanted the

strongest of messages at Wolfsburg's door. It could be left no longer; the GTI needed a boost to stave off the competition. Come September 1982 and the shadow boxing game with Ford and the others was finally over, the deed had been done, for Wolfsburg's GTI had a new, more powerful engine.

Volkswagen's generic Golf brochure for the 1983 models hyped up the GTI generally and its interior specifically, with the traditional two-page spread of earlier years becoming four overnight. Admittedly, the extra space was allocated to the car's creature comforts rather than its ability to leave the rest of the crowd standing in more ways than one, but that says more about the car's potential market than anything else. It was essential to cater adequately for the older, richer buyer, in general a person who demanded the status of a 0–60mph sprint in under 10sec, but an individual who, to be honest, would rarely use the GTI to its full potential. As a spin-off to such a philosophy, at least summary particulars of the new engine had to be included and, for that reason if no other, the 1.8 engine was afforded space of its own:

The ultimate hatchback?
If you feel a certain tingle of excitement when you look at this car (and even more when you drive it), we must admit that this was our very intention. And powered by a new 1.8-litre 112bhp fuel-injection engine, this slingshot hatchback takes another stride ahead of the competition in 1983. The new power-unit offers improvements to torque, acceleration and top speed – yet also offers more refined high-speed cruising characteristics.

Most will argue that there was much more to the 1800 engine than it simply being a bored-out version of the 1600. At the time of its release, the Mk1 GTI's days were strictly numbered, the original and now noticeably compact hot-hatch concept having been eclipsed in terms of available space by a whole series of marauding manufacturers. To retain its crown it was essential that the GTI should benefit from the engine designed with the next generation of GTI in mind. Refinement, especially in relation to the higher speed ranges, flexibility, both in terms of lower speed operation and general acceleration through the gears, plus cleaner combustion, were all key messages when the 1800 was considered.

With the bore up from 79.5mm to 81.0mm and the stroke similarly extended to 86.4mm from 80.0mm, at face value the slender 2ps gain in output, up from 110 to 112ps, coupled to the correspondingly slender 6lb ft uplift in terms of torque, which had shifted from 102.9lb ft to 109lb ft, seemed hardly worth the effort. Yes, the new 1800 engine delivered its maximum output at 5,800rpm, compared to 6,100rpm for the 1600, which in essence meant a little quieter running, but was this really significant? A little had been knocked off that all important 0–60mph time, the difference between the 1600 at 9.1sec and the brisker 1800 at 8.2sec amounting to just under a full second, but this was hardly earth-shattering. Likewise, top speed was fractionally improved, from the 180km/h (112mph) of the 1600 to the lofty heights of an additional 3km/h at 183km/h (114mph).

Although the 1800 engine used a different block, essentially it was of the same design as that of the 1600. However, both the cylinder heads and the pistons were truly innovative. While the 1600 engine had featured a flat head and 'bowl-in' piston combustion chambers, the new unit centred upon the majority of the combustion chamber being in the head, with only a relatively small part of it in the piston top. As a result, the compression ratio increased to 10:1. Valve sizes were increased. Serious rivals were still able to match, if not necessarily outclass, the GTI in straightforward terms of pace through the gears and in some instances could offer a better top speed, thanks to the already aging aerodynamics of the GTI, but with the arrival of the 1800 that is where it ended. Other cars lacked the smooth, yet spirited delivery of power and the resultant flexibility in the higher gears at correspondingly low crankshaft speeds. The essence of the 1800 was in its torque, the maximum now being

achieved at 3,500rpm instead of 5,000rpm, key to an important improvement in mid-range punch. Likewise, the new characteristics of the 1800 engine suited the five-speed close-ratio gearbox, just as much if not more than it had done with the 1600, while thanks to the need to change gear less often, overall fuel consumption got better. Improved lower speed flexibility ensured more so than ever that the GTI delighted in a split personality, changing as requested from a high-speed, hot-action motorway performer, to an equally relaxed and at-home town-centre shuffler.

Other changes were more or less restricted to a multifunction computer and the Golf Formel E's econometer and/or gear-change light. Essentially, this latter device took the form of a dashboard-mounted light, which only came on when it was appropriate to drive in a higher gear. As for the MFA (the *multifunktion anzeiger*, or multifunction indicator), this LED display at the bottom of the dashboard binnacle relayed elapsed journey time, trip mileage, average speed, fuel consumption, oil temperature and outside air temperature. All of this information was available by pressing a button on the end of the windscreen-wiper stalk. Most were of the opinion that here was an innovative, yet amazingly simple device that took technology several steps forward. If it had a downside it was relatively minor, in that the series of displays outlined above shared space with the clock function. To modern eyes, this would no doubt be an unacceptable travesty of confusion, but in the relatively naive days of newly burgeoning technology for the masses, all in all it was hardly an issue of any significance.

Almost as an aside, at least for the British market, the palette of trendy colour options had moved on by the time of the 1983 model year. While Black and Mars Red were still very much on the agenda, Alpine White had joined the list of paint options, while Diamond Silver had been replaced by Lhasa metallic.

Autocar's heading for its review of the 1800-powered GTI was transparent in its praise both for Volkswagen and for its latest offering. From

Golf GTI Mk1 1800, 1983

Engine

Type	Transversely mounted 4-cylinder in-line
Bore and stroke	81mm × 86.4mm
Capacity	1780cc
Compression ratio	10.0:1
Fuel injection	Bosch K-Jetronic
Max. power	112ps at 5,800rpm
Max. torque	109lb ft at 3,500rpm
Fuel capacity	45ltr (9.9gal)

Transmission

Gearbox	Five-speed all indirect with synchromesh	
Clutch	Single dry plate	
Ratios	1st	3.45
	2nd	2.12
	3rd	1.44
	4th	1.13
	5th	0.91
Final drive	3.65 to 1	

Suspension and Steering

Front	MacPherson struts, coil springs, anti-roll bar
Rear	Torsion beam, trailing arms, coil springs, anti-roll bar Suspension lowered by 15mm (0.6in) compared to other Mk1 Golfs

Steering	Maintenance-free self-adjusting rack and pinion
Tyres	175/70 HR-13
Wheels	5.5J × 13 alloys

Brakes

Type	Diagonally divided dual circuit with brake servo and brake pressure regulator
Size	Front 239mm (9.4in) diameter discs, internally ventilated Rear 226mm (8.9in) diameter self-adjusting drums

Dimensions

Track	
Front	1.404mm (55.3in)
Rear	1,372mm (54.0in)
Wheelbase	2,400mm (94.5in)
Overall length	3,815mm (150.2in)
Overall width	1,630mm (64.1in)
Overall height	1,395mm (54.9in)
Unladen weight	860kg (1,896lb) – quoted by Volkswagen for both the three- and five-door model!

Performance

Top speed	183km/h (114mph)
	0–80km/h (0–50mph) 6.2sec
	0–100km/h (0–62mph) 8.2sec

Runaway, Run-Out GTI

These days, it's a sure sign that a model is nearing the end of its lifespan when the words 'Match' or 'Highline', to name but two of Volkswagen's favourites, raise their heads above the automotive skyline. Easy to categorize by upgrades in alloy wheels and extras in comparative abundance, the trend, at least in Volkswagen's water-cooled era, started with a run-out model of the Mk1 GTI, a vehicle that is now highly sought after.

Christened the Campaign GTI in later years, this limited-edition sales booster was launched in May 1983 in Germany, a full two months and more before finally arriving in right-hand-drive form for the British market. To indicate the nature of its exclusivity, just 1,000 models were available for customers on this side of the Channel, the plan being to have completely sold out before the arrival of the Mk2 Golf in GTI form.

Variances in the specification between Britain and the rest of Europe were quickly apparent, but the essential elements of the Campaign model were distinguishable right across Europe and beyond. For several years there had been a lively aftermarket trade in four-headlamp conversions for the GTI. For the Campaign model this beefier package was thrown in as standard, improving the Golf's purposeful look no end. Attractive Pirelli 6J × 14 alloy wheels were instantly identifiable by their distinctive 'P-shaped' cut-outs. Best of all, though, was the upgrade from

continued next page

13 to 14in wheels, which in turn was conveniently linked to the tyres. From the standard GTI's 175/70 tyres, Campaign owners could not only boast of their Pirelli wheels, but also of 185/60HR 14 P6 rubber. Additionally, both a steel-sliding sunroof and tinted window glass were standard, while on the Continent, but not in Britain, the plastic wheel-arch extensions and bumpers (with the exception of the centre strip) were colour-coded to the main body of the car.

Volkswagen UK owns the Diamond Silver Campaign model GTI featured here. Built in October 1983, three months after the debut of the second-generation Golf, the car was first registered in January 1984 and would have cost its owner £7,156. The 1781cc fuel-injected engine developed 112ps at 5,800rpm and had a top speed of 183km/h (114mph). Volkswagen listed amongst its attributes the Pirelli 'P' 6J × 14 alloys with 175/70 HR13 tyres, lowered suspension, front and rear anti-roll bars, red-lined grille, twin halogens, front 'bucket' seats, multifunction computer and black/grey body 'stripes'.

A publicity shot of a Campaign GTI, on this occasion finished in black, a colour that shows off the red-lined grille and silver body stripes to perfection. (Photograph Courtesy of Volkswagen AG)

a starting point of 'Bettering the best', the magazine poured superlative upon superlative:

> The new GTI can be summed up by saying that it preserves all that was right about the old one, and adds even better performance. ... The old engine delighted with its smoothness and eagerness. The new one does too, resoundingly, and even more so ... the power unit is more flexible and certainly just as marvellously rapid ... the GTI never sags it just goes, gloriously ... As an example of safe high performance in a small car, the GTI always was very good: in this fuller-blooded but still very civilized 1.8-litre version it is even better.

Motor was similarly impressed and made considerable play on the dreaded subject of price – in Volkswagen's favour: 'VW have raised the capacity of the GTI's jewel-like single overhead cam "four" from 1.6 to 1.8-litres, given its stronger legs a longer stride, and installed a multifunction on-board computer – all without hiking the price.' The tester's conclusion must have warmed the cockles of the hearts of VW's people in this country and, providing the report filtered back to Germany, impressed no lesser a figure than the latest Director General, Carl Hahn: 'The GTI still rules. The best car in its class has been made better: quicker, thriftier, quieter.'

End Notes

Despite the introduction of a second-generation Golf in August 1983, production of the Mk1 continued for several more months, finally coming to a permanent halt on 31 December 1983. However, there are several aspects of the Mk1 GTI story that haven't been covered yet, each being worthy of more than a few lines. From mock GTIs and topless versions, to the awful state of affairs to be found at the time in the USA, plus the rise of a booted edition of the Golf, a new car that could well have had sporting pretensions, the Mk1 story isn't as yet quite complete.

Also, perhaps it's worth getting the GTI into perspective. The implication drawn has been clear; the GTI was popular from its inception and as a result it became the mainstay of Golf sales. Sadly, this is far from the truth, as the table indicates. Also, it's worth noting just how low UK sales were, even after the arrival of the GTI in right-hand-drive form.

		Comparative GTI Sales			
Year	*GTI Sales – Europe*	*GTI Sales – Britain*	*GTI Sales – USA*	*Total Golf Production*	
1976	10,366			527,084	
1977	31,746			553,989	
1978	42,293	22		714,947	
1979	58,252	1,573		833,625	
1980	68,599	1,449		831,527	
1981	72,394	3,834		799,287	
1982	62,529	3,830	8,074	656,359	
1983	71,002	6,148	36,375	626,797	

The owner of this second-edition Golf Driver has added attractive BBS alloys, making the car look even sportier despite its humble 1300 60ps engine. With a retail price in 1983 of £4874.94, plus £99.67 for metallic paint, the Driver represented exceptional value and went a good way to looking like the real GTI.

The GTI lookalike, the limited edition 1300 engine Driver, proved to be very popular. The cover of this special brochure produced to market the model relates to the 1979 edition as evidenced by the single headlamps. A less attractive brochure was produced to promote the second edition of the Driver in 1983.

Golf Driver

Without any shadow of a doubt, a proper sheep in wolf's clothing, the limited-edition Golf Driver launched in June 1979 for the British market was little more than a cosmetic package based on the 1.3 Golf designed at first glance to look like a GTI. That the brochure boasted about a 0–50mph (80km/h) time in 8.6sec quickly gives the game away, but GTI side stripes and black plastic wheel-arch extensions, larger 5½J × 13 wheels (if not necessarily pure GTI), a sports steering wheel and equally sporty looking seats, plus the GTI's black velour carpets and hallmark golf-ball-shaped gear knob, to name most of the perks, pandered to illusions of power. Even the fact that the Driver, like the GTI, was only available as a three-door model, served to strengthen the fantasy. Sadly, the biggest giveaway of all was in the exterior paintwork, in that two out of the three options available, namely Mandarin

The Golf Driver branding was used on the hatch as well as on the car front grille.

Orange and Santos Green, were not GTI colours in Britain. However, when finished in Mars Red, the Golf Driver with its special badge on the grille certainly went some way to looking the part.

Definitely a marketing success, the Driver was reborn towards the end of Mk1 production, the brochure issued at the time being dated April 1983. Again based on the 1.3-litre power plant, the aim once more was to produce a lookalike GTI. The brochure copy-writer referred to the Driver's 'strong sporting image with black beaded wheel arches, wide profile tyres, chunky side stripes and inside, a four-spoke sports steering wheel and golf-ball gear knob'. Particularly pertinent for 1983 was the apparent pre-empting of the Campaign model's 'twin front head and fog lamps'. Easy for an avid GTI fan to detect as not being what it might appear to be, this time around the Driver was available in six paint shades, only two of which were official GTI options at least in this country, none other than the ubiquitous Mars Red and the late arrival, Alpine White.

A Topless GTI

If for no other reason than that the niche-market Cabriolet version of the Beetle, introduced in 1950, remained within the confines set by its hefty price premium over that of the air-cooled saloon, eventually breaking the world production record of 331,426 cars in 1978, it was almost inevitable that there would be a soft-top Golf.

Unbeknown to the world at large, the coachbuilder Karmann of Osnabrück, the firm responsible for not only the Beetle Cabriolet, but also the air-cooled Karmann Ghias based on the Beetle and the larger VW 1500/1600 respectively, plus the sporty bodied Scirocco, had set to work on ripping the top off the Golf during the course of 1976. The result of their efforts was presented to the world at the 1979 Geneva Motor Show, signalling the end of the road for the soft-top Beetle that had out-lived German production of the Beetle saloon.

Compared to the comparative ease with which it was possible to adapt the separate chassis standard Beetle to open-top Cabriolet usage without losing rigidity, a modern mono-coque vehicle proved a far greater challenge. To add to Karmann's concerns, rumours were rife of an impending American safety legislation effectively dismissing all types of open-topped cars as inherently dangerous, in turn leading to a blanket ban on such vehicles.

To restore the necessary rigidity to the open-top Golf's structure, Karmann added both cross-members and reinforcements along the sills. The latter ran the length of the car between the front and rear wheel arches and were welded to the inner wings. The boot of the Cabriolet, already reduced considerably in size when compared to that of the normal hatch thanks to the need to store the hood, became smaller still, as a sheet metal box was installed with the purpose of bracing the rear of the car. Key amongst the cross-members was the hefty one welded in place under the dashboard, although the box section beam positioned behind the rear seats was also essential to the design. Additionally, the car's suspension turrets were also reinforced. Most important of all, however, was a rollover bar, which was welded both to the stiffening sills and the sheet metal of the car. Its inclusion enabled the Golf Cabriolet to defy US concerns, as the vehicle sailed through the strict rollover test for all saloons as dictated in the

A survivor from the early days of Golf Cabriolet production pictured at GTI International in the summer of 2007. Badged as a GLi, only the additional weight associated with its construction prevented the Cabriolet keeping pace with its tin-topped sibling. According to an update issued with the Cabriolet brochure dated August 1979, or the start of the 1980 model year, the open-top car was available in four paint options for the UK market. These were Brazil Brown Metallic, Diamond Silver Metallic and Black, while the fourth option, River Blue Metallic, is illustrated in the photographs. Brown and Black cars had sand-coloured hoods, the other options were offered with black roof fabrics.

United States Federal Motor Vehicle Safety Standard 208.

Unquestionably an element of the Beetle Cabriolet's enduring success had lain in the complex, many layered and comprehensively watertight hood, complete with a proper glass window, which in later years even extended to a demisting facility. Karmann saw the immediate advantage of fast-forwarding this arrangement to the Golf and in so doing further threatened the survival chances of the less well-prepared soft-tops built by other manufacturers. The copywriters had a field day when it came to describing the properties of the hood, as an extract from the UK launch brochure serves to illustrate:

Between closed and watertight there is a very fine difference, through which many an irritating draught and impertinent raindrop can slip. And because we know that this is the sort of thing that can get even the most dauntless convertible motorist down in the long run, we put a great deal of care and thought into this point in particular. Our efforts were well rewarded: a top made of five layers and ready to face all winds and weathers. In the centre there is a thick layer, which not only keeps it perfectly watertight, but beautifully warm as well.

As if to indicate that the Cabriolet version of the Golf wasn't really a sporting model, an automatic option was available.

Golf GLi Cabriolet 1980 Model Year

Engine

Type	Transversely mounted 4-cylinder in-line
Bore and stroke	79.5 × 80.0 mm
Capacity	1588cc
Valves	Two valves per cylinder
Compression ratio	9.5:1
Fuel injection	Bosch K-Jetronic
Max. power	110ps at 6,100rpm
Max. torque	102.9lb ft at 5,000rpm
Fuel capacity	55ltr (12gal)

Transmission

	Front-wheel-drive
Gearbox	Five-speed manual
Clutch	Single dry plate

Suspension and Steering

Front	MacPherson struts, coil springs, anti-roll bar
Rear	Torsion beam, trailing arms, coil springs, anti-roll bar
Steering	Maintenance free self-adjusting rack and pinion
Tyres	175/70 HR13
Wheels	5.5J × 13 Alloy

Brakes

Type	Diagonally divided dual circuit with brake servo and brake pressure regulator
Size	Front 238mm (9.4in) diameter discs, internally ventilated. Rear 180mm (7.1in) diameter self-adjusting drums

Dimensions

Track	
Front	1,404mm (55.3in)
Rear	1,372mm (54.0in)
Wheelbase	2,400mm (94.5in)
Overall length	3,815mm (150.2in)
Overall width	1,628mm (64.1in)
Overall height	1,395mm (54.9in)
Unladen weight	940kg (2,072lb)

Performance

Top speed	180km/h (112mph)
	0–100km/h (0–62mph)
	10.2sec

With the hood up, it was easy to imagine that the journey was taking place in a normal saloon; with the top down riding in the Cabriolet was the most enjoyable of experiences for the front seat passenger and driver. Inevitably, rear seat passengers were buffeted to some extent by the wind, while access for the third or fourth occupant was undoubtedly hindered by the presence of the hefty anti-roll bar. Like that of the Beetle before it, raising or lowering the hood was a very simple task, accomplished in a very short space of time. To drop the hood, all that was necessary was to release the two handles positioned above the windscreen, then push the material backwards, where it collected into a neat concertina-style file. Raising the hood was equally easy and involved freeing a safety catch, pulling the material towards the screen, releasing the handles and then pulling them taut once more.

The downside of producing the safest Cabriolet in the world was that it was inevitably going to be heavier than a normal tin-top model: indeed weightier to the tune of 136kg (300lb), a factor that would have a direct bearing on the car's performance.

The fun factor behind the Cabriolet undoubtedly lent itself to the inclusion of the hottest of engines in the options for most, if not all, markets. Indeed, the launch brochure for the UK market shows the 1588cc, 110ps offering to be the only one. However, Volkswagen had to acknowledge that the weight penalty imposed on the Cabriolet resulted in suppressed performance, with a quoted 0–100km/h time of 10.2sec. As the years went by, more options became available in the UK with a 1457cc GL, in both manual and automatic form, being added. As for the GLi, as the sporty version was known, when the 1800 engine became available, this was immediately offered in the Cabriolet, producing a claimed 0–60mph time of 9.0sec.

Harking back to the days of the Beetle once more, the Cabriolet had always benefited from the most luxurious specification available at the time and, as larger air-cooled engines were developed, it had been endowed with the most powerful version. Continuing that air of exclusivity, while it might have been inappropriate to move the trimmings of the metal-roof GTI lock, stock and barrel to the soft-top, the key elements were conveniently cherry-picked and blended with the deep-pile comforts of the then most lavish trim on offer, that of the GL:

Just take a look into the Golf Convertible. It is simply chock-a-block full of interesting and useful details: luminous cigarette lighter, ashtray and heating lever. A windscreen wiper with intermittent operation setting and automatic wash/wipe. An outside mirror that can be adjusted from inside. A padded instrument panel with rev counter and dimmable dial illumination. An elegant carpet covering the whole interior. Parking light, three-speed air blower, a shelf with the width of the whole instrument panel, a quartz clock, a trip mileage recorder. And so on and so forth. The Golf Convertible is, logically, available with these luxurious appointments, which are largely identical with those of the GL saloon. There's no need for us here to go into great detail about the engineering of the Golf Convertible. It suffices to say that it comes from the Golf saloon. And that tells you everything. About its quality, its performance and its durability. For your safety we have built a stable roll bar into the Golf Convertible. This roll bar is well padded all round and accommodates the upper anchorage points for the safety belts … Under the bonnet of the Golf Convertible GLi lies a 110bhp fuel-injected engine. This gives you a top speed of 112mph and gets you to 60mph in a quick 10.9sec. Safety to match performance is provided by a low-slung chassis. And internally ventilated disc brakes with a brake pressure regulator makes for instant braking power.

Press comments regarding the Golf Cabriolet were invariably in the form that would have been music to both Volkswagen and Karmann's ears. Placing the Golf head on against the Ford Escort Cabriolet 1.6i at just about the time when the Mk2 Golf was about to make

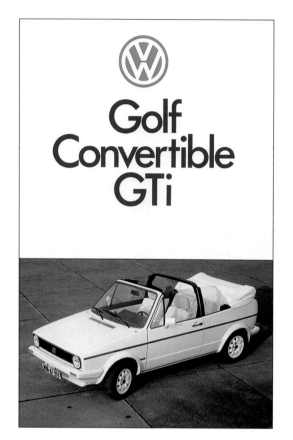

The cover of the special brochure designed to promote the all-white Cabrio, an attractive but somewhat impractical soft-top that could easily have been mistaken for a limited edition runout model. Note particularly the white wheels and colour-coded bumpers. The paint shade was known as Alpine White.

its debut, *Motor* praised the Ford most highly, but nevertheless plunged for the Golf as the better of the two cars:

> It's the way a car performs that's equally – perhaps more – important, and it's the Golf GTI Convertible that appeals to the driver's heart as well as head. It begs to be driven quickly, yet remains refined and discreet when touring. The engine never loses its zest, the chassis is always composed. The Golf rewards – give it the gun and its performance is scintillating, take it to the shops and it won't misbehave. … We have no hesitation in choosing the Golf. Those who value sheer driving pleasure beyond more mundane considerations will not be disappointed …

Come the time of the imminent end of the life of the Mk1 Golf and the arrival of the Campaign model GTI, it might have looked as though the Cabriolet was heading in the same direction. In Britain, 'a convertible even more desirable than the Karmann built convertible Golf' was on offer:

> This exclusive Alpine White Convertible has a matching hood, white bumpers, white interior, adjustable door mirrors, white front spoiler and white painted alloy sports wheels. Even inside, the front sports seats and rear seats are trimmed in an attractive white cloth with tastefully designed thin

This extremely attractive example of a Golf Cabriolet, which dates from the era of the Mk2 saloon, serves to demonstrate that Volkswagen decided to run the Mk1 bodyshell throughout the years of second generation production and did so successfully without obvious signs of an obsolete appearance.

black stripes running horizontally across the upholstery. The door and side panels are trimmed in white leatherette with cloth inset on the doors. … Matched to the elegance of the 'all white' Convertible is exhilarating performance provided by the renowned Volkswagen 1800cc fuel-injection engine – which has gained its reputation in the cult setting hard-topped Golf GTI. This engine powers the Golf Convertible GTI through its five gears to a top speed of 108mph and to 60mph from standstill in only nine seconds. All this performance without sacrificing economy – at a steady 56mph the 'all-white' Convertible will return over 46mpg.

While the 'all-white' Cabriolet was easy to mistake for a run-out model, nothing could have been further from the truth. The Mk1 Cabriolet was destined to stay in production for many years, indeed throughout the lifespan of the Mk2 Golf. The logic behind such a move was simple; producing a template for a Cabriolet was expensive, as only the front wings, bonnet and doors were carried over from the hatch when the Golf Cabriolet was introduced. While the car looked sufficiently modern and mechanical upgrades could be integrated with its body, Volkswagen or Karmann's designers could tinker with its specification. Far from being a run-out model, the 'all-white' Cabriolet was a forerunner of further special editions and foretold the overall appearance of the soft top over the next decade.

Rabbit, Rabbit

While space if nothing else precludes telling the story of Volkswagen's recurring misfortunes in America in the post air-cooled era, the very fact that the flagship GTI wasn't available in the USA until 1983 serves to indicate that all was far from well there in the years following the fall of the Beetle.

The Golf was introduced to North America in 1975 and branded as the Rabbit. Exactly why the change of name occurred is somewhat obscure, but as the Passat had become the Dasher, and even the Audi 80 had been renamed as the Fox, there was a precedent. The legend is that Rabbit was selected as a name implying an agile, fast creature, a theory that isn't entirely credible given the lop-natured personality of the beast. Fortunately, advertising gurus DDB turned the name to Volkswagen's advantage as only they could. Take as an example one of their adverts dating from the launch year, featuring a simple image of the Rabbit and the headline, 'No wonder Rabbits multiply so fast'.

Sales of the Rabbit were relatively healthy to start with, but well behind those of the Beetle in its heyday. Volkswagen's figures for total sales in the USA illustrate the point more than adequately. In 1968, 582,009 Volkswagens of all shapes and capacities were sold; three years later in 1971 that total had dropped fractionally to 532,904. In 1975, the year of the Rabbit's debut, total sales had slipped to a 268,751, a pattern that continued during the following year, when only 3,000 cars took Volkswagen over the 200,000 mark.

Sadly, the earlier Golfs imported to the USA were blemished with teething problems, most notably in the area of the carburettor (which led to both stalling and hesitation), oil-consumption issues and, worst of all, rust. Although some concerns were partially resolved, far greater issues lay just around the corner.

On 10 April 1978 the first Rabbit to be manufactured in the USA left the Westmoreland, Pennsylvania, assembly line, the purpose behind the move towards full manufacture being related to the comparative strength of the dollar against the deutschmark. Unfortunately, the homespun American Rabbit didn't capture the needs of the marketplace. Rectangular, rather than the circular headlamps of the Rabbit's European counterpart, may have been amenable to would-be purchasers, but the less supportive, poorly made and cheaper seats of US origins were definitely a cause for concern. Likewise, the colour-coded dashboard was of poor manufacture, leading to a

Background: Rabbit hatchback, Lago Blue. Foreground: Rabbit "L" 2-door hatchback, Sunbrite Yellow.

VW Rabbit.
The more you know it,
the more you like it.

Way back in 1974, Volkswagen reinvented the automobile. And ever since, we've been perfecting and improving our Original.

Today, Rabbit is among the most space-efficient cars you can own. And it is available in fuel-injected, gasoline engine models, as well as the popular Rabbit Diesel. Either way, our Original is available with VW's highly original passive restraint system.

The appearance of the American version of the Mk1 Golf, the Rabbit, as described and illustrated in a sales brochure dating from 1981, was always somewhat more cumbersome than that of its European counterpart. Rectangular headlamps and exceptionally heavy girder-style bumpers were the main contributory factors.

more general feeling of lower standards in quality. To make matters worse, US-manufactured Rabbits were more softly sprung, whilst also being heavier overall. Problems with valve guide seals led to the engines burning oil and, as Americans were used to driving long distances without resort to routine checking, premature engine failure.

Car and Driver's measured response to a few years of American manufacture was suitably damning: 'VW has soft-pedalled its German heritage in favour of an Americanized image. Suspension turned flaccid, seats became bench-flat, and the flash and filigree level rose alarmingly. If you wanted a German-style driver's car, you had to choose from one of the imported models on the dealer's floor, like the Jetta and Scirocco'.

In response to the growing wealth of frequently voiced criticism, in 1981 Volkswagen issued the Rabbit S, a car with stiffer suspension and sports seats amongst its attributes. The problem, however, was that it didn't possess a larger engine and as a result the better handling of the S model only served to emphasize that the car suffered from extra weight and a lack of appropriate power. To put it bluntly, VWoA's strategy had backfired and was damaging the brand. The American nadir came in 1982 when Rabbit sales fell by a staggering 50 per cent.

Motor Trend magazine was horrified that the Rabbit S was the best that VWoA was going to offer, even writing an open letter to them bemoaning the lot of the US Volkswagen owner, or would-be VW driver:

Volkswagen of America seems interested in selling economy only … It is our opinion that many Americans want more from a small car than just economy and would welcome a small high-performance gasoline-powered car. We don't subscribe to the notion that American car buyers are less demanding or sophisticated than the Europeans. So if the GTI is such a great success in Europe, why isn't it available in this country?

The US-made Rabbit S is really a detuned version of the GTI with a larger displacement engine. Both use a fuel-injection system. To equal the performance of a GTI, you would have to certify a new engine. Even if this cost you $250,000 dollars, and you sold only 20,000 cars, the cost of certification would add a mere $12.50 to the price of each car, an amount enthusiasts would gladly pay …

Introduction of a US GTI would be an inexpensive, yet effective, way of boosting the VW image here in America. So how about it, VWoA? Build us a Rabbit GTI and give Americans a reason to leave their Porsches at home.

Motor Trend's request was apparently heeded, for a GTI team was established under the wing of Duane Millar, VWoA's Vice President of Engineering. Two actions in Germany were fortuitous: the first, and by far the less significant, being the manufacture of an alloy wheel for the Quantum that was also suitable for a hot Rabbit; the second being the creation of an American specification version of the 1800 engine designed for European versions of the GTI engine.

Burdened with 5mph impact bumpers, emission controls and every American's expectation of air conditioning, the US specification GTI was some 90kg (200lb) heavier than its European counterpart. As a result the suspension of the two cars differed a little. Compared to the ordinary Rabbit the front spring rates were increased by 22 per cent, while at the car's rear, they were 29 per cent stiffer. The Rabbit GTI offered 90bhp at 5,500rpm, while maximum torque of 105lb ft occurred at 3,250rpm. The compression ratio stood at 8.5:1. Compared to a standard Rabbit the exhaust system was modified to accommodate a redesigned catalytic converter and a larger-diameter pipe. While the Rabbit GTI would have lost out to its European counterpart in a head-to-head race, nevertheless the much improved package, compared to that of the S or any of the US models, was quite spectacular. On a good run, 0–60mph was achieved in a respectable 10.0sec, falling away to 10.6sec on an average or poor one, while the car's top speed was confirmed to be 167km/h (104mph).

While Volkswagen was content simply to describe its new product and potential lifesaver as 'a wolf in sheep's clothing', journalists went to town, rolling out superlative after superlative, despite the 200lb weight penalty, the slower 0–60mph time and a fuel consumption figure of 11ltr/100km (26mpg). The very positive price of around $8,600 dollars undoubtedly helped, but the real key to the GTI's appeal in the USA was its ability not only to out-perform sporting vehicles that cost many thousands of dollars more, but also ones which showed little if any advantage in other ways.

Car and Driver magazine headed its preview test of the Rabbit GTI with the simple but effective heading, 'The car we've all been waiting for'. So thankful was the magazine that VWoA had finally seen fit to grant the overtly eager with the car they had been demanding, the report contained nothing but praise. An extract or two serves to convey the tone of the five-page report:

> Without further ado, allow us to introduce the latest autobahn panzer to grace our roads, the Volkswagen Rabbit GTI, from – wait a minute – Westmoreland County, Pennsylvania? That's right, Volkswagen of America is now producing a home-grown version of the little sedan we've been waiting for, the GTI – the perennial benchmark of high-performance European econoboxes. Better still, it works so well, you'd swear it came from Wolfsburg. … The new GTI is not a hard-edged street racer. The engine isn't shrill or peaky; the suspension doesn't jiggle or crash over the bumps. The GTI is far more sophisticated than that. It will stick like glue … but excellent roadholding is only half the story. It's also as composed and supple as the high-dollar brands over bad pavement, always on its toes through mountain switchbacks, and quick to answer your right foot at any speed. It never seems to breathe hard … What ultimately makes the GTI truly significant, however, is that it's the first car sold in the US to marry this level of driving satisfaction with the utility, compact dimensions, and fuel efficiency of an economy car … When it comes to sheer driving enjoyment, though, the new GTI currently stands in a class of one. True to its pedigree, it can make you feel great – and that's the best thing any car can do for its driver.

Road and Track's report, subtitled 'Street racer in a bunny suit', was equally fulsome in its praise of the late entry GTI. Amidst streams of superlatives however, *R&T* played the Joker with the message that the GTI was fun, and FUN in a big way. The following short extract not only includes the fun message, but also serves to illustrate the whole tone of the article:

> Let us tell you what really makes it different – the driving and simple, go-for-it fun, and we mean FUN! 'One quick trip around the block and you won't want to give this one up,' enthused one of our editors, while another described the GTI as a 'basic pocket-rocket street racer carried to subtle limits … The fun quotient in this sleeper is maximum!' And perhaps the most telling comment from one of us (keeping in mind that we each drive 80 to 100 different cars per year), 'Here's a car I would actually buy with my own money.'

Sales of the Rabbit GTI more than justified its existence; indeed, the vehicle proved to be a mainstay of VWoA's fortunes for a time. However, as the US story began, so must it conclude. Troubled times lay ahead for Volkswagen. The Beetle's unique characteristics had allowed VWoA greater leeway. When it came to so-called modern cars in the USA, while quality and performance were important factors, recognition that a saloon was by far higher in the preference stakes than ever a hatchback would be demanded action and so – belatedly in the scheme of Mk1 activity – the Jetta was born.

Golf with a Boot

With the emphasis being on performance, there isn't a great deal to say about the booted version of the Mk1 Golf, named in true Volkswagen style as the Jetta. Pre-empting succeeding chapters, the point is worth making that only in America – where the passion was, and remains, for a traditional three-box saloon – has the Jetta name survived throughout. After two generations of Jetta in Europe, both variations of which were obviously Golfs with boots more or less welded on, Volkswagen decided that a rebranding exercise was essential and

THE VOLKSWAGEN JETTA
The new VW Jetta   Volkswagen's important new entrant into the traditional medium-sized saloon market.
Pictured here the top of the range GLi version with its 1600cc 110bhp fuel injected engine.
Issued by the PR Dept, Volkswagen (GB) Ltd, Yeomans Drive, Blakelands, Milton Keynes. Tel: 0908 679121

The sporty version of the first booted Golf, branded as the Jetta. Denied full GTI status, the car was designated as a GLi. Volkswagen's press shots of the day didn't extend to colour.

promptly named the third-generation model saloon as the Vento. Disappointed once more despite the Vento's less obvious Golf ancestry, Volkswagen decided that the Mk4 Golf should be supplemented by yet another new name, this time the somewhat unfortunate designation, at least to British ears, of Bora. Despite the elegance of this particular car and reasonable sales, the name remained strictly a one-off.

Press releases pertaining to the launch of the Mk5 notchback make interesting reading and unintentionally confirm where loyalty to the booted concept has always remained steady. Typical is the release from the British Press Office dated 2 December 2005, written some two months before the UK launch in February 2006:

The Jetta replaces the Bora, and signals the revival of the Jetta name in Europe. By introducing a worldwide, uniform name for its compact saloon, Volkswagen decided to adopt the one already used in the USA, where the Jetta is not only the company's best-selling car, but also the top-selling European car outright.

Equally significant is the realization that the US version of the Jetta came onto the market ahead of its European counterpart by many months and, astonishingly to those resident on this side of the Atlantic, ahead of the Mk5 version of the Golf. However, browsing through selected years of sales of the Jetta in the USA compared to those of the hatch helps to explain a great deal.

By 1991, Volkswagen was firmly in the doldrums in the USA. Just 96,736 vehicles were sold during the year. Of these 38,017 were Jettas, while the combined total for the Golf and GTI amounted to just 14,340 cars, outclassed by the Passat at 16,139 and within a whisper of being eclipsed by the Brazilian-built Fox at 13,463. Come 1993, and the nadir as far as sales in America were concerned, of the mere 49,533 Volkswagens sold, 14,582 were Jettas, compared to 4,554 Golfs and just 139 GTIs. Fast-forwarding to the days when the New Beetle galvanized Volkswagen's revival, in 1999 total sales amounted to 315,563 cars. Of these 130,054 were Jettas, 13,816 Golfs and 5,174 GTIs, demonstrating that despite the renaissance, the pattern of preference for a boot rather than a hatch continued.

Introduced at the Frankfurt Motor Show in September 1979, the 164.9in Jetta (compared to the 150.2in Golf) was available from the start with a sporty engine as well as the more mundane 60ps 1300 and 70ps 1500 offerings. Presented as both a two-door and four-door in Germany, in Britain the Jetta was only offered with the family-friendly option of more, rather than less, doors. As has already been mentioned, in Germany the Golf GTI was offered as both a three- and five-door hatch, but in the UK only the single, young and unattached option was available. Somewhere along the line, the decision had been taken that a three-box saloon suited older, more conservative, family owners.

While every now and then, clever marketing slogans such as 'the boot's in the back; the kick's up front', were bandied about, the launch brochure for the Jetta in Britain shows in comparatively few words how little focus was paid to the prospects of the car as a hot saloon:

> There is a choice of three powerful engines. The 1300cc with a top speed of 92mph, the 1500cc which accelerates from 0–50mph in 8.5sec or the 1600cc fuel-injected GLi which develops 110bhp

and doesn't hang about – it gets the Jetta to 50mph in a quick 6.4sec.

With reference to the 880kg (1,940lb) Jetta's 0–60mph time of 9.5sec being relegated to the small print, and after all that was only marginally slower than the lighter 810kg (1,786lb) kerb-weight GTI at 8.8sec, the sporty package, identical in terms of both the engine and alloy wheels was dismissed in just one brief sentence: 'In addition, the fuel-injected GLi has alloy sports wheels and a five speed sports box.'

Even in the technical specification, or other footnotes, it was either difficult or impossible to find mention of anti-roll bars front and rear, brakes encompassing ventilated front discs, go-faster stripes along the lower parts of the doors and plastic wheel extensions – all characteristics of the GLI's specification and important to a sporting design.

If there was one area in which the GLi was inferior to the GTI, it had to be the interior, for here there was nothing to indicate anything other than a higher-end level of trim for the family man. Not only was the GTI's three-spoke steering wheel missing, but also the GLi didn't have sports seats, was deprived of the GTI's black headlining in favour of the normal light-coloured one and, most important of all, lacked the GTI's temperature gauge.

In the greater scheme of things, the GLi seems to have been little more than an irritant: a sop to a voice or two calling for a hot saloon, or an unnecessary specification level in most respects. Perhaps it wasn't a great surprise when, for the second year of Jetta production, the GLi was dropped. The speculative reason was that demand for the fuel-injected 1600 engine was so strong that Volkswagen was having difficulty producing enough. No higher-powered Jetta to consider and life became considerably easier almost at a stroke.

3 Two: Sprinting Ahead

Getting the New Golf (GTI) Right

Volkswagen's hierarchy of the later years of the 1970s bore no relation to the team in place a decade previously. Everyone, and most noticeably Director General and ex-Ford man, Toni Schmücker, took it for granted that the best-selling Golf would be replaced by an improved model within a comparatively short period of time, in line with the *modus operandi* of other successful manufacturers. One question that did arise was whether Volkswagen's in-house designers, under the leadership of Herbert Schäfer, would be allotted full responsibility for this most important of projects, or if the expertise of freelance stylists such as Giugiaro should also be requested to enter submissions. As early as November 1978 there were ten concepts to choose from, but after studying the responses of a group of 500 specially invited participants at a series of customer clinics, Volkswagen's management decided to progress one of their own in-house designs. Prototypes sufficiently advanced to be roadworthy were available during the course of May 1980. Once general testing and specific crash analysis had been completed,

During the eight-year production life of the Mk2 GTI a great deal happened. At the start a trend was set, with the decision to retain the overall visual appearance of the first Golf in the new car. Each subsequent generation would take the concept forwards, invariably accompanied by an increase in the overall size of the vehicle. Nevertheless, the last of the Mk5 GTIs was still recognizable as coming from the same stable as the first of the Mk1s. However, it was in terms of power development that the Mk2 will best be remembered, with the successive introduction of a 16-valve engine, a limited-edition permanent four-wheel-drive supercharged Golf and finally a similarly aspirated production model, but without four-wheel drive, a car that gave Continental customers the choice of three GTIs.

twenty-two examples of the new Golf were despatched to Volkswagen's proving ground in Ehra-Lessien, where they were later joined by a number of vehicles from the first pre-production batch of 300 cars. Between them, they covered some 3,700,000 miles.

Curiously, after such determination to move with the times and introduce a new model before the original Golf was anywhere near its sell-by date, the selected design bucked the general trend and bore a strong visual resemblance to its predecessor; a trait that would be perpetuated at least as far as Volkswagen's mainstay went for the next twenty years and more. Schäfer told the world that 'The Golf must remain a Golf. Therefore the new Golf will inherit the look of the Mk1 Golf with its typical shape.' The original Golf had two noticeable shortcomings: the first related to insufficient legroom for even the average-sized rear seat passenger; the second was with regard to luggage-carrying capacity, even though this was far more generous than it had been for Beetle owners. The task therefore was to make the original car both longer and wider, while also adding extra height. In the interests of improving aerodynamics – an important consideration when it was virtually inevitable that the new larger Golf would be heavier than the original – the design edges needed to be rounder, with the more obtrusive features melded wherever possible into the overall shape.

Using like-for-like GTI model specifications, the skill with which Schäfer and his team accomplished the task set is quickly appreciated. Crucially, the new Golf had a longer wheelbase, measuring 2,475mm (97.4in) compared to 2,400mm (94.5in), or an increase of 75mm (2.9in). This helped to accommodate an overall increase in length to 3,985mm (156.9in) compared with the Mk1's total of 3,815mm (150.2in) in its big-bumper format. The width of the older GTI was recorded as 1,630mm (64.1in), while that of the new model showed a growth of 50mm (2in) to 1,680mm (66.1in). To keep the record straight if not to draw all-in comparisons, the new Golf GTI stood at a height of 1,405mm (55.3in) contrasted with the old model's measurement of 1,390mm (54.7in), while its lowered suspension meant that it sat squatter than the rest of the new model range by 10mm (0.4in). As previously, the Mk2 GTI had a wider front and rear track than the rest of the range, most models' statistics coming out at 1,413mm (55.1in) front and 1,408mm (54.9in) rear, compared to the Mk1 GTI's of 1,432mm (55.8in) and 1,429mm (55.7in), respectively.

The resultant increase in weight took the Mk2 two-door GTI to 920kg (2,029lb) from a previous figure of 860kg (1,896lb) (the four-door model weighed in at 940kg/2,072lb, the extra doors costing 20kg/44lb as Volkswagen ensured the cars were as rigid as each other), but this didn't necessarily equate to a slower Golf, or one that used more fuel. For the UK market, Volkswagen produced a promotional pamphlet entitled, 'The new Golf. Or how to make a best-seller still better', a brochure that sold the story particularly well, and an ideal document from which to draw a few words:

> Volkswagen presents: the new Golf. Not a futuristic experiment in an early stage of its development. But a logical progression of the world's most successful automobile concept of the last ten years. Once again, setting new standards for an entire class of motoring by means of an impressive list of design improvements.

Covering all aspects of the car, from three brand new engines (the GTI's was subtly modified but not sufficiently enough to warrant a mention in the brochure) to a larger fuel tank, from improved corrosion protection through, for instance, the use of over 2.3kg (5lb) of hot wax to flood the lower body cavities and plastic front wheel-arch linings, to a new design of tail light to enable a wider tailgate opening and the consequent ability to load larger objects more easily. Key, though, and particularly so to the performance-leading and top-of-the-range specification GTI, was the following, neatly summarized in the opening gambit Mk2 brochure:

> Better: lower interior noise level ... down by 3 dB in the new Golf. ... Better: ... the rear seat backs have been heightened for added back support and rear seat passengers have more legroom behind and beneath the front seats. ... Better: sheer space. The new Golf is bigger. It is longer and wider. This larger exterior has particularly benefited the interior passenger area. There is more legroom, headroom and shoulder room. And doors are bigger for easier entry and exit. ... Better: driving safety. The new Golf incorporates still greater occupant safety features: a strong passenger compartment structure that remains intact on impact, energy absorbing zones at the front and rear ... Better: luggage space. 30 per cent more space. ... Better: rain channels. They are plastic and integrated into the roof of the new Golf to aid good aerodynamics. ... Better: aerodynamics. With a Cd value of only 0.34, the new Golf leads its class.

Succinctly, the new Golf's similarity in shape to that of the Mk1, noticeably the retention, or even of enlarging, the characteristic wide C-pillars, belie noticeable improvements. Although the frontal area was slightly larger, a combination of the new model's more slippery shape, its adoption of recessed rain gutters, side glass that

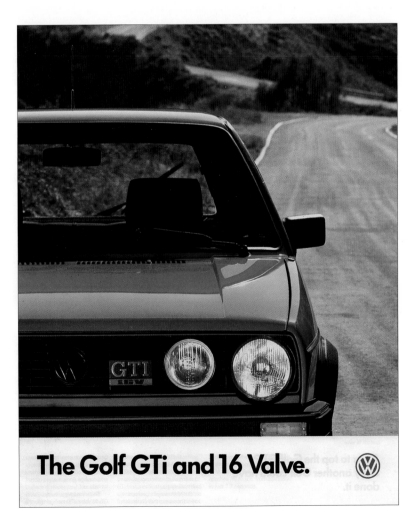

Understandably proud of the 16-valve GTI, Volkswagen displayed its badge prominently on the cover of its brochure. For many years Wolfsburg overlooked the erroneous description of the GTI as a GTi!

The Golf GTi and 16 Valve.

This very original Mk2 GTI 8-valve was on show at GTI International in 2007. Only the alloys are noticeable additions to the standard specification. The car is finished in Medium Blue Metallic, one of eleven options open to purchasers of 1990 model year cars in the UK.

was flusher to the body, and an underbody deflector that pushed airflow around the silencer, ensured that drag coefficient improved from a respectable 0.42 to a class-leading 0.34.

Carrying the engine, gearbox, suspension and steering on a rubber-mounted subframe not only had the effect of providing additional insulation from both mechanical and road noise, but also improved the torsional stiffness of the front end. The section of the torsion cross-beam was changed to an open channel from an inverted L-shape, one effect being that the GTI's anti-roll bar could run inside, while the design of the rear attachment points and bushes was amended to cater for an increased degree of rear suspension wheel travel, thus creating a more comfortable ride. As the size of the engine bay was larger, there was scope to accommodate power steering, although this wasn't done until the 1986 model year, and also to ensure that owners of RHD Golfs had appropriate brake servo and wiper systems.

Specifically GTI

As already indicated, the new GTI was powered by the same 1.8-litre engine as the latter-day Mk1 hot hatch. However, Volkswagen had made a couple of fine-tuning improvements. First, the twin butterfly throttle body had been upgraded to a 35/52mm unit with the effect of developing low-speed torque, while helping the engine to breathe better at high revs. A new manifold and air-shrouded injectors resulted in improved fuel-mixture control at lower speeds, while the effect of both measures was to boost torque from the Mk1's utmost of 109lb ft at 3,500rpm to 114lb ft at 3,100rpm. Although maximum power remained the same at 112ps, the number of revs at which this was achieved dropped from 5,800rpm to 5,500rpm. Finally, of note in this field, the oil cooler had become water-cooled, which both ensured a faster warm-up time and stabilization of engine temperature at higher speeds.

For would-be GTI owners, the all-important top speed and the equally, if not more so,

0–100km/h sprint figure, made interesting reading. Volkswagen's official documents indicated a maximum for the Mk1 of 183km/h (114mph), while the heavier Mk2 GTI was shown as being capable of 192km/h (119mph). However, the blast through the gears didn't look quite so good for the Mk2, particularly as the goalposts had been changed somewhat. The Mk1 was shown as having achieved 60mph in 8.2sec, whereas the 9.7sec time for the new car was based on the continental norm of a 0–100km/h gallop. *Motor* magazine got its hands on a new GTI ready for publication of the full test details in the May 1984 issue, and first suggested that the old model could cover 0–60mph in 8.1sec, before trimming the difference for the new car right down to just 0.2sec, allocating a 0–60mph sprint of 8.3sec to the Mk2 GTI. As for *Drive* magazine, the in-house publication for AA members, it was content to note that the Mk2 could blast its way up 160km/h (100mph) in under 25sec, while suggesting that maximum speed was no more than 187km/h (116mph) and that the 0–60mph figure was no better than 8.9sec. *Autocar*, which ran a Mk2 GTI on one of its well-known long-term tests, might have had a Friday afternoon car, for even after it had been given more time to loosen up, this particular GTI wouldn't budge away from a rather leisurely 0–60mph amble of 9.2sec, while its maximum speed was a slightly under par 185km/h (115mph).

Apparently against the odds, fuel consumption was certainly no worse than that of the Mk1 GTI, with a recorded urban figure of 10.3ltr/100km (27.4mpg), 5.8ltr/100km (48.7mpg) at a steady 90km/h (56mph) and 7.6ltr/100km (37.2mpg) at a law-breaking 120km/h (75mph). Wheels and tyres on the Mk1 GTI, at 5.5J × 13 and 175/70 HR 13, respectively, became larger and meatier at 6J × 14 for the former, shod with 185/60 HR 14s.

What was undeniable to all, and a great relief to many, was the decision to abandon the cost-cutting and life-endangering practice of fitting the GTI with drum brakes on its rear wheels instead of offering discs all round.

Golf GTI Mk2 8-Valve 1984

Engine		Tyres	185/60 HR 14
Type	Transversely mounted 4-cylinder in-line	Wheels	6J × 14 – alloys standard on five door – optional on three door
Bore and stroke	81mm × 86.4mm		
Capacity	1781cc	**Brakes**	
Compression ratio	10.0:1	Type	Diagonally divided dual circuit
Fuel injection	Bosch K-Jetronic		with brake servo and brake
Max. power	112ps at 5,500rpm		pressure regulator
Max. torque	114lb ft at 3,100rpm	Size	Front 239mm (9.4in) diameter
Fuel capacity	55ltr (12.1gal)		discs, internally ventilated –
			single piston sliding caliper
Transmission			Rear 226mm (8.9in) solid disc
Gearbox	Five-speed all indirect with synchromesh		and single piston sliding caliper
Clutch	Single dry plate	**Dimensions**	
Ratios	1st 3.46	Track	
	2nd 2.12	Front	1.413mm (56.2in)
	3rd 1.44	Rear	1,408mm (56in)
	4th 1.13	Wheelbase	2,475mm (97.4in)
	5th 0.89	Overall length	3,985mm (156.9in)
Final drive	3.67 to 1	Overall width	1,680mm (66.1in)
		Overall height	1,405mm (55.3in)
Suspension and Steering		Unladen weight	920kg (2,029lb) three-door;
Front	MacPherson strut and lower wishbone, 18mm (0.7in) anti-roll bar		940kg (2,072lb) four-door
		Performance	
Rear	Torsion beam, trailing arms, 20mm (0.78in) anti-roll bar	Top speed	192km/h (119mph)
			0–80km/h (0–50mph) 6.5sec
Steering	Maintenance free self-adjusting rack and pinion		0–100km/h (0–62mph) 8.3sec

A Medium Blue Metallic 8-valve GTI pictured with the optional 6J × 14 alloys of a two-door model, which were fitted as standard on some four-door cars.

At 239mm (9.4in), the ventilated front discs were identical in size to those on the Mk1 GTI, while the new solid rear discs measured 226mm (8.9in).

A Good-Looking GTI

When it was launched on the UK market shortly after the rest of the Mk2 range in the spring of 1984, the GTI was available in the expected shades of Black, Mars Red and Diamond Silver metallic, plus the later Mk1 classic of Alpine White, to which was added the somewhat conservative colour of Atlas Grey metallic. Although the first brochures depicted the GTI with single headlamps, errata stickers noted amongst other non-GTI related matters that twin headlamps were indeed standard. Early models could also be distinguished by a second generation of Pirelli 'P' alloy wheels, but it wouldn't be all that long before three-door GTIs would be fitted with steel wheels, alloys being reserved for the five-door model, when that option was first introduced at the beginning of 1985 to the UK market. (Later still, all cars came with steel wheels as standard – a retrograde step that would be unprecedented in years to come.) Of the other external items Volkswagen listed as being standard to the GTI, but over and above the specification of the GL, all were carry-overs from

Mk1 days, but nevertheless still possessed enough sway to make the GTI stand out from the crowd. These additions came in the form of black wheel-arch extensions, a rear hatch spoiler, black vinyl surround fitted to the rear window of appropriately light coloured vehicles, black or silver side stripes – again depending on the car's paint shade – matt black body trim, an enlarged but subtly redesigned front spoiler, and of course the hallmark 'red trim strips on radiator grille'.

Inside, the car was also instantly recognizable as a Golf GTI, although it did incorporate some of the features attributed to the run-out Campaign model. Apart from the gloomy black headlining, which to be honest the majority of fans appeared to approve of, other old familiars included the golf-ball gear knob and sports seats that amazingly were covered with the same loosely woven striped material

---

Mk2 GTI Paintwork Options 1984

In addition to the original choices of black, red and silver, all three of which were still offered in their original hues of Black, Mars and Diamond, respectively, the Mk2 GTI could be specified in Alpine White and Atlas Grey metallic. However, the total number of paint options available on the UK market for one model or another totted up to fourteen.

Although the superstitious might be wary of a green car, GTIs like this late model 8-valve GTI finished in Oak Green Metallic have always proved popular.

as those of the Mk1. The four-button sports steering wheel, an MFA trip computer and gear-change indicator were additional items that demonstrated the GTI's higher than average specification.

Initial Verdicts

With the undoubted benefits afforded by hindsight, we all know that the Mk2 GTI is assured of a reputable place in history. Admittedly, its greatest glories came at least part-way into its production run, but to relive some of the contemporary reviews of first-year Mk2 GTIs it could be easily assumed that Volkswagen had committed something of a *faux pas*. *Autocar*, for example, couldn't quite make its mind up about the car, blowing from hot, even boiling, one minute, to lukewarm, bordering on cold, the next: 'Our long-term GTI has been so reliable it is almost boring, were it not for the fact, of course, that it is an extremely exciting motor car.' In addition:

> On the plus side is the beautifully balanced handling combined with a ride that always leaves me impressed. The quality of build is also high and, to some extent, justifies the higher than most rivals price tag. ... On the minus side are the ... lack of

rear intermittent wipe facility, ... [while] another minor niggle concerns the rather smart looking Pirelli alloy wheels which are vulnerable to kerbing with their almost flush fit ... Compared to the Mk1 Golf GTI, the Mk2 is only marginally improved. It is a little quieter at speed but still generates a lot of exhaust noise ... Compared to the new Astra GTE, the Golf GTI looks perhaps a little ordinary, but it certainly makes up for any deficiencies here in just about every other area of design ...

Motor was definitely not impressed by Volkswagen's claimed top speed of 192km/h (119mph), only being able to force a meagre 183km/h (114mph) out of the example they test drove, while price was a further concern:

> When you consider that the old car managed 112.4mph it is clear that while the new model's paper aerodynamic advantage is real it is not that significant ... Accelerating from rest, the new GTI matches strides with its predecessor up to 40mph, but lags to 60 (8.3 against 8.1 sec) and 70 mph (11.0 against 10.6 sec) ... A better GTI? Maybe. But can it really be worth £7,607? Most direct rivals undercut it by margins it's hard to ignore. For instance the MG Maestro 1.6 – which has five doors – costs just £6,775 ...

Not necessarily high on the list of favourite GTI colours, when well looked after an Alpine White Mk2 GTI 8-valve looks good with its distinctive black trim.

While *Motor*'s report was far from condemnatory throughout, with a good deal of praise emerging for a variety of attributes, its conclusion could hardly have set potential GTI buyers' hearts pounding, or for that matter sent Volkswagen's marketing people into shrieks of ecstasy.

> There is little doubt that the new GTI's virtues extend its appeal – as a family express it is certainly an improved car. Equally, as a driver's car it still feels the same – it has lost none of its magic. But in seeking a wider audience, VW have taken no more than a sideways step. For the existing GTI owner who drives solo, better brakes and improved efficiency alone are, perhaps, not quite enough to justify the upgrade.

Volkswagen Audi Car, the two-marque magazine hardly renowned for criticizing its lifeblood, nevertheless felt duty bound to report that the Mk2 GTI was 'softer and less exciting than its predecessor'. However, full glorification of the GTI as an unparalleled deity came from the AA:

> Unlike most of its rivals, the Golf GTI will do absolutely nothing for your ego when it's standing at the kerb or when the inquisitive peer inside. But

once under way it proves to be the master of the understatement. It's versatile, civilized and well built, but most of all it's exciting, which is what a hot hatch is all about. We aren't sure who put about the malicious rumour about the GTI's grey hairs but as far as we're concerned the Golf GTI rules ... OK.

Early Days Revamp

With effect from 1985, not only could the GTI be ordered as a three- or five-door model in the UK, but both versions were the subject of a makeover, breaking to some extent the direct

There's always something extra special about well-looked after black paint on a GTI.

links with the vehicle's Mk1 ancestry. From the rear, the GTI now sported angled and meatier looking twin exhaust pipes, as well as a red trim strip towards the upper edge of the bumper, a feature that was naturally extended to the front of the car as well. Down the side, the black or silver stripes disappeared, to be replaced by a wide black side moulding, genuinely capable of resisting damage to body from minor obstacles. A sliding steel sunroof became standard rather than an extra-cost option, although unlike the one fitted to the Scirocco of the day, it didn't tilt. As previously mentioned, three-door GTIs were now fitted with steel wheels as standard, but the five-door model retained the Pirelli-style alloys. The only other change was to the interior of the car, with the arrival of a new design of material to cover both the front sports and rear passenger seats. Available as previously in either black, grey and red, or black, grey and silver, the latter option being selected when the car was finished in Diamond Silver, the new look was considerably bolder than previously with very distinct stripes of colour. Bordering on garish it might have been, but apart from making a statement that here was a new Golf not to be confused with the Mk1 GTI, the material was more in keeping with a sporty heritage.

Two GTIs for the Price of One – Arrival of the 16-Valve

Good, but hardly glowing in most instances; that would probably be Volkswagen's verdict on the collection of press reviews gathered after the release of the Mk2 GTI. In some ways, Volkswagen only had itself to blame. The GTI had been a unique concept when it was launched in 1976. Escalating sales obviously excited the attention of rival manufacturers, who rightly saw that there was money to be made out of a hot hatch. At the end of Mk1 GTI production, in excess of 400,000 GTIs had been sold, but others had not only created their own hot hatches, they had also started to close the gap with cheaper cars, vehicles

dripping in appealing gadgetry and crucially with motors that were just as fast as the Volkswagen. Even more of a challenge were the likes of Ford's RS Turbo Escort and the new Opel Kadett 2.0 GTE.

The answer for Volkswagen was to up the specification by adding a second string to its GTI bow, leaving prospective purchasers with the option of a fast, well-trimmed, well-built hatch, or an equally well-constructed vehicle, with high-quality decor plus an even more powerful engine. The arrival of the 16-valve in late 1985, a GTI that made its way to the UK in early 1986, created a precedent that would stay the course for the remaining years of Mk2 production and that would at least initially cause consternation at the start of the third generation's run, due to the absence of the more powerful sibling. The notion of dual GTIs was set to wither with the advent of the Mk4 Golf, albeit that in the UK Volkswagen endeavoured to keep what was now a fantasy alive by badging a good car, but not a GTI, as just such a model.

The debut of the Mk2 GTI 16-valve had Volkswagen's fans cheering with delight, while across the rest of the motoring world the boffins were immediately put to work, their collective task being one of catching the hare once more before they went to the dogs!

Volkswagen had considered various ways to make the GTI more powerful. One such would have been to go down the route of turbocharging, but for a mass-production company like Volkswagen, whose reputation for reliability had always ranked high, potential dealer servicing difficulties and long-term dependability were both issues where the risk was too great. The questions surrounding turbo-lag and heat-soak problems only intensified the potential perils of such a course. Porsche might have gone down that route in the 1970s, but essentially it was not a mass manufacturer. Supercharging, too, wasn't a practical proposition at the time; a satisfactory level of development only arrived towards the end of the Mk2's production run, as will be revealed shortly.

With the arrival of the Mk2 GTI 16-valve, in theory the original GTI became the poor relation. However, at least visually there was little to distinguish the two cars, the red 16V attachment to the GTI badge on the front grille being the more powerful car's most notable means of identification.

Sixteen-valve technology had already found a tentative home with Volkswagen courtesy of Volkswagen in France and its relationship with the German tuning firm of Oettinger and its Okrasa 16-valve aftermarket kit, and although too complex in nature to produce at a reasonable cost, it was undoubtedly a way forward. Amazingly, the task of producing a 16-valve engine was started as long ago as November 1981, indeed at the same time as the 8-valve 1800 that made its debut in the Golf during September 1982, for the 1983 model year.

The new 16-valve engine was exhibited at the Frankfurt Motor Show in 1984, but behind the scenes engineers were still frantically working on the design to iron out, amongst other things, why heads kept cracking; in all probability this was due to exhaust-valve cooling

issues. Only when Volkswagen was fully satisfied that the 16-valve would be as reliable as the 8-valve was the new model made available, a delay of nearly a year therefore ensuing.

Made of alloy, the 16-valve's new crossflow cylinder head had twin camshafts, one to operate the sets of two 32mm inlet valves, the other to work the dual 28mm exhausts. With the Golf's transverse layout the inlet ports were at the front, with the throttle chamber at the rear. As a result, four large cast-alloy inlet pipes passed over the top of the engine, affording instant recognition to the 16-valve. Volkswagen was taking no chances, though, as a combination of letters and figures cast onto the top of the manifold spelled out 'VW DOHC – 16V'. Due to the limited space available, Volkswagen's engineers retained but strengthened the standard GTI's toothed belt drive to a single camshaft, while slaving the other shaft to it with a short drive chain linking two small sprockets and both camshafts at the other end of the engine. For the first time, the tappets became hydraulically operated, primarily to ensure consistent

Something to boast about: the twin overhead camshaft 16-valve engine as installed in the Mk2 Golf GTI, good for 0–100km/h in 7.9sec and a top speed of 208km/h (129mph).

valve clearance, but also as their relative inaccessibility would have made them difficult to adjust. Compared to the single 40mm (1.6in) inlet and 33mm (1.3in) exhaust valves of the original GTI engine, the 4 valves per cylinder arrangement allowed in the region of 20 per cent more gas flow. The 16-valve layout wasn't symmetrical, for the inlet valves leaned 25 degrees away from the centre line of each cylinder, while the exhaust valves stood upright, but were offset. This arrangement was not only conducive to better airflow, but also made the manufacturing process easier and therefore cheaper to effect. The exhaust valves were hollow-stemmed and filled with sodium to assist with the quelling of heat and to aid longevity as a result.

Although the cylinder head was new, much of the rest of the standard 1781cc GTI engine was retained; bore and stroke remained at 81 × 86.4mm respectively and the compression ratio stayed at 10.0:1, all of which went to demonstrate the distinct advantages of the extra valves per cylinder. Maximum power rose to 139ps at 6,100rpm, a sizeable jump from the existing GTI's 115ps at 5,500rpm; similarly, torque increased from the standard engine's 115lb ft at 3,100rpm to 123.5lb ft at 4,600rpm.

The result, as might have been anticipated, was a much faster GTI, a car capable of outperforming its rivals once more, and one entitled to retain the Golf's crown as the finest of hot hatches. The GTI's top speed rose by 16km/h (10mph) to 208km/h (129mph), and the 0–60mph time improved by 0.4sec, clipped from 8.3 to just 7.9sec. Those were the key figures, as the difference between an 8-valve and a 16-valve in terms of both 30–50 in third and 50–70 in fourth, was more or less negligible, going some considerable distance to suggest that the major gains in power were only achieved at higher rev ranges, certainly above 4,000rpm. However, different driving techniques were required to bring the best out of the two engines – with the 16-valve, greater use of the gearbox and the right gear for the occasion ensured that it was considerably faster

than the 8-valve. Unlikely to be of vast interest to a great number of potential purchasers, the 16-valve wasn't all that much thirstier either considering its extra power. Volkswagen's official figures indicated 10.6ltr/100km (26.6mpg) for the 16-valve and 10.3ltr/100km (27.4mpg) for the 8-valve on the urban cycle, 6.1ltr/100km (46.3mpg) and 5.81ltr/100km (48.7mpg) respectively at a constant 90km/h (56mph) and 7.9ltr/100km (35.8mpg) compared to the 8-valve's 7.6ltr/100km (37.2mpg) at a steady 120km/h (75mph).

Volkswagen sold the 16-valve's story well in a series of brochures that now took the GTI away from the rest of the Golf family:

> Volkswagen's swift Golf GTI has entered a new era, thanks to the development of a sophisticated new 16-valve engine. Designed to increase driver appeal as well as take the GTI into an even higher-performance league. The new 16-valve engine is the most powerful in its class ... The 16-valve engine at the heart of the Golf GTI 16V is the most advanced unit Volkswagen has ever built. The result of four years of development – over and above that which went into the normal Golf GTI engine on which it is based ... Combined with the car's light weight, the 16-valve engine gives the Golf GTI 16V class winning speed, and enough performance to embarrass many sports cars costing twice as much. Yet, such is the advanced nature of the engine, it is also very economical. At a steady 56mph, the GTI returns 46.3mpg.

To accompany the increase in performance, Volkswagen provided the 16-valve with new anti-roll bars, dampers and stiffer springs, 10 per cent more so at the front and 20 per cent at the back, while the height of the car was dropped by a further 10mm (0.4in). Although the brakes were initially the same size as those of the 8-valve, the master cylinder bore size was increased to 22mm (0.86in). To give that extra bit of grip, while the 8-valve continued to be shod with 185/60 HR 14 tyres, the 16-valve was endowed with 185/60 VR 14 low-profile rubber.

Golf GTI Mk2 16-Valve 1986

Engine			**Rear**	Torsion beam, trailing arms, 20mm (0.78in) anti-roll bar
Type	Transversely mounted 4-cylinder in-line Belt and chain driven twin overhead camshaft with two inlet and two exhaust valves per cylinder		Steering	Maintenance free self-adjusting rack and pinion
			Tyres	185/60 VR 14
			Wheels	6J × 14 alloys
Bore and stroke	81mm × 86.4mm		**Brakes**	
Capacity	1781cc		Type	Diagonally divided dual circuit with brake servo and brake pressure regulator
Compression ratio	10.0:1			
Fuel injection	Bosch K-Jetronic		Size	Front 239mm (9.4in) diameter discs, internally ventilated – single piston sliding caliper Rear 226mm (8.9in) solid disc and single piston sliding caliper
Max. power	139ps at 6,100rpm			
Max. torque	123.5lb ft at 4,600rpm			
Fuel capacity	55ltr (12.1gal)			
Transmission				
Gearbox	Five-speed all indirect with synchromesh		**Dimensions**	
			Track	
Clutch	Single dry plate		Front	1.427mm (56.2in)
Ratios	1st	3.46	Rear	1,422mm (56in)
	2nd	2.12	Wheelbase	2,475mm (97.4in)
	3rd	1.44	Overall length	3,985mm (156.9in)
	4th	1.13	Overall width	1,680mm (66.1in)
	5th	0.91	Overall height	1,405mm (55.3in)
			Unladen weight	960kg (2,117lb)
Final drive	3.67 to 1			
Suspension and Steering			**Performance**	
Front	MacPherson struts and lower wishbones, 18mm (0.7in) anti-roll bar		Top speed	208km/h (129mph) 0–80km/h (0–50mph) 6.0sec 0–100km/h (0–62mph) 7.9sec

The arrival of the 16-valve on the market didn't trigger a wave of visual changes to distinguish the two GTIs either externally or internally; far from it! For the UK at least, the 16-valve was only available as a three-door model initially, although the rule that alloys were standard to the five-door only was disregarded. As far as alloys went, the new Montreal design – also standard to the five-door 8-valve, with its large centre cap or disc and negligible, near invisible, fifteen spokes was one of the most discreet ever to hit a hot hatch and in later years might easily have been mistaken for nothing more than a plastic wheel trim.

Likewise, although the 16-valve sported a new style of slightly larger front spoiler with rectangular ducts cut into either end, this was also part of the 8-valve package when it was introduced at the beginning of the 1986 model year in the summer of 1985. However, three features, two of which easily caught the eye, were unique to the 16-valve. Gone was the wing-mounted radio aerial, to be replaced by a distinctive bee sting style on the car's roof, while status-attracting black-out-of-red '16V' badges were appended beneath the GTI insignia on both the radiator grille and the rear of the car. The third exclusive came in the form of heat-

Towards the end of production the Mk2 Golf GTI 16-valve appeared as beefy as ever.

**Mk2 GTI Paintwork Options
1986 and 1987**

The 1986 model GTI could be specified in six shades of paint, which included all the old favourites, ranging from Black, Mars Red and Diamond Silver to Alpine White. Atlas Grey Metallic and Jade Metallic made up the rest, although for the 16-valve only there was a seventh colour, Monza Blue Metallic.

For 1987, and bearing in mind the model years ran from August to July, the first casualty from the original trio of paint colours emerged, with Tornado Red replacing Mars Red. While red might be red, even casual observers would have noticed that the new colour was less orange in its tone and all the more attractive for it. Respected motoring journalist, Laurence Meredith, even went so far as to condemn Mars Red as a 'splendid example of German lack of appreciation of colour'.

---

insulating green-tinted glass. Inside, the 16-valve's identity was broadcast to passengers via a red '16V' badge on the glovebox lid, electric front windows, the normal location for the winder handle having been blanked off, and central locking.

Both the 8- and the 16-valve cars could be fitted with power-assisted steering at extra cost, while other optional equipment included headlamp washers, air conditioning and leather upholstery.

Most motoring magazines of the day seemed reasonably happy to award the new 16-valve GTI gold-star ratings, although in the best tradition of journalism writers were eager to earn their keep by finding at least something irksome on which to report. *Motor*'s test of December 1986 was typical:

> The extra power is there, all right, but the engine has to be revved hard to unleash it. Upper range acceleration is much stronger with the 16-valve car, so too is the top speed. But though the measured 124.6 mph mean figure is better than that of the 8-valve car's 115.4mph and fully competitive with that of most rivals ... it is a little disappointing in the light of

Volkswagen's 129mph claim. ... With more power, there are times when the steering becomes edgy, and the driver is left in no doubt as to which end is driven. But that aside, the marked torque steer that the 8-valve car suffered from has been cured ... It is fair to say that the new 16-valve engine does not represent a quantum leap forward for the Golf GTI; the 8-valve car is far too good for that. But for the hard-driving enthusiast, the extra top-end power does give the GTI that extra sparkle that's needed to take on the rapidly improving competition. It is capable, seamless, mature; strong on all-round ability and long-term desirability. All told, it's still the best.

Autocar's James Baker covered 27,350km (17,000 miles) with a 16-valve GTI, finding few real grievances with regard to its road behaviour:

> It doesn't take long behind the Golf's wheel to understand that this is a car designed and built to be driven rapidly. Its sporty nature isn't ideal for town driving – the ride is hard and the steering heavy at low speeds. But most keen drivers will soon decide that this is an acceptable compromise for the sheer pleasure experienced when unleashing the car along a quiet country road. The joy of the 16V is its sparkling performance.

But, of the few minor irritations listed, one really annoyed the otherwise unruffled Mr Baker:

> The visibility is ... poorer than you would expect, hampered by vast pillars and ridiculous quarter-light windows which seem to force VW to position the door mirrors six inches further back than they should be, craning your head forward to get full mirror vision is dangerous in heavy traffic conditions ....

As for an overall verdict, Volkswagen wouldn't have been unduly worried by what was written:

> Our Golf has given commendable service, few problems and a huge amount of entertainment. It is a driver's car, demanding a spirited style to discover its true personality. While it happily tolerates city driving, put it on an empty country road and you'll find out just how pleasing it can be.

The Mk2 GTI 16-valve is seen here finished in black, although the eagle-eyed will notice that two cars have been photographed to make this single cameo. Note on the image of the GTI taken from the rear the bee-sting aerial, originally the exclusive preserve of the 16-valve and much coveted by owners of 8-valve models.

As with the first generation GTI, time, effort and often a great deal of money has been spent on personalizing or customizing their cars by enthusiastic owners. The white car features a full-blown body kit. Most noticeable with the other two cars are the aftermarket alloys.

Years of Improvement

Compare a run-out Mk2 GTI with the 1986 model year cars that saw the debut of the 16-valve vehicle and quite a few differences can be found, both of a visual and mechanical nature, without too much of a struggle. Although the 16-valve had become the top of the range GTI, work didn't automatically grind to a halt on the development of the 8-valve model. During 1986, hydraulic tappets were included, providing both adjustment-free operation and

For the moment at least the second generation GTI is the one most likely to have time and money spent on it by owners wishing to enter a classic Concours event. The cars depicted on this page and overleaf, all of which are finished in Tornado Red, clearly have loving owners who spend many hours polishing their vehicles to perfection. All are 8-valve examples, although by the time Mk2 production came to an end it had become increasingly difficult to distinguish such a model from the more expensive 16-valve. Apart from the merging of the red-trimmed grille with the rest of the car, no finer-looking colour than hot Tornado Red could be selected for the Mk2 GTI.

a greater degree of quietness, the valve timing was changed, a larger sump was fitted, increasing capacity by half a litre, and a new exhaust manifold was brought in.

In 1987, for the 1988 model year, the 8-valve's K-Jetronic method of continuous ignition was replaced by Digifant electronic management, a more sophisticated data-controlled system with mapped fuel and ignition, a knock sensor and an airflow meter amongst its attributes. While this had no effect on the GTI's maximum power of 112ps, it was now able to run

Twin halogens and GTI grille badge.

GTI initials were countersunk into the side trim and always highlighted in red.

Smoked rear lenses, black vinyl around the rear window and identifying GTI badge.

BBS alloys became standard on the Mk2 GTI 8-valve in the final days of the model's production run.

Far from exclusive to the GTI, the VW roundel was fitted to the rear of all Mk2 Golfs.

on low-octane unleaded fuel, although while Volkswagen listed the torque figure as 117lb ft, an increase of 2lb ft, this was only achieved at the higher rate of 4,000rpm, compared to the original figure of 115lb ft at 3,100rpm. Interestingly, the 16-valve retained the K-Jetronic system and would do so until the end of Mk2 production.

The 1988 model year also saw changes affecting not just the GTI but all members of the Golf family. At the car's front the grille was altered, the new version having both wider slats and a larger VW logo than previously, while at the rear the VW emblem was repositioned to a

The classic steel wheels fitted as standard to many a Mk2 GTI 8-valve.

central location, the accompanying Volkswagen script of the older badge being dropped. A more substantial design of side rubbing strip helped not only the car's appearance, but also provided more effective protection. Much more significant, though, was the removal of the front quarter-light, creating a full-size wind-down window and, even better, the option to relocate the door mirrors further forward where they were of greater use. Inside, new column controls ran throughout the range, while the GTI's upholstery was changed; the bold, broad stripes of old being replaced by a restrained sports check in grey/blue or grey/red. The four-button steering wheel had also run its course and was replaced with what might best be described as a wheel that would rapidly take on a new corporate look, a four-spoke affair with a diagonal line pattern moulded into the central horn pad. While neither outstandingly exciting nor horrifically downmarket, the new wheel was hardly inspirational, particularly so for the GTI buyer, who had come to expect something openly sporty.

The 16-valve's front discs were enlarged from the 239mm (9.4in) of old to 256mm (10.1in) in late 1988, while larger calipers were fitted. While obviously bringing the car to a halt in a shorter time, they also increased fade resistance.

The 1990 model year saw the last major set of cosmetic changes for the Mk2 Golf in general and the GTI in particular. The GTI's

bumpers were further enlarged at both the front and rear. Integrated with a deep spoiler at the front, which was designed to accommodate a pair of DE fog lamps, at the rear the plastic was extended, forming a mock valance. The intention was to give the GTI a more modern look, something in which Volkswagen succeeded, particularly as the new set-up was partially colour-coded. If there was a downside it came in the form of a shared package with the most upmarket of the other models, the 1.8 GL, which was now also allocated the GTI's sports steering wheel and the option of Recaro seats, an extra cost choice with the GTI for a number of years. Even chunkier side rubbing strips were added and these came complete with a red-out-of-black GTI logo embedded into the plastic on the front door closest to the wheel. Sixteen-valve models, which for the UK market were at last available in both two- and four-door forms, looked particularly attractive due to 6 × 15 BBS cross-spoke alloys becoming standard. Shod with 185/55 15 tyres they made the 16-valve stand out from the 8-valve, which still came with steel wheels, although alloys could be purchased at extra cost.

Changes of a mechanical nature included enlargement of the manifold pipes, although the effect of this modification on performance was considered debatable by some, but by far the most important was the inclusion of power steering as part of the standard specification

Volkswagen UK owns this 8-valve Mk2 GTI, which was built in August 1991 (taking it into the 1992 model year). Its black exterior is complemented with 'Rainbow' cloth upholstery and 6J × 15 BBS alloys shod with 185/55 VR-15 tyres. Volkswagen listed its attributes to include: central locking, electric windows, power-assisted steering, multifunction computer, lowered suspension, steel sliding sunroof and the inimitable red-rimmed front grille. While not all such attributes were included in the specification of early 8-valve models, a reasonable percentage was. Run-out models of the Mk2 8-valve GTI still offered no more than the 112ps of the Mk1 a decade earlier, but such cars certainly looked the part.

rather than charging for it as an extra-cost option. Volkswagen even referred to its attributes in its latest brochures: 'The steering will feel light and responsive at low speeds whilst giving you plenty of "feel" on the road, thanks to the well-balanced Volkswagen power-assisted steering.'

Inside the 1990 model year 16-valve, the upholstery was changed once more and, while the new pattern was considerably more apt than the previous sombre check, a cloth that was still attributed to 8-valve cars, the striped pattern wasn't unrealistically garish either, encompassing a predominantly grey background interspersed on both the swab and the backrest, with

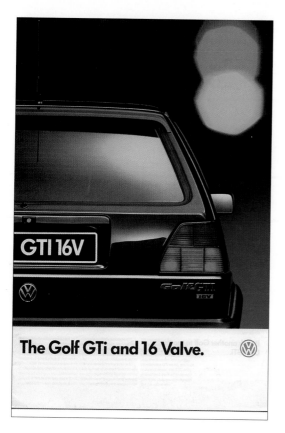

The cover style of brochures produced to promote the Mk2 GTI changed as the years went by. This example, dating from 1990, has been included to compare with the covers of both the Rallye Golf and G60 brochures, each of which is illustrated on later pages.

a single burst of three relatively dominant stripes, one in red, a second in blue, with the third coming in green.

As the end of the line approached for the Mk2 8-valve it was afforded more and more of the items normally reserved for the 16-valve. Apart from its upholstery, the GTI 8-valve was also allocated electric windows, the sought-after BBS alloy wheels and even the highly coveted bee-sting aerial.

The Extra Special Golf Rallye

In order to compete in World Championship rallies, Volkswagen had to build 5,000 road-going examples, the minimum required for motor sport homologation, of the car it intended to race. In the late 1980s there was a belief that sales of the 8- and 16-valve GTI could be given a significant boost if a rally version was seen to make its presence felt on the scene. That Volkswagen got nowhere, thanks partly to the imposition of an inlet restrictor on all cars by the sport's governing body, a move which had considerable effect on a supercharged engine but not so much on a turbocharged one, was irrelevant, even if the decision to pull out was taken as quickly as it been entered into. The marketplace got what it wanted – 5,000 highly sought-after high-performance Golfs. All the cars, known as the Rallye Golf, were built at the Volkswagen factory in Brussels during 1989; all were left-hand-drive models, but the UK market was nevertheless allocated eighty such cars, which were available as a special-order item only. Volkswagen even went to the lengths of having a brochure prepared in, or at least translated into, English.

Essentially, the Rallye Golf combined elements from the 8-valve GTI, the Corrado G60 and the Golf Syncro, to produce a supercharged, four-wheel-drive car, with a maximum power of 160ps at 5,600rpm and maximum torque of 166lb ft at 4,000rpm, although 145lb ft or more was available from 2,400–5,600rpm. Official figures confirmed a top speed of 209km/h (130mph) and a

The 5,000-strong band of Rallye Golf models could be distinguished from all other Mk2 GTIs, including the forthcoming G60, by unique rectangular headlamp lenses, larger colour-coded bumpers, a deeper front spoiler with built-in foglamps, extended all-metal wheel arches, much wider sill panels, and a special radiator grille amongst other items. Confirmation of the car's identity came in the form of a Rallye Golf badge on the car's rear.

0–100km/h acceleration through the gears of 8.6sec. Quick reference to the 16-valve GTI's top speed confirms that the Rallye Golf had only one extra mile per hour up its sleeve, so while the car had better mid-range torque and better road adhesion, it was no faster than the 16-valve. The driving factor behind this was undoubtedly weight, for the Rallye Golf bumped its way up to the maximum with a very hefty 1,195kg (2,635lb), the GTI 16-valve

---

The Rallye Golf 1989

Engine

Type	Transversely mounted 4-cylinder in-line Five-bearing crankshaft; valve control through toothed belt-driven single ohc. Mechanical supercharger (G60-charger) with charge pressure control. Intercooler operated by airflow G60 supercharger runs at 1.7 times engine speed, delivering 0.65 bar (9.4psi) maximum boost
Bore and stroke	80.6mm × 86.4mm
Capacity	1763cc
Compression ratio	8.0:1
Fuel injection	Digifant
Max. power	160ps at 5,600rpm
Max. torque	166lb ft at 4,000rpm
Fuel capacity	55ltr (12.1gal); different location than other models

Transmission

	Permanent four-wheel drive with slip-dependent power distribution to front and rear wheels. Drive to front wheels via differential and half shafts with constant velocity joints. Drive to rear wheels via bevel gears, three-piece propeller shaft and viscous coupling. Final drive with freewheel integrated between bevel gears and differential	
Gearbox	Five-speed manual	
Clutch	Single dry plate	
Ratios	1st	3.78
	2nd	2.11
	3rd	1.34
	4th	0.97
	5th	0.80

Final drive	3.68 to 1

Suspension and Steering

Front	MacPherson struts and lower wishbones, coil springs 23mm (0.9in) anti-roll bar
Rear	Semi-trailing wishbones, coil spring struts, 21mm (0.82in) anti-roll bar Lowered by 20mm (0.78in) compared to ordinary models
Steering	Maintenance-free power steering self-adjusting rack and pinion
Tyres	205/50 15 VR
Wheels	6J × 15 Sebring alloys

Brakes

Type	Diagonally divided dual circuit with brake servo and load sensitive brake pressure regulator. Electronic Teves Anti-lock Brake System (ABS)
Size	Front 280mm (11.0in) diameter discs, internally ventilated Rear solid disc from the Polo front fitted with Golf calipers

Dimensions

Track		
	Front	1,429mm (56.3in)
	Rear	1,434mm (56.5in)
Wheelbase		2,479mm (97.6in)
Overall length		4,035mm (158.9in)
Overall width		1,700mm (66.9in)
Overall height		1,399mm (55.1in)
Unladen weight		1,195kg (2,635lb)

Performance

Top speed	209km/h (130mph)
	0–80km/h (0–50mph) 5.6sec
	0–100km/h (0–62mph) 8.6sec

---

three-door being a mere lightweight on the scales at 960kg (2,117lb) by comparison.

Essentially, the Golf Rallye's engine block was the same as that of the GTI 8-valve, although the bore had been reduced from 81.0mm to 80.6mm, the net effect of which was to reduce capacity from 1781cc to 1763cc. The purpose behind this apparently odd decision was to avoid the Rallye being forced to move up one category in motor sport classifications, due to the multiplication factor applied to forced-induction engines – 1763cc ensured that it remained conveniently under the 2.5-litre class limit.

Although Volkswagen's initial involvement with superchargers dated back to 1973 and an air-cooled engine, it was only when engineers came across the work of Frenchman Louis Creux, whose invention, patented in 1905, had only failed due to the poor casting techniques then available, that progress became significant. His creation essentially compressed air between a pair of G-shaped metal scrolls, hence the name of G-Lader (shaped) supercharger. Having satisfied itself that modern techniques would ensure that the precise tolerances required were achieved, Volkswagen tested the market with a short production run of the Polo 1.3, named the G40. The designation was derived from the depth of the working chambers on either side of the supercharger, hence when the 1.8-litre car was so endowed it became the G60. Although the G-Lader supercharger placed less stress on the engine than would a turbo, steps were taken to ensure reasonable longevity for it. These included: the application of heat treatment to the cylinder head in order that it withstood the thermal stresses of a higher output; sodium-filled exhaust valves as per the GTI 16-valve; forged, rather than cast, pistons with thicker wrist pins; and a reduction in the compression ratio to 8.0:1.

The supercharger ran at 1.7 times engine speed and delivered a maximum boost pressure of 0.65bar. Air entered the car's filter, passed through the fuel-injection metering unit, the supercharger and the large intercooler in front of the radiator, which reduced the temperature by up to 55°C, and into the inlet manifold at the back of the engine. Volkswagen proved eager to explain that there was more to the Rallye Golf than just a supercharger:

Two aspects of the Rallye Golf lift it head and shoulders above the crowd – the G-charger and the Syncro four wheel drive system. One creates the performance, the other allows the driver to use it! The beauty of the mechanically driven supercharger is that it develops its power, particularly in the low and mid range bands, with none of the lag that besets the exhaust driven turbo. And that is matched by the efficiency of the Syncro system.

Despite the fact that the Rallye Golf would only be imported into the UK in small numbers and all examples were in left-hand-drive form, Volkswagen still produced an English version of the brochure designed to generate a quick turnover in sales of this limited production car.

The Rallye Golf's four-wheel drive arrangement came directly from the Golf Syncro, a vehicle that went into production in February 1986. It was intended to give either off-road capabilities, or maximum stability in all road conditions, to its owner, rather than any form of sporting pretension. Volkswagen explained the system and its merits in the brochure dedicated to the model:

> The unique Syncro system operates not through complex electronics, but by means of a viscous coupling. For the first time, it has been integrated directly into the drive train to provide many different functions simultaneously. In particular, it provides slip-sensitive power distribution between the front and rear axles, ensuring that the driving force is always highest on the axle which has the best adhesion to the road surface ...

In straightforward Rallye Golf terms, this meant that only on the occasions when the significant power of the engine might have caused the front wheels to spin was drive transmitted to the rear wheels, a feature which instantly gave it an advantage over the GTI 16-valve.

In addition to the Golf Syncro's four-wheel-drive system, the Rallye Golf acquired its suspension, which was promptly lowered by 20mm (0.78in) and fitted with both stiffer springs and dampers, as well as thicker anti-roll bars. As such, the rear suspension was fully independent, with semi-trailing wishbones and coil spring struts.

The Rallye Golf was endowed with the 02A gearbox as fitted to the latest Passat. Both lighter and more compact than many boxes produced previously, it was selected on account of its ample strength to cater with the power of the supercharged engine. Power steering was, as might have been expected, standard, as was an anti-lock braking system (ABS), while the 280mm (11in) ventilated disc brakes on the Rallye Golf's front wheels were those fitted to the Corrado, the rear ones were Polo front discs mated to Golf calipers. The car ran on 6J × 15 Sebring alloys, which were shod with ultra-low-profile 205/50 VR-15 tyres.

To allow space for the rear wheel drive-train, the fuel tank had to be relocated and the exhaust system adjusted. The net result was that the floor of the boot had to be raised, cutting the carrying capacity with the rear seat backrest in position down to just 8.1cu.ft compared to the GTI's 14.4cu.ft.

As might have been anticipated the Rallye Golf could not be regarded as economical. Volkswagen's fuel consumption figures indicated 23.2mpg on the urban cycle, 38.7mpg at a steady 90km/h (56mph) and 29.1mpg at a constant 120km/h (75mph).

Visually, at first glance the Rallye Golf appeared to be fitted with the rectangular headlamps of the Jetta and an aftermarket customizing body kit, but this was far from the case. The unique bodywork, very much in the style of the Audi Quattro of the day with semi-angular extended wheel arches, was of all-steel construction. (The Rallye Golf measured 1,700mm/66.9in in width; the GTI 1,680mm/66.1in.) Greatly extended sill panels, bigger and fully colour-coded bumpers, a larger, deeper front spoiler with built in DE fog lamps, again colour-coded, a painted rear spoiler, and what Volkswagen described simply as a 'special radiator grille, painted in vehicle colour' with unique rectangular headlamp lenses housing twin broad-beamed halogen lights, more or less completed the distinguishing aspects of the car's exterior.

Inside, the emphasis was on sporting luxury, although many aspects of the Golf GTI, for example the standard sports steering wheel, albeit leather-clad, were retained. Leather extended to the door and side panels, the handbrake and gear-lever gaiters, the gear knob, plus the seat headrests and side bolsters. The remaining parts of the sports seats were trimmed in an attractive grey and red stripe cloth, while both could be adjusted for height. The rear seat and backrest were of the deluxe one-third, two-thirds split folding type. Other items, such as the multifunctional digital computer, an interior courtesy light with delay action, green-tinted heat-insulating glass, while not the province of

The Rallye Golf Paintwork Options 1990

The Rallye Golf was available in Black, Tornado Red, Pearl Effect Blue, Pearl Effect Green and Graphite Metallic – a less extensive collection of shades and different in nature to colours offered on a contemporary GTI, with the exception of the non-metallic, non-pearl colours.

The Rallye Golf photographed here has been fitted with the optional 6.5 × 15 BBS alloys instead of the standard 6 × 15 Sebring wheels.

a base-model Golf, were certainly to be found on the GTI 16-valve.

Over and above the standard fitments, would-be owners could opt for electrically heated and adjustable colour-coded door mirrors, central locking, a manual sliding sunroof and electric windows. Further extras were available for the German market and these encompassed 6.5 × 15 BBS alloys, rear head restraints and Recaro seats.

The Golf GTI G60

A third regular member of the GTI family made its debut at the Frankfurt Motor Show in September 1989 and by the end of the year it was on sale in Germany. This was the Golf GTI G60, in essence a higher volume development of the Rallye Golf. As such, would-be UK buyers eagerly anticipated the day they would be able to purchase a right-hand-drive version of the car, but in such aspirations they were to be thwarted. Rumour persisted that there were problems mating the G60 engine to the cable shift gearbox, as described for the Rallye Golf. However, Volkswagen UK chose not even to import the car in left-hand-drive form, leading many to believe that the company feared that the position of the best-selling Corrado G60 would be jeopardized.

To all extents and purposes the Golf GTI G60 looked like any other GTI, red G60 badges on the front grille and rear panel being one of very few giveaways as to the car's real identity. However, while the GTI G60 inevitably lacked the greatly extended wheel arches of the Rallye,

its wings were wider than standard and this wasn't achieved merely by fitting larger plastic extensions. Amazingly, if Volkswagen's measurements are to be believed, the Rallye and the GTI G60 both measured 1,700mm (66.9in) in width, compared to the GTI's 1,680mm (66.1in). Thanks to the designer's skill, the difference was subtle, but it was there nonetheless, as was a variation on the GTI's ride height. While the 16-valve GTI sat 10mm (0.4in) lower all round than the 8-valve, the GTI G60 was a further 10mm (0.4in) lower at the front. It also had thicker anti-roll bars, 23mm (0.9in) at the front and 22mm (0.86in) at the rear, compared to the 20mm (0.78in) and 18mm (0.7in)

One of Volkswagen's many highly attractive press shots covering the G60. (Photograph courtesy of Volkswagen AG)

The power behind both the Rallye Golf and the Golf GTI G60, the G-shaped supercharger merged with the GTI 8-valve engine.

diameters for the other GTIs. Additionally, the G60 sported Passat-style dampers and the gearbox already referred to, while the final-drive ratios differed from those of the two other GTIs. ABS was standard, while EDL (Electronic Differential Lock) could be specified at extra cost. One more visual signature worthy of mention was the wheels, even though the exact nature of the alloys, or in the very early days, steel, varied from market to market. The G60 ran on 6J × 15 wheels, shod with 185/55 R15 V tyres, or later, when BBS alloys seemed to be

Mk2 GTI G60 1990

Engine

Type — Transversely mounted 4-cylinder in-line Valve control through toothed belt-driven single overhead camshaft. Mechanical supercharger (G60-charger) with charge pressure control. Intercooler operated by airflow G60 supercharger runs at 1.7 times engine speed, delivering 0.65bar (9.4psi) maximum boost

Bore and stroke — 81.0mm × 86.4mm
Capacity — 1781cc
Compression ratio — 8.0:1
Fuel injection — Digifant
Max. power — 160ps at 5,800rpm
Max. torque — 166lb ft at 3,800rpm
Fuel capacity — 55ltr (12.1gal)

Transmission

Gearbox — Cable-shift, five-speed manual
Clutch — Single dry plate
Ratios —
1st	3.78
2nd	2.12
3rd	1.34
4th	0.97
5th	0.76

Final drive — 3.67 to 1

Suspension and Steering

Front — MacPherson struts and lower wishbones, coil springs 23mm (0.9in) anti-roll bar
Rear — Semi-trailing wishbones, coil spring struts, 21mm (0.82in) anti-roll bar

— Lowered by 20mm (0.78in) at the front and 10mm (0.4in) at the rear compared to ordinary models
Steering — Maintenance-free power steering self-adjusting rack and pinion
Tyres — 185/55 R 15V, or 195/50 R 15V
Wheels — 6J × 15 steel, or 6.5J × 15 BBS Alloys

Brakes

Type — Diagonally divided dual circuit with brake servo and load sensitive brake pressure regulator. Electronic Teves anti-lock brake system (ABS) EDL optional
Size — Front 280mm (11.0in) diameter discs, internally ventilated Rear solid disc from the Polo front fitted with Golf calipers

Dimensions

Track
Front — 1,433mm (56.4in)
Rear — 1,428mm (56.2in)
Wheelbase — 2,475mm (97.4in)
Overall length — 4,040mm (159in)
Overall width — 1,700mm (66.9in)
Overall height — 1,400mm (55.1in)
Unladen weight — 1,080kg (2,381lb) two-door; 1,105kg (2,436lb) four-door

Performance

Top speed — 216km/h (134mph)
0–80km/h (0–50mph) 5.7sec
0–100km/h 0–62mph 8.3sec

ABOVE AND BELOW: *This G60 may or may not be one of the exclusive Edition One cars. The wheels at least suggest it isn't, but as such cars revolved purely around a special trim package only the owner would know!*

LEFT: *To the frustration of UK GTI fans, the GTI G60 never made British waters, although rumours of an English-language version of the brochure abound. The cover of this G60 brochure not only confirms that in appearance the car was similar to both the 8-valve and 16-valve Mk2 GTIs, but also that France was one of the many countries to sell the car.*

The Edition One G60 can be distinguished by its combination of BBS RM alloys, chromolux tinted windows, clear front indicators and special badges on the wings and bonnet. This example is finished in Metallic Black paint.

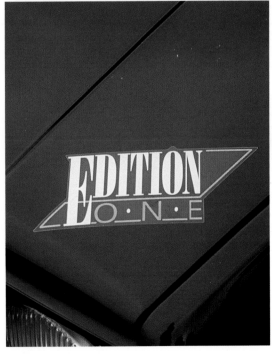

Mk2 GTI Paintwork Options 1991

As the new decade started to gather a little pace it was obvious to all that the age of the metallic was upon Volkswagen. For the 1991 model year, UK GTI purchasers were offered a choice of eleven paint shades. Four of these were solid colours and included the staple diet of Black, the new-look red in the form of Tornado and the relatively well-established option of Alpine White. One additional plain colour was the would-be owner's lot: the hardly inspirational option of Blue-Black.

In metallic shades Diamond Silver continued to lead the field, but was now accompanied by such desirables as Capri Green, Royal Blue, Pearl Grey, Oak Green and Bright Blue, while there was even the option to go down the road of a metallic black car, with the arrival of Brilliant Black Metallic.

Oak Green Metallic was a particularly attractive shade for any driver without a superstitious fear of the bad luck engendered by any green-coloured car.

---

more or less standard, the meatiness increased further to 6.5 × 15 with 195/50 tyres.

Unlike the Rallye, the GTI G60's engine had a capacity of 1781cc, but maximum power was the same at 160ps, although this was achieved at 5,800rpm rather than 5,600rpm. Maximum torque was also identical to that of the Rallye Golf, at 166lb ft at 3,800rpm. Without the benefits of four-wheel drive, the GTI G60 lacked the traction of the Rallye, but as it had both a full-size boot and a less complex exhaust system, there were compensations. Thanks to the inevitable reduction in weight caused by the absence of the paraphernalia of four-wheel drive, the GTI G60 stood at 1,080kg (2,381lb), compared to the Rallye's 1,195kg (2,635lb), a factor that made it faster, with a top speed of 216km/h (134mph) and a 0–100km/h romp of 8.3sec. The car was also faster than the GTI 16-valve, even though it weighed more and had greater torque throughout the range.

With the Mk3 Golf on the near rather than distant horizon, Volkswagen seemed to be determined to pull out all the stops with the G60. In February 1991, a syncro version of the Golf GTI 60 was added to the range, essentially a Rallye Golf in a standard bodyshell. There was even an Edition One GTI G60 and, while this was purely a trim package rather than a go-faster G60, its appeal was considerable. Sporting BBS RM alloys, Recaro seats trimmed in blue cloth, chromolux tinted windows, clear front indicators and Wolfsburg Edition badges on the wings and bonnet, the Edition One was available in a choice of three colours: Metallic Black, Pearl Grey and Dark Burgundy Pearl Effect.

First of the Celebratory Specials?

The summer of 1988 saw the ten millionth car bearing the name Golf roll off the assembly line, an achievement Volkswagen were keen to commemorate. Cynics were eager to point out that the second Golf was a totally different car from the first one, and as such the hype surrounding the occasion was little more than a way of engendering publicity and additional sales! Whatever the truth of the matter, Volkswagen duly celebrated with a limited-edition GTI, referred to occasionally and erroneously as a Campaign model. Although a fully fledged GTI, the trim package was based on the German market GT and included smoked rear lights, tinted glass, broad seven-spoke 15in Le Castellet alloys and low-profile tyres and, for the interior, a unique multicoloured upholstery. Available as either an 8-valve or 16-valve, three paint options were offered – Black, Helios Blue and Oak Green, all of which were metallic finishes.

In Perpetuity – Cabriolet Style

As was indicated in the previous chapter, there was no Mk2 version of the soft-top Golf, but the original Cabriolet continued to be produced by Karmann throughout the production run of the second-generation saloon. At the top of the range was a Cabriolet known as the GTI; a model possessed of the 1781cc,

The Cabriolet built by Karmann soldiered on with its Mk1 body throughout the era of the Mk2 Golf. At first glance the car pictured appears to be an example of the 'All White' special edition Golf Cabrio, but the black hood, if nothing else, reveals that it isn't.

Snippets from America

Inevitably behind Volkswagen AG, the Westmoreland plant in the USA began production of the Mk2 in September 1984 and, unlike the Mk1, it was decreed that from day one it would be known as a Golf rather than a Rabbit. Available initially with a diesel engine, or with a 1.8-litre fuel-injected petrol engine producing 85bhp (SAE) at 5,250rpm and 96lb ft maximum torque, the latter car could accomplish 0–60mph in 10.3sec and had a top speed of 172km/h (107mph). The US version of the GTI, known like its predecessor as the Volkswagen GTI, developed 100bhp SAE and was 11 per cent more powerful than the first-generation model. The 16-valve GTI only became an option in the USA in 1987 and upon its arrival in US guise was capable of the 0–60mph sprint in 7.9sec and a top speed of 199.5km/h (124mph).

However, Americans were more interested in a hot Jetta and in 1988 the 16-valve engine made its way into the GLI, where it remained as a genuinely sought-after option. During the course of 1991, the 2.0-litre Passat engine was adapted to accept a 16-valve head and became the key engine for the US GTI. Developing 134bhp at 5,800rpm and 133lb ft of torque at 4,400rpm, although equipped with a catalytic converter the car went a long way to offering American fans performance compatible with that of European models. Sadly, by this time Volkswagen's general sales were in a spiralling decline and even this model could not account for more than a few thousand cars throughout America per annum. The Mk2 GTI in America was finally replaced by the Mk3 in March 1993.

The American version of the Mk2 Golf GTI, known simply as the Volkswagen GTI, looked different to the European version thanks to its rectangular headlights.

Golf GTI Cabriolet 1991

Engine

Type	Transversely mounted 4-cylinder in-line
Bore and stroke	81.0 × 86.4mm
Capacity	1781cc
Valves	Two valves per cylinder
Compression ratio	10.0:1
Fuel injection	Bosch K-Jetronic
Max. power	112ps @ 5,800rpm
Max. torque	113lb ft at 3,500rpm
Fuel capacity	55ltr (12.1gal)

Transmission

	Front-wheel drive
Gearbox	Five-speed manual
Clutch	Single dry plate

Suspension and Steering

Front	Suspension struts and lower wishbones
Rear	Combined trailing arm torsion beam axle at rear
Steering	Maintenance-free self-adjusting rack and pinion
Tyres	185/60 HR 14
Wheels	6J × 14 Alloy

Brakes

Type	Diagonally divided dual circuit with brake servo and brake pressure regulator
Size	Front 24mm (0.9in) diameter discs, internally ventilated. Rear 18mm (0.7in) diameter self-adjusting drums

Dimensions

Track	
Front	1,404mm (55.3in)
Rear	1,372mm (54.0in)
Wheelbase	2,400mm (94.5in)
Overall length	3,890mm (153.1in)
Overall width	1,640mm (64.6in)
Overall height	1,410mm (55.5in)
Unladen weight	966kg (2,138lb)

Performance

Top speed	174km/h (108mph) 0–100km/h (0–62mph) 9.4sec

112ps engine and a sporty trim package. Due to the luxury nature of all Cabriolets it wasn't unusual to find some elements of the normal GTI package included on other models, sports seats being one example. Typical GTI extras at the beginning of 1986 might have been: trim around the grille; an air blade on the driver's windscreen wiper; alloy sports wheels; and a multifunctional computer. With the introduction of the 1988 models, there was a growing realization that steps had to be taken to keep the Cabriolet looking reasonably up to date. Colour-coded body kits and, where possible, use of the latest accessories to GTI identity were adopted, as Volkswagen's marketing people were keen to advise customers. Having sold the open-top driving story generally, they confirmed that:

> There is no better way to experience those delights than in the car that – more than any other – was responsible for the trend back to open-top motoring, the Volkswagen Golf Convertible GTI. …
>
> Especially as it has been refined still further for 1988, with a sportier appearance and GTI performance from the 1.8-litre injection engine. It has changed inside and out to take this proven favourite into a new era. The … range … features many of the innovations of the new hard-top Golfs, plus even more stylish, fashionable colour co-ordination. The GTI is specified inside and out for performance motoring …

A Further Generation of the Jetta

Despite the relatively poor sales performance of the Mk1 Jetta it was always planned that there would be a second-generation booted saloon. The Mk2 Jetta was launched in Germany in January 1984, arriving in the UK in September of the same year. Although the second-generation Jetta didn't appear in the USA until the last months of 1985, the Mk1 Jetta had kept the flag flying, being endowed with the American specification GTI engine. In the UK, after a comprehensive overhaul of the range in 1985, a new model, the GT, complete with red badge on the front grille, bumpers and side trim strips with red inserts, black wheel-arch extensions, black door sills, centre roof pillars and rear number plate surround, a boot top spoiler, plus, key to it all, the 112ps engine from the Golf GTI, made its debut in 1986. Volkswagen sold this special Jetta as 'The driver's sports saloon', making big play of the car's uprated suspension and its all-round disc brakes, 'to match the car's performance'. Only marginally slower than the Golf GTI, both in terms of top speed and 0–100km/h perform-ance, perhaps at last the stubborn problem of poor sales figures for the booted saloon might have been rectified.

Volkswagen in the UK must have been pleased with what it saw in the GT as with the availability of the 16-valve engine, a new model was introduced, the Jetta GTI 16-valve, while the 8-valve model was similarly rebranded as a GTI. This was the first occasion when the booted saloon had carried the ini-tials GTI, even though in Germany the boot-ed 16-valve model was known as the GTX. Brochures produced to market the Golf GTI and to proclaim the virtues of the Jetta GTI were virtually identical, even down to depict-ing the 8-valve models with the same style of optional extra alloys!

In terms of specification the two cars were very similar. Using the 16-valve Golf and Jetta as examples, each benefited from lowered sus-pension and had sports seats with identical trim, both were fitted with low profile VR rated tyres, had GTI 16V badges on the front grille, a rear panel and attached to the glovebox lid, while together they shared a bee-sting aerial. Where there was a difference and always had been was weight. The unladen 16-valve two-door Golf was shown as weighing 960kg (2117lb), 40kg (88lb) more than the equivalent three-door 8-valve model. Accepting that the Jetta was only available as a four-door car, the 16-valve stood at 1,010kg (2,227lb), 50kg (110lb) more than the 16-valve Golf. Inevitably then, the Jetta would be slightly slower, despite the two cars being recipients of identical engines. The Jetta 16-valve offered its owner a top speed of 204.3km/h (127mph), in contrast to the Golf's 207.6km/h (129mph), and powered its way from 0–60mph in 8.3sec, compared to the Golf's 7.9sec. Few, if any, would accept that this slight disparity in performance cost the Jetta GTI 16-valve literally thousands of sales. Nations may have liked the Jetta, but they cer-tainly preferred the Golf, and by the last months of 1991, despite updates concurrent with those on the Golf GTI, the range, not just the hot elements of it, had been discontinued.

4 Three: A Change of Direction; Gains in Weight

Launch Pad

Launched at the Frankfurt Motor Show in September 1991, the Mk3 was still recognizably out of the Golf stable, but changes to its appearance were much more apparent than had been the case when the Mk2 replaced the Mk1. Additionally, Wolfsburg had adopted two new approaches to guarantee the Golf's continuing success; one linked to events in which they had little or no control, the other, however, was entirely of the company's own making. The net result for followers of the cult of the hot hatch was an 8-valve GTI, which, apart from a certain loss of identity, was apparently slower than its predecessor, coupled to a new breed of performance car, the VR6, which not only cost a great deal of money, but also seemed geared to a different market than the one catered for by both the Mk2 Rallye Golf and GTI G60 of recent history. The temporary absence of the more powerful 16-valve GTI for reasons

Thanks to the non-appearance of the 16-valve version of the Mk3 GTI when the car was launched, the lack of an extra-dynamic hot-house option like the Mk2 GTI G60, the gains in weight associated with additional safety precautions taken in the construction of the new Golf, plus the rather soft, wallowing suspension, the third-generation GTI did not get off to the best of starts. Additionally, not everyone cared to understand the message behind the ultra-powerful, but not necessarily overtly sporty VR6. Once denigrated, for some the Mk3 GTI was forever the black sheep of the family. In reality, the car sold just as well as its predecessors and by the time production ended in 1997, most if not all of the early problems associated with it had long since been ironed out.

which weren't entirely clear did little to quell the fears of fans, although even the most dispirited recognized that in the Mk3 Golf Wolfsburg had created a greatly superior car for the family market.

Taking the Mk2 GTI 16V in its last model year and comparing its size with that of the Mk3 Golf, most would have been surprised to discover that there was little difference between the two. The older car was 4,040mm (159in) in length, 1,700mm (66.9in) in width and 1,405mm (55.3in) in height, against the Mk3's 4,020mm (158.3in) length, 1,710mm (67.3in) width and an identical height of 1,405mm (55.3in). Comparison of the two vehicles' respective wheelbases went some way to explain the similarity, as both measured 2,475mm (97.4in). The difference in body styling between the angular Mk2 and the Mk3, the newer car appearing pleasingly chunkier and more rounded according to its advocates, or bulkier, possibly even bloated, to its critics, undoubtedly contributed to the illusion that the new Mk3 was considerably larger than its predecessor.

While the contents of the brochures launching the Mk3 GTI might have concentrated on the subject matter, the cover certainly did not, if anything giving most prominence to the outgoing Mk2 GTI!

Against the trend of the time, the Golf Mk3 retained its substantial C-pillar and in certain circles Volkswagen was criticized for its decision to perpetuate this potential blind spot. To have lost it, though, would have been to detract from the new Golf's general air of opulence; a feeling generated through bumpers, valances, sill mouldings and side rubbing strips of a more sizeable appearance and encouraged through the more substantive design of most of the panels. The most radical departure from the general look of the two previous generations came at the front of the car, where the traditional combination of round headlamps and an elongated rectangular grille was dispensed with in favour of single near-oval lenses and a much condensed two-bar grille. And if those lenses were something of a disappointment to GTI fans they were also an illusion too, for higher-ranking models, naturally including both the VR6 and the GTI, continued to feature twin headlights; they were simply housed under single lenses. The creation of a slippery and aerodynamic body not only cut down wind noise, but also had the effect of reducing drag coefficient to figures between 0.30 and 0.33 dependent on the model selected, or a 10 per cent reduction compared to that of the Mk2.

Sadly, the Golf's new frontal appearance did little to sustain the distinctive nature of the GTI brand. Twin headlamps, although not exclusive to the GTI in Mk2 guise, or inclusive of all members of the hot-hatch family, had nevertheless made a contribution to the generally and genuinely sporty stance of the car. Crucially, though, the distinctive red trim line surrounding the grille had now been banished, as realistically the latest design lacked sufficient substance to accommodate it, while no attempt had been made to lodge the hot-hatch red hallmark elsewhere. Bumpers made of plain black plastic with colour-coded valances could have housed a token red stripe; even the reasonably large chromed GTI grille badge, or the chunky side rubbing strips were candidates for some form of identification mark, but nothing was forthcoming.

The most controversial aspect of the latest Golf undoubtedly related to its weight. Using the GTI 8-valve as the example, the unladen weight of the Mk2 two-door model stood at 920kg (2,029lb) and the four-door at 940kg (2,072lb), while the Mk3 model tipped the scales at 1,035kg (2,282lb) and 1,060kg (2,337lb), respectively. The significance of the new and ground-breaking VR6's unladen weight of 1,150kg (2,536lb) in two-door guise, and 1,180kg (2,602lb) with four, will become apparent shortly and is definitely worth mentioning here.

Although the American market no longer dominated Wolfsburg's thinking as it had both in the Beetle's heyday and during the time of the ill-fated Rabbit, it was still important. Imports may have declined dramatically – by the end of the 1980s they were down to 129,705 cars and looked set to fall further – but Volkswagen had no apparent intention of throwing in the towel just yet. To ensure that the Mk3 Golf was suitable for the USA in the 1990s, account had to be taken of the tough occupant protection legislation, which would come into place during the course of 1993. In so doing, Volkswagen created one of the strongest and safest hatchbacks in the world at the time. Significant space in every brochure produced was allocated to safety:

> Immense efforts have been made by Volkswagen to ensure that the new Golf meets not only current safety regulations but, as far as possible, future laws as well. As a result it has been crash-tested to both current US standards (which themselves are more stringent than present European testing) and to a new and tougher US level which will only become law in America with the 1994 models. The new Golf passed all the tests, putting it firmly ahead of its competition ...
>
> *(UK launch brochure, January 1992)*

Practical, but weight-attracting, examples of Volkswagen's safety commitment with the Mk3 Golf were spread throughout the car's body. Sills and central door pillars were strengthened,

The Mk3 Golf 8-valve as portrayed in one of Volkswagen's many publicity shots. (Photograph Courtesy of Volkswagen AG)

while side impact was also resisted more effectively to the tune of some 30 per cent through reinforcing members within each of the doors. Resistance to side collisions was also improved due to a rigid box-section beam, which ran behind and below the dashboard, while a second was positioned under the front seats. The longitudinal struts were formed in a new and ground-breaking technique called 'mash-seam welding'. This was a process in which metals of differing thicknesses were welded together, assisting cushioning in a frontal accident through deformation in a particular way.

Volkswagen even went to the length of translating and reprinting an *Auto Motor und Sport* article entitled 'VW Golf Crash-Test' to 'sell' the new car's greatest attribute to would-be purchasers:

> The offset crash is undoubtedly the hardest test of the bodyshell's structure. Its strength and quality determine whether the survival area remains intact and if there are sufficient crumple zones. The bodyshell construction of the new Golf takes particular account of these factors. The front lower side frame member, which takes the main impact in such a crash, dissipates the majority of the energy into predetermined fold points. A front located cross member ensures that the side not involved in the collision also takes part in the deformation. Additional side members in the upper sections of the wings absorb further deformation energy and route the forces to the A-pillar. This side-member construction is continued in the doors beneath the window edge to the rear panels. Reinforced door sills support this structure and reduce at the same time the risk of injury in a side impact. The new Golf is also protected against the results of a side-on collision by protective bars located in the doors. A rigid cross member in the vehicle's floor increases the stability and safety reserves of the vehicle's body.

And the results, leading to the simple conclusion that, 'the new Golf is not only better than its predecessor, it is also safer', were: 'after the impact, the bodyshell of the new Golf looked

Although the GTI as a concept had lost a little of its identity with the Mk3, thanks to the deletion of the famous red-edged front grille, the car was still recognizably a Golf. In confirmation of which model is which, the red car in the three photographs is the Mk3, the black car is a Mk2 GTI and the silver car is the equally anonymous Mk4. Note particularly the wide C-pillar where this is visible, a feature whose origins can be traced to the Mk1.

in visibly better condition than that of its predecessor'; 'the passenger cell of the new Golf was found to be considerably more rigid compared with its predecessor'; and 'the safety measures incorporated into the design of the new Golf also proved their worth in the interior'; which permitted the additional statement that, 'these positive results lead to the lowest HIC- value (Head Injury Criterion) which *Auto Motor und Sport* has ever recorded in an Offset crash ...'.

Although not contributing to the overall weight of the vehicle, Volkswagen's whole-hearted commitment to safety was demonstrated further by: the fitting of anti-submarining seats that prevented drivers and passengers from sliding underneath their lap belts during a collision; the design of the steering wheel to include a much improved energy-absorbing structure; a further developed steering column that increased the deformation limit by some 50 per cent; and seat-belt tensioners, which were created to tighten to the best possible position against the body in the event of a collision.

If Volkswagen was committed to safety, the burgeoning interest in the environment led the company to consider measures in that field too. The use of recycled plastic was widespread, with items ranging from bumpers to inner wheel-arch liners all being so manufactured. Laudable though such measures were, none did anything to reduce the Golf's weight; indeed, attempts to reduce noise pollution through fitting more insulating material, 10kg (22lb) in total, positively contributed to the car's heavier stance.

Finally, with reference to weight, Volkswagen had reassessed its market. Gone were the days when it was looking to produce a simple people's car, dismissed was the notion that the average GTI owner's only wish was for outright power and that the spartan trim was actually favoured by such drivers. Abandoned too was the assumption that the vast majority of GTI owners would be aged under thirty-five. The Mk3 was a more luxurious Golf than its predecessors, with models like the GTI bordering on the opulent. Indeed, the newly introduced VR6 flagship might best have been described as lavish, at least in Volkswagen terms, without of course demonstrating the ostentatious nature of some of the products of rival manufacturers. And it was through the upgrade in trim levels that a further gain in weight was inevitable, with the VR6 attracting more kilos than any other model.

Eight-Valve GTI

When the Mk3 Golf range made its debut in Britain in February 1992 there were two notable exceptions to the range announced in Germany a few months earlier. Absent was the 90ps GT, but this was a conscious decision on the part of the UK importer; missing also was

one of the two GTIs, the 16-valve model, although it was promised for the summer. In reality, the more powerful of the GTIs would be absent not only in the UK but across Europe and beyond until the last months of 1993, despite its inclusion in many a brochure, and therein lay the roots of the often held view then and to some extent still held now, that the Mk3 was the least successful of Golfs produced to date. A reliance on the smaller-engined GTI, burdened by extra weight, yet downgraded in terms of identity, and a still-to-be introduced issue of handling, all conspired to give credence to such opinions.

To say that the Mk3 GTI 8-valve benefited from a new engine was not entirely correct, although it was the first 2.0-litre unit to power a car badged with those legendary three letters. For the Mk3 GTI 8-valve's 1984cc engine, developing 115ps, which was achieved by increasing the bore and stroke to 82.5 and 92.8mm respectively from the 1781cc, 112ps engine's figures of 81.0 and 86.4mm, with a corresponding increase in compression ratios up to 10.4:1 from 10.0:1, was essentially the same unit that had powered the Mk1 Golf GTI some fifteen years earlier. Designed originally for the Audi GTE, the displacement had gone up to 1800cc towards the end of the life of the Mk1 GTI and now it had increased once more. Recalling the engine's early days, most would soon realize that maximum power had only increased by 5ps over the years and that the latest boost had only added 3ps to the score. A relatively leisurely 0–100km/h time of 10.1sec compared to the often quoted Mk2 8-valve's zip to the target in 8.3sec, was further exacerbated by a rethink on the part of Volkswagen, which proceeded as a result to recalculate the sprint time to a yawningly drawn-out 10.9sec. For the saddened, angry or simply curious, Volkswagen's UK press office explained that official performance figures were now calculated on the basis of a half-laden car, and as a result, 'might appear conservative when compared with data obtained by other means'.

Unlike both of its predecessors, the Mk3 GTI and the rest of the Golf range did not undergo any major facelifts during the production run, making model year identification more difficult. Equally tricky and particularly so as the years have gone by, with owners having changed the standard specification wheels, is the task of distinguishing between an 8- and a 16-valve car. However, there is one significant clue! An 8-valve car lacks a '16V' badge on the rear. The GTIs pictured are finished in Flash Red, a new shade that replaced Tornado Red in the latter part of the Mk3's run.

Mk3 GTI 8-valve 1992

Engine

Type	Transversely mounted 4-cylinder in-line
Bore and stroke	82.5mm × 92.8mm
Capacity	1984cc
Compression ratio	10.4:1
Fuel injection	Digifant
Max. power	115ps at 5,400rpm
Max. torque	122lb ft at 3,200rpm
Fuel capacity	55ltr (12.1gal)

Transmission

Gearbox	Five-speed manual	
Clutch	Single dry plate	
Ratios	1st	3.45
	2nd	1.94
	3rd	1.29
	4th	0.97
	5th	0.81
Final drive	3.67 to 1	

Suspension and Steering

Front	MacPherson struts and lower wishbones, coil springs, 20mm (0.78in) anti-roll bar
Rear	Torsion beam, trailing arms, track correcting mountings, coil springs, and 20mm anti-roll bar 'Plus suspension' – lower ride height 10mm (0.4in) at the front and 20mm at the rear
Steering	Maintenance-free power steering, self-adjusting rack and pinion
Tyres	195/50R 15V
Wheels	6J × 15 Le Mans Alloys

Brakes

Type	Diagonally divided dual circuit. ABS optional extra
Size	Front 280mm (11.0in) diameter discs, internally ventilated Rear 226mm (8.9in) diameter solid discs

Dimensions

Track		
	Front	1,462mm (57.6in)
	Rear	1,444mm (56.9in)
Wheelbase		2,475mm (97.4in)
Overall length		4,020mm (158.3in)
Overall width		1,710mm (67.3in)
Overall height		1,405mm (55.3in)
Unladen weight		1,035kg (2,282lb) two-door; 1,060kg (2,337lb) four-door

Performance

Top speed	198km/h (123mph)
	0–80km/h (0–50mph) 6.7sec
	0–100km/h (0–62mph) 10.1sec

However, all was not doom and gloom, for not only was the Mk3 GTI's top speed of 198k/h (123mph) up by 6.4km/h (4mph) on that of the Mk2 car, but also there was an improvement in torque. The 1.8-litre engine in the Mk2 GTI had a recorded maximum torque figure of 115lb ft, which was achieved at 3,100rpm – in itself good in comparison to earlier days, when to achieve a decent performance the engine had to be revved reasonably harshly. However, with the 2.0-litre engine maximum torque rose to 122lb ft at 3,200rpm, while at least 110lb ft was available from 1,900rpm all the way up to 5,400rpm; its broad spread

making it feel both more refined and flexible than its predecessor, if not exactly sporty. That the same engine found its way into vehicles as diverse as the Passat, Sharan and Corrado might go some way to reaffirm its generally relaxed nature, while nevertheless being a unit that could perform strongly when required.

That the GTI achieved the performance it did in such an unflustered manner did nothing for its street credibility. Journalists expected a car bearing the GTI brand to be gruffer, harsher and noisier. They found it difficult to come to terms with Volkswagen's notion of smooth, high-speed transport for rising executives and were overly critical of the new car's characteristics, with which they weren't as yet completely *au fait.*

Fuel consumption, as might have been anticipated with such an engine, was generally thought to be good with an average of 8.1ltr/100km (35mpg) being readily achievable even if a percentage of hard driving was included. Less convincing was the Mk3 GTI's handling, variously described as 'flabby', 'soggy', or simply 'less impressive' than that of its predecessors, while steering too appeared to some to be 'lacking in response'. Again seen as a victim of Volkswagen's brand realignment, the latest GTI appeared to be angled towards comfortable cruising, rather than the desired optimum in handling, despite the 'plus' specification outlined in numerous pieces of print:

> Performance suspension – front: the independent front suspension lowered by 20mm, features MacPherson struts, coil springs, telescopic dampers and an anti-roll bar. The 'plus' suspension package, standard on the GTI, includes geometry changes and a stiffer power-assisted steering, giving the car impressive stability. Performance suspension – rear: featuring a torsion beam axle, coil springs, telescopic gas-filled dampers and an anti-roll bar, the rear suspension has been lowered by approximately 20mm ...

Intended to iron out potholes, humps and bumps on the more minor roads, the GTI felt agile enough in town driving, but once away from that environment most were convinced that the steering and damping both needed to be firmer. Volkswagen took heed of the comments and adjusted the match between springing and damping as the years went by, with the result that a late Mk3 GTI felt considerably better than an earlier one. Sadly, mud sticks and few members of the general automobile press took the trouble to revise their original opinions. Indeed, writing in the summer of 1994, *Autocar & Motor* remained unconvinced, even when testing no lesser a model than a VR6:

> Its body control and general cornering composure are no longer as good as they should be in a 140mph car. But more worrying still is the disconcerting corkscrewing motion at the rear end through fast corners, highlighted by any broken or undulating surface ... No matter how much more involving the Golf is down a twisting B-road, such fundamental failings cannot go unpunished.

However, the specialist magazines who returned to the Mk3 GTI on a regular basis should have the last word on the subject of suspension, if for no other reason than the Mk3's reputation many years after the event. Paul Harris of *Volkswagen Audi Car* wrote in 1995 of the Mk3 not having got any lighter, and of it still being 'podgy in comparison with the Mk2 cars', but at least 'the handling was no longer in the rice pudding category'. A year later he had much more to say:

> Volkswagen has not told anyone what it has done to the suspension of the GTI, but someone has been working behind the scenes to smarten up a system which, originally, did not do the car justice. The major difference is the degree of damping, now much firmer than before. It keeps the wheels more under control on bumpy roads and limits the amount of roll. The net results may not be firm enough for extremists, but the average GTI driver will find it a good compromise between ride quality and precise handling.

Inside, the Mk3 GTI was more luxurious than its predecessor, although in the process it lost some of its hot-hatch identity. The dashboard was both attractive and well laid out, but its image was of luxury rather than sportiness and there were few distinguishing marks to herald it as the facia of a GTI, while the design of the three-spoke sports steering wheel was such that only those making a direct comparison with the equally well-padded four-spoke affair offered in the GL, or the slightly simpler but still plush wheel of the lesser models, would have understood that here was the sportier version. Gone was the hallmark golf-ball gear

---

Mk3 GTI Paintwork Options 1992

Check out the paintwork listing in a brochure produced to promote the attributes of the newly launched Mk3 GTI and, at first glance, it appears that just three shades of paint were on offer and, curiously, that most traditional of GTI colours, silver, wasn't one of them. Standard colours then were Tornado Red, Black – now coupled to the code 9,000 – and Alpine White. Optional colours available at extra cost included all the metallic shades and two pearl-effect hues. Perhaps the biggest news was that Diamond Silver had at last been replaced by a new shade given the apt name of Satin Silver. This metallic option, which would last through the remainder of the Mk3's run and into the early days of Mk4 production, had a silky sheen to it, sometimes mistaken for a milky or even neglected look.

The full list of options in 1992 in addition to the plain colours already mentioned was as follows: Windsor Blue Metallic; Montana Green Metallic; Brilliant Black Metallic; Dusty Mauve Pearl Effect; Satin Silver Metallic; Indian Red Pearl Effect; and Pearl Grey Metallic.

---

knob, while the sports seats were trimmed with a particularly attractive Jacquard Classic material in black with mauve, green and blue darts, which would have been ideal for any executive saloon. Yes, the letters GTI were embroidered into the backrests, but Volkswagen's own choice of both 'tasteful' and 'discreet' as descriptions for their once loud, vibrant and outgoing interior undoubtedly confirmed once more the direction in which the company had moved. Curiously, the GT, which as has already been mentioned wasn't on the UK specification list, hit the German market in both standard and special guise; the latter sporting the most GTI-like upholstery for several years. Known as French-Karo, on a base of black, the material featured bright red, green, blue and grey stripes!

Although nowadays drivers would take for granted such items as a central locking system that automatically closed both the windows and sunroof, a mileage recorder which also

advised when the next service was due and a pollen filter, in the early 1990s these goodies, all of which were standard on the new GTI, were strictly the preserve of the luxury class and particularly so when factory-fitted options included ABS, airbags, rear head restraints, front fog lamps and manual air conditioning. All of these items would lead directly to a new flagship model, conceivably a truly executive GTI with performance to match, or possibly simply a luxury car designed to suit the American buyer. However, the truth of the matter was that the VR6's role in life was neither.

'The New Golf VR6. In a Class of its Own'

When Volkswagen launched the Golf GTI it created a new breed of car – the 'hot hatch'. With the VR6 Volkswagen has again created a new class of car – one which combines luxury and effortless performance with all the practicalities of a hatchback.

(Launch brochure 1992)

To be blunt, nothing in Volkswagen's Europe-wide marketing suggested that the VR6 was a GTI, but perhaps due to the absence of a 16-valve version of the GTI at launch more than a few erroneously attributed it with such credentials, undoubtedly to Volkswagen's considerable, but silent, annoyance. After all, for example, in Britain the VR6 was the first Mk3 Golf to tread rubber on UK soil when it made a guest appearance at the Earls Court Motorfair held in October 1991. In February 1992, when the Mk3 went on sale in the UK, the VR6 headed the list of models available. The car cost in excess of 30 per cent more than the GTI 8-valve and was possessed of a 174ps engine capable of a top speed of 225km/h (140mph). Accustomed to two breeds of GTI for the last few years and the flagship Golf always being a GTI since the first-generation model joined the then range in the long distant 1970s, what were people expected to think?

As a part of the emerging brand strategy Volkswagen wanted a V6 engine, not just for

Unless the image of a VR6 under observation is a late model, only the car's alloys and VR6 badges readily distinguish it from the Mk3 GTI. The owner of this VR6 has either added or inherited the red bumper piping, a feature of the rather lowly Golf Driver, or the sought-after Mk3 Anniversary GTI. To some, the effect might be one of making the car look cheaper, but to the hot-hatch enthusiast, it is pure magic.

the Golf, but also for the largest model in the family, the Passat. The goal was not to encroach on GTI territory, the absence of a really powerful 16-valve GTI being of an accidental nature rather than a deliberate strategy, but to capture a good part of the lucrative market held by BMW. Renowned for the superior, smooth and yes, sporting performance of their 6-cylinder engines, BMW reaped the benefits of people willing to pay considerably more for cars so endowed. Mercedes and Opel had also been developing similar cars and successfully extending their respective customer bases; Volkswagen needed to act swiftly.

Sister company Audi was already well ahead in the V6 game, even though Volkswagen had seemingly been half-heartedly experimenting with such technology for a number of years. Sadly, the Innsbruck engine at the time wasn't suited to either the Passat or particularly the Golf in terms of its size. What was required was an engine that was a good deal shorter than an in-line six and considerably narrower than a conventional V6. After all, at least in the case of the Golf and preferably both models, the engine would be mounted transversely. Again, this was essential if both the Golf's short bonnet and small turning circle were to be maintained,

107

Compare this VR6 with the car on the previous page and this one can be identified as the later of the two vehicles by the absence of plastic wheel-arch trim. Although this feature was retained on the GTI, at least to modern eyes the VR6's overall appearance is improved by the deletion of unnecessary plastic.

while to guarantee good crash protection the engine needed to be narrow enough to leave a sufficient safety zone at the front of the car. The solution was an in-line V, or VR6, the German word *reihen* translating as in a row or line, and confirming that two banks of three cylinders were at an angle of 15 degrees contained in a single cast-iron block and served by just one aluminium cylinder head. The 2 valves per cylinder engine was given the designation of

VR6 DOHC on its valve cover, and whilst it carried two overhead camshafts, one operated both the intake and exhaust valves for a single bank of three cylinders, while the other did the same for the remaining bank.

Clearly the most powerful Golf to date, the 2.8-litre, 2792cc VR6 had a bore and stroke of 81mm and 90.3mm respectively, a compression ratio of 10.0:0, and developed 174ps at 5,800rpm. Peak torque of 173lb ft was achieved at 4,200rpm, but that was only a part of the story of the VR6, as it possessed a very broad

Mk3 VR6 1993

Engine

Type	Front 15-degree V6 transversely mounted. Single light alloy cylinder head. Chain-driven single camshaft per bank. 2 valves per cylinder
Bore and stroke	81.0mm × 90.3mm
Capacity	2792cc
Compression ratio	10.0:0
Fuel injection	Bosch motronic
Max. power	174ps at 5,800rpm
Max. torque	173lb ft at 4,200rpm
Fuel capacity	55ltr (12.1gal)

Transmission

Gearbox	Five-speed manual	
Clutch	Single dry plate	
Ratios	1st	3.30
	2nd	1.94
	3rd	1.31
	4th	1.03
	5th	0.84
Final drive	3.68 to 1	

Suspension and Steering

Front	MacPherson struts with lower wishbones, coil springs and anti-roll bar
Rear	Torsion beam, trailing arms, coil springs and anti-roll bar 'Plus suspension' – lower ride height 20mm (0.78in) at both the front and rear
Steering	Maintenance-free power steering, self-adjusting rack and pinion
Tyres	205/50R 15V
Wheels	65J × 15 BBS Alloys

Brakes

Type	Diagonally divided dual circuit. Servo-assisted. ABS and EDS (Electronic Traction Control)
Size	Front 280mm (11.0in) diameter discs, internally ventilated Rear 226mm (8.9in) diameter solid discs

Dimensions

Track	
Front	1,464mm (57.6in)
Rear	1,448mm (57in)
Wheelbase	2,475mm (97.4in)
Overall length	4,020mm (158.3in)
Overall width	1,695mm (66.7in)
Overall height	1,417mm (55.8in)
Unladen weight	1,210kg (2,667lb) two-door; 1,240kg (2,734lb) four-door

Performance

Top speed	225km/h (140mph) 0–100km/h (0–62mph) 7.8sec

torque curve with 147lb ft or more available from as little as 2,000rpm right up to 6,000rpm. Volkswagen's figures for the 0–100km/h sprint varied a little over the years and of course were now measured 'with half payload', but nevertheless suggested a crisp surge accommodating a time of anything between 7.6 and 7.8sec and a top speed hovering around 225km/h (140mph). The key to its success, however, lay in its mid-range performance where it was noticeably quicker than the GTI 8-valve and would also be faster than the 16-valve when that joined the family.

The VR6's performance was variously described as 'silky,' or 'smooth'; the result of 6-cylinder technology linked to power being readily available from the point of ignition upwards and right through the ranges. Volkswagen captured the moment in its promotional literature after first noting both the 0–100km/h time and maximum speed: '... Even more impressive is the manner in which it performs – quiet and smooth, it has a level of refinement not normally associated with such performance.'

Ventilated front discs measuring 280 × 32mm (11 × 1.25in) at the front and solid 226

× 10mm (8.8 × 0.4in) ones at the rear ensured that even a car of the VR6's capabilities could be brought to a halt swiftly, while it was also the first Volkswagen to be fitted with Electronic Differential Lock (EDL), also known as TCS, or Traction Control System, in addition to ABS, a clever arrangement where in the event of one wheel starting to spin, power was automatically transferred to the remaining one. Although not available for the British market, the VR6 could be specified with syncro for those demanding even more in the way of sure-footedness.

Not surprisingly, the only real criticism of the car's mechanical attributes came with regard to its suspension, which was of the same basic 'Plus' arrangement as that of the GTI. Fitted with stiffer front springs than the GTI to compensate for the extra weight of the engine, the shock absorbers remained the same as those fitted to the hot hatch and, while its anti-roll bar had a 20mm (0.78in) diameter compared to the GTI's 18mm (0.7in) version, nevertheless there was a feeling that it was under-damped, particularly when coping with rougher roads. Potentially, passengers were likely to complain of the ride being too bouncy, while at worst handling might easily also have been affected.

The other potential issue with the VR6 related to fuel consumption. Official figures gave an urban-cycle reading of 12.6ltr/100km (22.4mpg), while at a constant 90km/h (56mph) 7.3ltr/100km (38.7mpg) was recorded. However, common-sense reality was a little harsher, with one magazine suggesting figures starting with a miserably low 16.7ltr/100km (17mpg) after a relatively short stretch of hard driving, rising to 11.3ltr/100km (25mpg) when great care had been taken to make little use of the right foot. However, considering the car's purchase price, would most owners have been concerned? In modern-day terms does a slightly higher rate of road licence fund pinch the pocket of the owner of a £40,000 Touareg? In reality, the only occasions when fuel consumption became an issue was when a second-

hand VR6 was snapped up by an enthusiast who wanted to make full use of its electric power, treating it like a double-gold GTI.

Inside, the VR6 was inevitably the most luxurious Golf yet available, its price, if nothing else, demanding this! Fitted as standard with the same sports seats as the GTI, the VR6 might be trimmed either in Black or Mauritius Blue Jacquard cloth, but it was not unusual to find cars with either black leather throughout or Recaro front seats. At the time of the VR6's launch, appendices containing comprehensive equipment listings seemed out of favour in Volkswagen's literature, but amongst the VR6's interior goodies were a height-adjustable steering column and leather-covered wheel, an MFA trip computer, a reading light and courtesy light delay, plus a pollen counter.

Otherwise, green-tinted heat-insulating glass, an electrically operated glass tilt and slide sunroof, electric windows front and rear, electric mirrors, variable interval wipers and front fog lights were all standard, as were 6.5J × 15 BBS cross-spoke alloys, shod with 205/50R 15V tyres, while it was taken for granted that colour-coded bumpers, door mirror housings and front grille, black sills and spoilers, plus darkened rear light lenses would be standard.

As for paint options, the VR6 was available in all the classic GTI colours, ranging from Tornado Red, Alpine White, Black and Saturn Silver, through to another more upmarket shade referred to as Brilliant Black Metallic, while this option gave a clue to a further spectrum of exotica, ranging from Montana Green Metallic, to Indian Red Pearl Effect, Dusty Mauve Pearl Effect and Windsor Blue Metallic. Not that Volkswagen was trying to create an elite paint range for the VR6, for all the aforementioned colours plus one more, Pearl Grey Metallic, were also available as GTI shades.

When the time came to analyse sales the big question regarding the VR6 had to be one of assessing Volkswagen's success in what it had set itself to do. Was BMW quivering and quaking in its well-heeled shoes? Had other manufacturers thrown in the towel? Probably even for

A VR6 finished in Alpine White is not seen all that often. The colour highlights the general styling of the higher-ranking Mk3s of this vintage, so despite the car being in partial shade the photographs were taken. Note the darkened rear lenses and the tailgate spoiler and bee-sting aerial.

Volkswagen the jury remained out on the subject of the VR6. As will be revealed when the Mk4 Golf comes under scrutiny, there was no straightforward replacement for this breed of Golf. However, there was both a V5, which shared many of its characteristics, and eventually there was a V6 4MOTION that appeared to inherit more still, but also seemed to be the choice of caravan owners. Of course, some might say the late entry Mk4 R32 was the real VR6 successor, but also a direct descendant of the Mk2 Golf Rallye. Perhaps the simplest solution to the VR6's fate was to describe it as a victim of a further change in direction, brought about by the arrival in 1993 of a new and very determined Director General, Ferdinand Piëch.

But even if Volkswagen wasn't entirely sure of what it had done, the motoring press appeared to have drawn its own encouraging conclusions.

Autocar & Motor was congratulatory of Volkswagen's initiative: 'Like all the best ideas, installing a muscular V6 engine in a regular family hatch body and creating an overnight classic seems, in hindsight, such a simple and obvious concept to execute.'

The magazine, like others before and after it, also tackled head-on the issue that Volkswagen had brought to the boil, by posing the ultimate question, 'Is VW's 6-cylinder Golf just an expensive GTI for grown-ups or a sporting car the equal of even BMW's wonderful 325i? What a confrontation ...'. After considerable debate, *Autocar & Motor*'s conclusion was indisputable:

> The BMW remains a potent force, and there are people who, like us, will go on adoring it for that.

The 1996 Golf VR6

This late in the production run, the brochure confirms that the VR6's looks were improved through the removal of the plastic wheel-arch trims, which were retained on the GTI.

The Golf VR6 Highline

Perhaps the special edition Highline's luxurious interior should have graced the cover of the special insert brochure designed to promote its attributes, as only the real enthusiast would be able to distinguish the car from the exterior.

But in performance, refinement and handling the VR6 shows that much of the 325i's potency is achievable in a smaller, less expensive package …

Victory, in the end, is unequivocal. The Golf VR6 is faster, more economical, more fun to drive, especially for those brought up on front-wheel drive cars, more refined in several key ways and potentially cheaper by up to £4,000. It is easier to drive fast or slow, it has more room inside, a heap more day-to-day practicality and an engine that's just as characterful. Perhaps most telling of all, in no area does it lag noticeably behind the 325i …

16-Valve – Back with a Vengeance?

In the global picture of the history of hotter Golfs, many would have thought placing the VR6 chronologically before the Mk3 16-valve

Even though the Mk3 GTI 16-valve's arrival was delayed quite considerably, all brochures contained full details about it. This style of cover, dating from the mid-period of the car's production run, would have been one of the first to include legitimate details regarding the 16-valve.

If in doubt, check the back of the car! Here's the official red '16V' badge, the sole preserve of the 16-valve GTI.

GTI to be a little curious. However, reality was that in partnership with the Mk3 GTI 8-valve, the VR6 had to fly the flag for some considerable time following the latest Golf's launch, for, to put it simply, despite Volkswagen's assurances and pretty pictures in brochures, a new 16-valve engine was nowhere near ready. Frustration mounted – the VR6 was doing what it had been designed to do but it wasn't a GTI; the 8-valve model had its own problems relating to health and safety weight issues, while it had never been intended that it should replace both the 8- and 16-valve Mk2 models.

Few would have thought it possible that when the Mk3 GTI was launched in the autumn of 1991 that it would be two full years before the 16-valve version was available. Volkswagen insisted that the delay was the result of a problem with the engine assembly line, while cynics argued that it was a devious ploy by the marketing department to avoid any form of distraction from the newly launched VR6 in the shape of an additional performance-oriented engine, while rumours persisted that the root cause was the development of the engine itself. For the planned 2.0-litre 16-valve wasn't just an upgrade of the Mk2's K-Jetronic from 1.8 to 2.0 litres, nor was it the same catalyst 16-valve developing 136ps that had already been used in both the Passat and the sporty Corrado. Instead, this was a completely new engine designed specifically for the Mk3 GTI. Amongst the differences with this 2.0-litre, tall block, Digifant, later Simos, injection engine, were its new design cylinder head, larger valves and alternative option cams.

The net result was a 1984cc engine that developed 150ps at 6,000rpm, offered a 0–100km/h sprint of 8.7sec and roared its way

---

Mk3 GTI 16-valve 1994

Engine

Type	Transversely mounted 4-cylinder in-line
	Twin overhead camshafts driven via a toothed belt. 4 valves per cylinder
Bore and stroke	82.5mm × 92.8.4mm
Capacity	1984cc
Compression ratio	10.4:1
Fuel injection	Digifant
Max. power	150ps at 6,000rpm
Max. torque	133lb ft at 4,800rpm
Fuel capacity	55ltr (12.1gal)

Transmission

Gearbox	Five-speed manual	
Clutch	Single dry plate	
Ratios	1st	3.35
	2nd	1.94
	3rd	1.31
	4th	1.03
	5th	0.84
Final drive	3.68 to 1	

Suspension and Steering

Front	MacPherson struts and lower wishbones, coil springs, 20mm (0.78in) anti-roll bar
Rear	Torsion beam, trailing arms, track correcting mountings, coil springs and 20mm anti-roll bar 'Plus suspension' – lower ride height 10mm (0.4in) at the front and 20mm at the rear EDL traction control system

Steering	Maintenance-free power steering, self-adjusting rack and pinion
Tyres	205/50R 15V
Wheels	6.5J × 15 Monte Carlo Alloys

Brakes

Type	Diagonally divided dual circuit. ABS
Size	Front 280mm (11.0in) diameter discs, internally ventilated
	Rear 226mm (8.9in) diameter solid discs

Dimensions

Track	
Front	1,462mm (57.6in)
Rear	1,444mm (56.9in)
Wheelbase	2,475mm (97.4in)
Overall length	4,020mm (158.3in)
Overall width	1,710mm (67.3in)
Overall height	1,405mm (55.3in)
Unladen weight	1,165kg (2,568lb) two-door; 1,195kg (2,634lb) four-door (Weights taken from Volkswagen's own literature – note, general text suggests different unladen weights partly as Volkswagen now included the driver.)

Performance

Top speed	216km/h (134mph)
	0–100km/h (0–62mph) 8.7sec

Volkswagen UK's Mk3 GTI lacks a grille badge, but at least the eagle-eyed will be able to spot that this is a 16-valve car from letters and initials on the rear. Built in 1997 and listed as a 1998 model year car, according to VW the car's specification was high. Amongst the goodies a potential owner would have obtained for his or her purchase price of £16,575 would have been: EDS; 6.5 × 15 Long Beach alloys with 205/50R 15V tyres; darkened rear light lenses and front fog lights; suspension lowered by 10mm at the front and 20mm at the rear; electric windows and electrically heated and adjustable door mirrors; height adjustable Recaro sport seats finished in Black Cockpit upholstery; body-coloured bumpers and radiator grille; plus a double lock central-locking system. It is worth noting that the listing is based on Volkswagen's own specification document and in one or two instances contradicts the brochure details for the same model year.

up to a maximum speed of 216km/h (134mph). Maximum torque of 133lb ft was achieved at 4,800rpm. Clearly this was a big improvement on the 8-valve's 10.9sec to 100km/h, plus its top speed of 198km/h (123mph), and virtually guaranteed driver satisfaction, as did the healthy growl emitted by the 16-valve when it approached anything near 6,000rpm. Key to this was the much broader power curve, which guaranteed 125lb ft torque availability all the way up from 2,000 to 6,000rpm. (In comparison, the Mk2 GTI's maximum torque stood at 123.5lb ft at 4,600rpm.) On the downside, the 16-valve weighed more than the 8-valve even according to Volkswagen's own figures. Comparative unladen weights were respectively 1,045kg (2,304lb) for the 8-valve and 1,090kg (2,404lb) for the 16, and as both cars were considerably heavier than the Mk2 for reasons with which we are now entirely conversant, some testers felt that even the Mk3 16-valve's performance wasn't entirely blistering.

Paul Harris of *Volkswagen Audi Car* even went so far as to criticize the latest addition's gearing, while admitting that overall he had 'mixed feelings about the GTI 16V'. He went on to say:

> Because of the engine characteristics, you find that you need to be in a lower gear than you'd expect if you want the engine to pull hard. On bends which we would normally take in third gear, we were dropping down into second to get the needle above 4,000rpm ... The ratios of the 8V's gearbox seem to be much better suited to the engine. The boxes are entirely different, the 8V relying on the long established 020 with its rod gear change linkage ... [while] ... both the 16V and VR6 versions use the cable operated box ...

Autocar & Motor, however, needed little convincing of the Mk3 16-valve's merits:

> While it's more tractable than the old engine and the power delivery is essentially seamless, there's a small but still palpable increase in acceleration,

accompanied by a hardening of the exhaust note from 4,000rpm as it squirts to the 6,900rpm red line. Any harshness has departed and above 5,000rpm the new engine is noticeably quieter without losing all of what one VW marketing man calls 'the Italian sound' ... Far more responsive than the 8-valve GTI, this is an endearing engine that sounds just right for a car wearing a GTI badge ... Significantly, ... the 16V has the performance to enhance the Golf's chassis. ... Accurate, precise steering combines with neutral handling, beautifully controlled body movements and secure grip to give impeccable manners ... After building 1.14 million GTIs, VW has moved the goalposts on the 16V ...

As an added plus point, owners were keen to report back on fuel consumption, for the 16-valve wasn't a great deal thirstier than the 8-valve and, of course, in a different league to that of the VR6. Using Volkswagen's own figures, on the urban cycle the 16-valve only lost out to the 8-valve by 236ltr/100km (1.2mpg), while at a steady 90km/h (56mph) the difference was still only 98ltr/100km (2.9mpg). At a constant 120km/h (75mph) the Mk3 GTI 8-valve recorded 7.4ltr/100km (38.2mpg) compared to the 16-valve's 7.9ltr/100km (35.8mpg). *What Car?* suggested 9.6ltr/100km (29.4mpg) overall, while *Audi Driver* on two separate tests came up with a figure of 9.3ltr/100km (30.4mpg).

Volkswagen certainly missed a trick, however, when it trimmed the new 16-valve. Customers were paying an additional £2,000 for the more powerful engine, but visually the two cars were virtually indistinguishable. The 16-valve did sport slightly larger wheels, 6.5J × 15 Monte Carlo alloys, a broad five-spoke design already in use on both the VR6 and Corrado and shod with 205/50R 15V tyres, compared to the 8-valve GTI's 6J × 15 Le Mans alloys, which in turn ran on 195/50R 15V rubber, but the only other external distinguishing mark came in the form of a small '16V' badge below the standard 'Golf GTI' moniker at the rear of the car. At least this

badge marked the return, albeit in a minor way, for the GTI's hallmark colour of red, while later in the 16-valve's run the shiny GTI insignia on the car's grille was replaced with a second and somewhat larger red 16V emblem. Inside the 16-valve, only someone with an encyclopaedic knowledge of the brochure specification would have been aware of the car's identity through the inclusion of a front brake pad wear indicator in the instrument panel and a slightly different model of radio cassette.

Of real merit, the 16-valve's disc brakes, identical in size to those of the 8-valve at 280 × 22mm (11 × 0.9in) (vented) at the front and 226mm (8.9in) (solid) at the rear, not only came with ABS, an extra-cost option for the smaller engine car, but also with Traction Control System (TCS).

This reasonably late Mk3 GTI 16-valve sports has the large red 16V emblem close to the headlamp cluster.

Production Changes

In October 1994 both Mk3 GTIs were specified with a driver's airbag as standard, while front passengers could be similarly protected at extra cost. ABS was added to the 8-valve's specification and both cars were fitted with an electronic engine immobilizer. The once-standard electric sunroof became an optional extra, while the upholstery was changed from restrained Jacquard Classic cloth to equally sober Cockpit material, basically black with occasional patches of fine red and blue thread blended in. The 8-valve was endowed with a new design of wheels, the nine-spoke 6.5J × 15 Long Beach, taking it to the same size, if not appearance, of the 16-valve. For the 1996 model year, the front brake discs were enlarged to 288 × 25mm (11.2 × 2in), encompassing both larger pads and calipers, while the 16-valve from this point shared the Long Beach alloys with its less powerful sibling.

As for the VR6, twin airbags had become standard in 1994, but in order that this could be accomplished for the front passenger, at least in the case of right-hand-drive models, the glovebox had to be dispensed with. However, the biggest development in the VR6's production span was entirely in keeping with its purpose; the arrival of the ultra-sumptuous Highline in the summer of 1995, an introduction which coincided with a relatively minor but nevertheless interesting body makeover for the VR6 as a whole.

Scan through the pages of a Mk3 brochure, preferably a German edition where more models are depicted, and it soon becomes noticeable that rules had been set with regard to plastic wheel-arch trims. Hence, the lowly CL inevitably, plus the more elegant GL possibly surprisingly, lacked this form of trim, but the GT, GTI and VR6, the brand leaders, possessed it. Conceivably, at least a modicum of sporting credentials were key, for expensive oddities like the Golf syncro, which had a very different role to play, tended to be bracketed

with the likes of the GL. Special models, such as a further incarnation of the Driver GTI lookalike, might have had an assortment of extras thrown in, in that instance 6J × 14 Orlando alloys shod with 185/60 R14H tyres, darkened rear light lenses, an electric glass slide and tilt sunroof, a tailgate-mounted rear spoiler, and amazingly considering the situation with the genuine item, red pin striping on both the front and rear bumpers, but wheel-arch trims were not included. Breaking the rules previously set, concurrent with the launch of the Highline option of the VR6, the flagship car lost its wheel-arch trims, not to mention the previously intrusive flank badges, but gained fully colour-coded bumpers, mirror housings and side rubbing strips, making it appear somehow both more modern and gracefully attractive.

The 1997 Golf GTI

1997 and the end of the line! Even though the Mk3 lacked the red-line technology of previous generations it did sport a GTI badge on its grille.

With little in the way of visual changes to the Mk3 GTI to illustrate, the opportunity is taken to present a brief gallery of personalized Mk3 GTI models, cars which range from the simple expedient of different alloys, meatier exhausts and extra dark lenses, to fully fledged body kits and easy to accomplish badge removals.

The Golf GTI Colour Concept

The Mk3 GTI Colour Concept finished here in disarmingly bright Jazz Blue and trimmed with Votex accessories. (Photograph Courtesy of the Volkswagen UK Press Office)

The Colour Concept notion was undoubtedly something that appealed to the German car-buying public, with customers eagerly snapping up not just GTIs so bedecked but also other Golfs, not to mention other models in Volkswagen's repertoire. For the 1996 model year UK buyers wanting a rather special GTI could join in the alleged fun of what was essentially a sales-boosting exercise. The Colour Concept was produced, according to Volkswagen's marketing people, in five 'vibrant' paint shades, three of which had been 'developed exclusively' for this trim package. These were Salsa Green, Jazz Blue Pearl Effect and Yellow, to which were added the appropriate shade of Flash Red and the oddball in the pack, Diamond Black Pearl Effect.

Having duly trimmed the steering wheel with black leather, a first for any Mk3 GTI, Volkswagen then proceeded to apply generous amounts of the external paint shade around the car's interior; the effect was loud to say the least. Matching leather on the seats, both front and rear, contrasted with the black bolsters, while the same effect was gained on the side trim panels. Both the gear knob and gaiter, plus the handbrake lever, were similarly trimmed in colourful leather, while the black carpet mats and the aforementioned steering wheel were bound in colour-matched leather in the first instance, or stitched with colour-matched thread in the latter case. Even the VW roundel stamped into the plastic of the airbag steering wheel pad was adorned with colour.

Externally, the Colour Concept could be further identified by reasonably discreet in size, if loud in content, logos at the rear end of each side rubbing strip, plus darkened side indicators, while the 6.5 × 15in Solitude alloys, until now only mentioned in the context of the VR6 Highline, were part of the standard package. Silver-faced dashboard instruments were gimmicky and so were front seats that could be adjusted for various levels of heat on a winter's morning, but when this device was attached to the Recaro name few, if any, were going to complain.

The Golf GTI Colour Concept

The popular but loud Colour Concept GTI warranted its own mini brochure. However, it was to be read in conjunction with the standard VW literature.

This Yellow Colour Concept has been modified, but at least it leaves a lasting impression when it comes to the intensity of its colour.

The Colour Concept logo towards the rear wheel on the side rubbing strip.

The Mk3 GTI Colour Concept's interior, on this occasion trimmed in yellow, was undoubtedly a matter of personal taste. (Photograph Courtesy of Volkswagen UK Press Office)

Basically, the Colour Concept was a love it, or loath it, package, with some sexists proclaiming that it was greatly favoured by lady owners. Costing £1,650 more than the standard GTI, it may have appeared a great deal of extra money to pay to receive in return a little fun with colours and no form of mechanical enhancement, but when the Recaros at £551 and the leather upholstery at £1,283 were each taken into account, it was obvious that Volkswagen had trimmed their prices to present such a special, while the conservative purchaser wishing to take part in such a good deal but reluctant to be seen behind the wheel of a Salsa Green car, had recourse to safe and sound black.

The success of special edition was such that the Colour Concept remained an option until the end of Mk3 production, while Jazz Blue Pearl Effect paint became a standard element of Volkswagen's colour range.

The idea of a Colour Concept was reincarnated for a couple of years during the production run of the Mk4 Golf. In the UK, and as a factory-fitted option only, would-be owners could specify paintwork in Jazz Blue, Green Collection, Berry Red, Yellow, or what Volkswagen opted to describe as a 'more distinguished black'. As with the Mk3 Colour Concept, the exterior colour of the car was translated to its interior, affecting the centre panels of the seats, the gear-lever gaiter, the front leather section of the handbrake lever and the surround of the controls on the driver's door. Stitching on both the leather steering wheel and seats as well as the binding on the carpet mats, were also finished in the same colour. Externally, the Colour Concept cars were fitted with 16in Montreal alloys, while Recaro front seats were standard. Sadly, on this occasion the package was only extended to the 2.0-litre GTI and not the more powerful 1.8T. The top of the range diesel Golf and the V5 could also be specified as Colour Concept models.

The red option on the Colour Concept theme. This is Flash Red, a popular choice into the current century, at least while such coloured cars were in vogue.

The Highline was available in just two colours, Diamond Black Pearl Effect and Purple Violet Pearl Effect, while the interior was trimmed with corresponding shades of leather, either Black with black paint, or Blackberry with purple paint. The manual version, many such cars being automatics, had an American Walnut gear knob, while all Highline models, whether two- or four-door, came with heated front sports seats and manual air conditioning fitted as standard. A further distinction came in the form of 6.5 × 15 six-spoke Solitude alloys.

20 *Jahre* Golf GTI

In Germany it was the 20 *Jahre* Golf GTI, in the UK simply the Golf GTI Anniversary model, although brochure references to 21 years of GTI 'engineering excellence' abounded. To most, though, it didn't really matter if Volkswagen was celebrating the Frankfurt Motor Show debut of the GTI in 1975, or the start of production in June 1976, for while the limited-edition model sported no mechanical additions, it offered purchasers the chance to own a GTI trimmed in the way that many thought it should have been since the lacklustre Mk3 design package arrived on the scene in late 1991.

The Anniversary model, limited in the UK to 600 8-valve models and just 150 16-valve cars, was available in five colours, four of which were classic GTI shades. These were Black, to which was added Diamond Black Pearl Effect, Flash Red, the latest in Wolfsburg's unbroken line of strikingly bright red options, plus Satin Silver metallic. The fifth offering, Mystic Blue Pearl Effect, bore no reference to GTI heritage; just as a sixth shade offered on the German market, Moonlight Blue Pearl Effect, didn't either.

The Anniversary model sported particularly attractive wheels, 7 × 16 sixteen-spoke BBS RX 11 split-rim alloys, which were shod with 215/40 tyres. Perhaps slightly more difficult to keep pristine than many an alloy, while sadly

rumours of corrosion problems abounded, these wheels had one big advantage over the standard GTI 6.5 × 15 rims, as being fatter and meatier than the norm, road adhesion was improved. Visible behind the alloys were red-painted calipers, just one of several measures to reinstate red hot-hatch hallmark trim. The GTI badge, or '16V', on the front grille was painted red, as was every element of the insignia at the rear of the car. Enthusiasts were delighted to see the reappearance of red on the body of the car too, with piping on both bumpers and on the lower part of each side rubbing strip. These mouldings also carried red GTI initials just forward of the rear wheels. Other external features included the slightly deeper front spoiler previously allocated to the VR6 and, rather larger than normal, chromed

The Golf GTI Anniversary.

Compared with its German counterpart, the English version of the Anniversary brochure was a slender publication amounting to half the number of pages, although the covers were more or less the same.

An official press image of the Mk3 Golf GTI Anniversary. (Photograph Courtesy of Volkswagen AG)

Mk3 GTI Paintwork Options 1997

At the time that the Mk3 GTI was about to bid *adieu*, paint options had multiplied considerably, with a total of thirteen options now readily available. Of these colours, four were plain, although only one was instantly recognizable, as Tornado Red had been replaced by the brighter and louder Flash Red, while Alpine White had melted into Candy White. New on the plain colour front was Maritime Blue, leaving Black as the old-timer. Metallic options had been trimmed back to just three colours, namely Storm Grey, Electric Green and Satin, leaving plenty of scope for the new wave of pearl-effect hues. These were: Pacific Blue; Red Chilli; Mystic Blue; Twilight Violet; Dragon Green; and Diamond Black.

twin tailpipes. Tinted front fog lamp and indicator lenses, which only later became standard on all GTIs, were part of the package, but an electric sunroof, which was standard on German 20 *Jahre* models, came as an extra-cost option in the UK.

The interior of the Anniversary model put the standard GTI in near identical 8- and 16-valve guise to shame. Gone was the sombre mood; this car looked like a hot hatch! The sports seats were covered in a special Sportline fabric of near black and red checks that included the GTI logo, while the classic golf-ball gear lever made a welcome return, now being made of a combination of aluminium and black plastic. Volkswagen's marketing department had thought of everything!

Although the Mk3 Golf GTI Anniversary model offered no more power than a standard 8-valve or 16-valve, the cars on which it was based, its special trim package went more than a little way to restoring red-hot-hatch branding and credibility. On the car's grille a red GTI badge appeared in place of the normal shiny version, while at its rear even the 8-valve Anniversary could proclaim red-line technology in the form of more painted letters. Rear lenses looked mean and sporty simply because they were darkened. Red piping on the bumpers doesn't show particularly well on this car, but any enthusiast would have been delighted to see its return. The 16 in BBS alloys were particularly attractive and only partially masked the red painted brake calipers. Beefy twin tailpipes could hardly be described as unique, but they still added to the overall external appearance of the car. Inside the Anniversary there was special black and red check upholstery with the initials GTI woven into the cloth, red seat belts, a leather-covered steering wheel, gear gaiter and handbrake cover, each held in place with red stitching, a gear knob in the form of the original GTI's iconic golf ball with red GTI letters, plus striking white-faced instrument dials.

Racing red, what else? As you may expect from a car with such sporting heritage, red trim has never been so suited to a car. The black and red checked seat facings are complemented by red stitching to the leather coverings of the steering wheel, gear lever and handbrake which also has a red release button. The theme continues with red seat belts and red bordering to the luxurious black floor mats. Even the instrument needles are red, contrasting with the silver face of the dials.

In Germany, the 20 *Jahre* model could be specified with leather upholstery and, rather surprisingly, as a 110ps *Turbo-diesel-Direkteinsritzer, kurz TDI* (TDI), a sign of things to come. Cost-wise, the premium for the Anniversary model in the UK totalled just £700; apart from the attractive nature of the package, turning the car into a vehicle with genuine GTI appeal, this also amounted to a generous discount on the prices for the component parts that were involved.

Topless Golf: When Three Became Two!

Amazingly, the original Cabriolet version of the Golf survived throughout the era of the Mk2 Golf saloon and looked set to continue into the era of the Mk3. However, in 1993 the last GTI-based models found their way to the UK, respectively badged as the 'Sportline' and 'Rivage', although in the latter instance a leather-trimmed version, openly branded as the top of the range model, was only offered with a 95ps 'cat' engine.

Over the years, the Cabriolet had developed considerably, more often than not to mask the shortcomings of its aging body. The final incarnations of the GTI engine models are best described by means of two extracts from the brochure produced in 1993 to promote them:

Golf GTI Sportline. With 112ps available driving through a five-speed gearbox, performance is sparkling. Wide 6J × 15 BBS alloy wheels, with uniquely finished black centres and low profile

It must seem remarkably odd to someone unaware of the story of the Golf Cabrio to find what appears to be a Mk1 soft top nestling alongside Mk3 technology. The costs of creating what was essentially a niche-market model were extensive and between Volkswagen and Karmann it was decided not to tool-up for a second-generation Cabrio. However, by the time of the advent of the Mk3, and despite valiant updating attempts, the angular Cabrio was looking decidedly out of date.

Inevitably, the Volkswagen-Karmann partnership produced some enticing run-out models, one of which was the Golf GTI Sportline pictured here. Amongst its visual attributes were 6J × 15 BBS alloys and attractive Sportline decals. Inside, every attempt was made to make the Cabrio as upmarket as possible, moves which included leather trimmings and Recaro seats.

185/55 R15 tyres help to complete the picture. The smart, well equipped interior includes 'red on black' jaquard [sic] sport upholstery with Recaro front sports seats, a leather-bound steering wheel rim, a multifunction computer and a stereo radio cassette system. …

Golf GTI Rivage. Using the same high-performance engine and transmission as the GTI Sportline, performance levels are similar. Smart 6J × 15 Le Castellet polished alloy wheels, a cloth

hood and metallic paint add to the distinctive appearance of the GTI Rivage. Inside, electric windows, a multifunction computer, heated front sports seats and a stereo radio cassette system help to provide comfortable and relaxed travel for driver and passengers alike.

Powered by the now redundant 112ps engine as last used in the Mk2 GTI, both cars had a top speed of 174km/h (108mph) and accelerated

The cover of the brochure for the Mk3 Cabriolet fails to sell this niche market product effectively. Designed to match and blend with the material produced to promote both the GTI and VR6 models of similar vintage, unfortunately it is far from clear to a casual observer that the car photographed is a soft-top model, the image depicting the vehicle's front rather than a side or rear elevation.

The new 1994 Golf Cabriolet.

between 0–100km/h in 10.1sec, only the Cabrio's extra weight preventing a more stunning performance. Volkswagen had already turned to Karmann once more to deliver these cars' successor.

Apart from adding two vibration dampers, one in the form of a precision-calculated weight at the rear of the car, and the other amounting to 200kg (441lb) attached to the engine/transmission block, both designed to neutralize the effects of the scuttle shake that all convertibles are prone to, the new Cabrio was once again a mass of reinforcements, affecting the floor, the area under the dashboard and inevitably the car's

front and rear ends. The result of Karmann's endeavours was, as previously, a class leader in both torsional rigidity and stiffness.

Simply badged as the 'Golf Cabriolet', the UK market was initially granted two options; one powered by the 90ps 1800 engine, the other branded, at least on paper, as the Avantgarde and sporting the 1984cc, 115ps engine of the 8-valve GTI. Available with both a manual or automatic box, weight took its toll on performance figures, with the 0–100km/h sprint being accomplished in 11.2sec in the former case and 12.3sec in the latter. Top speeds of 190km/h (118mph) and 186.6km/h (116mph),

The three generations of Volkswagen Cabriolet: the evergreen Beetle; the long-lived Golf based on the Mk1 body; and the newcomer – a car that was destined to have a much shorter production run than either of its successors and a vehicle that would also be subjected to a frontal upgrade when the Mk4 Golf came along. (Photograph Courtesy of Volkswagen AG)

129

respectively, confirmed that the Avantgarde wasn't destined to win any races. With the lack of any reference to the GTI brand and a lavish but hardly all-out sporty specification, 6J × 14 Orlando alloys being one very typical example, it was clear that Volkswagen's intention was simply to offer the Cabriolet as a reasonably powerful, even exotic, means of transport to those with sufficient funds to be able to afford it.

The arrival of the Mk4 Golf saloon posed something of a quandary, as the tooling costs of creating a new version of the Cabrio were always substantial. Volkswagen's answer was to meld the frontal appearance of the new car into the design of the Mk3, something that was achieved with more than a modicum of success. Dubbed the Golf Mk3.5 by some wits, the giveaway to its origins came in the form of the swage lines and, albeit in a slightly revamped form, the Mk3 dashboard. The revamped Cabrio inevitably retained the Mk3's running gear and, of course, the old GTI 8-valve engine. Top of the range was the Avantgarde Colour Concept, but by the summer of 2002, although stocks were still available, the car was no longer in production.

Golf Cabriolet 2.0 Avantgarde 1994

Engine
Type	Transversely mounted 4-cylinder in-line
Bore and stroke	82.5 × 92.8mm
Capacity	1,984cc
Valves	Single overhead cam – 2 valves per cylinder
Compression ratio	10.4:1
Fuel injection	Bosch Digifant
Max. power	115ps at 5,400rpm
Max. torque	123lb ft at 3,200rpm
Fuel capacity	55ltr (12.1gal)

Transmission
	Front-wheel drive	
Gearbox	Five-speed manual	
Ratios	1st	3.45
	2nd	1.94
	3rd	1.29
	4th	0.97
	5th	0.81
Final drive	3.67	

Suspension and Steering
Front	MacPherson struts with lower wishbones and 20mm (0.78in) anti-roll bar. Track stabilizing steering geometry
Rear	Torsion beam trailing arm with track-connecting bearings. Anti-roll bar
	Suspension lowered by 10mm (0.4in) compared to other models
Steering	Power-assisted, maintenance-free rack and pinion
Tyres	185/60 R14H (Spare – temporary)
Wheels	6J × 14 Orlando alloys

Brakes
Type	Diagonally split circuits. Servo-assisted. Load-sensitive brake pressure regulator
Size	Front – vented 280mm (11.0in) discs with single piston sliding caliper
	Rear – solid 226mm (8.9in) disc and single piston sliding caliper

Dimensions
Track	
Front	1,478mm (58.19in)
Rear	1,462mm (57.56in)
Wheelbase	2,475mm (97.4in)
Overall length	4,020mm (158.3in)
Overall width	1,695mm (66.7in)
Overall height	1,410mm (55.5in)
Unladen weight	1,205kg (2,657lb)

Performance
Top speed	186.6km/h (116mph)
	0–100km/h (0–62mph) 12.3sec

This side view of the Cabrio based on the third version of the Golf somehow conveys small-car status, much more so than the equivalent tin-top. (Photograph Courtesy of Volkswagen AG)

Volkswagen produced various specifications for the Golf Cabriolet both in terms of engine power and trim levels. However, in true Mk3 Golf style, the average man or woman in the street wouldn't have been able to distinguish one model from another. (Photograph Courtesy of Volkswagen AG)

Golf with a Boot

Following disappointing sales with the Mk2 Jetta in most countries except America, new tactics were employed with the third version of the Golf with a boot. Having struggled with the booted version of the Polo, known as the Derby, Volkswagen landed on the idea of simply calling its small saloon the Polo Classic. As that notion failed too, any thoughts of referring to the booted Mk3 version of the Golf in similar terms were summarily dismissed. The car was presented with a new brand identity and became in true Volkswagen style the Vento, the Portuguese term for wind.

In the hotter stakes, the Vento was available in the UK with either the 115ps engine of the Mk3 Golf GTI 8-valve, but wrapped up in a GL specification package, or endowed with the VR6 engine. Despite this last mentioned model's luxury specification and power, it, like the rest of the obtainable options, failed to make any great impact, despite a near deluge of excellent reviews. Volkswagen gave in once more and changed the name of the booted Golf again when the Mk4 version made its way onto the market.

The Mk3 GTI in the USA

Just as the new Mk3 Golf was starting to penetrate European markets, VWoA hit an all-time low. Dwindling from a grand total for all models of Volkswagen sold of just 91,700 cars in 1991, the 1992 figure dropped to 49,553. Volkswagen's best offering for the USA was the 115ps 8-valve. But this engine powered all Golfs sold there, not just the GTI, and as such the once hot-hatch car was seen as little more than a trim package. Volkswagen's longer term answer was the VR6, which it introduced in 1995 badged as the GTI VR6. To confuse matters, a sports version of the ordinary Mk3 clad in VR6 clothing, but lacking its engine, brakes and other attributes, was also launched in 1995. The following year it was renamed as the GTI.

During 1997, 500 special 'Driver's Edition' GTI VR6s were made available, in colours ranging from Yellow and Jazz Blue, to Red, Black and White. The interiors were trimmed with special cloth that accentuated the car's external colour. Mimicking the European 20 *Jahre* model, aspects of the interior were highlighted in red, while the legendary golf-ball gear lever made a comeback. Of more importance, handling was upgraded and the suspension made stiffer.

Finally, although the primary interest has to be in the Golf, in the USA sales were dominated by the Jetta, with more than 60 per cent of the total being accounted for by this one model. Heading the specification list was the GLX, a Jetta powered by the VR6 engine and launched in the USA in 1994. Needless to say, the Jetta name remained in use throughout the lifespan of the third-generation model.

5 Four: The Most Refined Hot Hatch of Them All?

No Change, but All Change

First publicly aired at the Frankfurt Motor Show in September, the fourth-generation Golf had previously been presented to the world's automotive journalists at the international press launch in Bonn during the summer of 1997. No doubt to the amazement of the many that came to know and love the Golf Mk4, the initial response was hardly universal in praise of the car. Design engineers were confronted by a section of the assembled journalists demanding to know why there had been little progress with styling. At more than just a first glance, they complained, the new Golf looked the same as its predecessor. Volkswagen's response was that this was what customers wanted – a car similar in format and shape, but naturally much better. Following an all too short first test drive, virtually all went away not only placated, but suitably enraptured by the new car.

While the Mk4 GTI, at least in 1.8T guise, might well be heading for high rankings on the classic car list in a number of years time, for illustrative purposes this Golf is even more difficult to identify from its siblings than its predecessor. With giveaways limited to little more than alloys and discreet badges on the rear of the car, the inevitable result is a series of pictures that appear repetitive to all but the most experienced of enthusiasts. Fortunately, a little light relief comes near the end of the chapter with both the Anniversary Model, depicted here, and the R32. While far from extreme, at least there are sufficient variances on the general theme to warrant more than a few images.

The model shown is a 1.6SE with genuine VW accessory alloys. With the exception of the black trim on the bumper, this car could easily be a GTI.

For the UK launch at the London Motor Show held in October 1997, the Golf's steady evolution was suitably illustrated through a carefully orchestrated display of all four generations side by side. The subtle message was apparent to all but the dullest of spectators, that the radical chops and changes preferred by some manufacturers in the quest to reach the top of the greasy sales pole were not the method favoured by Volkswagen. Two short exerpts from early British press releases pertaining to the Golf Mk4 confirm the strategy. Under the heading, 'Volkswagen announces first details of the new Golf', the story was one of the 17 million such cars having been produced 'since the first example appeared in 1974'. The punchline was that the 'latest Golf retains many of the styling features that have made the model so successful – the recognizable "Golf-look" is quoted by customers as one of their prime reasons for choosing the car'.

That release was written at the end of July 1997, while what follows provided the basis of many a press feature article in mid-September. The theme remained undeniably constant: 'Though completely new and longer, wider and more spacious than its predecessor, this is still unmistakably a Golf and follows the same formula that made the car a European best-seller with production now well over 17 million.'

Similarly, an extended release, containing by definition a lengthier story, but one that reiterated the same basic message, was offered to journalists to get their teeth into:

> Research conducted amongst Golf owners throughout the world indicated that the car's recognizable and classless look was one of their prime reasons for choosing the model. Hence the decision was taken to retain many of the Golf styling cues in the fourth-generation car. For example, the oval headlights continue, though now the twin headlights, front turn indicators and front fog lights are housed within single front glasses on each side.

Adding a further spin to the story, an attempt was made to sell Volkswagen's corporate look, carefully even using the latest and most highly regarded Passat as a marketing tool for its smaller cousin: 'Elements such as the curved A-pillar, door handles and pronounced wheel arches provide a link with the Passat and forthcoming New Beetle'.

A pre-launch brochure for the British market, produced specifically for Volkswagen UK and entitled 'The New Golf – Reinventing a Classic', told the same story again, and, if anything, even more eloquently:

> Now there's a new Golf. The Mk4 version of Volkswagen's enduring classic. Yet despite being completely new, it's instantly recognizable: solid, sure, dependable, poised and practical. But beneath the reassuringly familiar shape it's been completely rethought, re-engineered and refashioned. Although the elegant proportions remain, the new Golf is bigger all round: wider, longer and taller. The car's legendary build quality is improved. …
> Reassuringly an icon. Still.

On the theme of change but no change, the picture depicts the rear end of the first four generations of GTI. Closest to the camera is the Mk4 and furthest away is the ancestral Mk1.

The new car was predictably bigger than the vehicle it succeeded. As this was an era in Volkswagen's management of share and share alike, the platform was borrowed from that of the Audi A3. Compared to its predecessor the wheelbase was extended by 40mm (1.6in) to 2,513mm (99in), the length of the car by 110mm (4.3in) to 4,131mm (163in) and the width by 40mm to 1,735mm (68.3in). (For the adept both at mathematics and feats of memory, the figures recorded for the Mk3 and Mk2 G60 suggest an inaccuracy of one or two millimetres along the way, other than with the width, where the apparent discrepancy was much greater. However, when taken into account that both the G60 and the Mk3 GTI possessed extended wheel arches compared to the more basic Golfs at 1,695mm/66.7in, all is then explained.) Volkswagen was keen to point out that the bodyshell's exceptional rigidity was achieved by 'ultra-modern manufacturing techniques such as laser welding and special adhesive bonding', while excellent build quality was demonstrated in extremely tight gap tolerances.

While the old maxim of bigger is better definitely applied to the Mk4 Golf, one consideration acted as a damper on an otherwise blissful state of affairs. The Mk4 Golf was noticeably heavier than its immediate predecessor once again, leading to the unavoidable conclusion that as the pounds piled on a further slice had been taken out of the performance cake. Unfortunately for followers of simplicity, Volkswagen's sets of scales were changed with monotonous regularity. Some took into account the necessity of a driver at the controls to make the car function, others didn't. Direct comparisons become increasingly awkward under such circumstances, but most would agree that not only was the Mk4 some 25 per cent heavier than the Mk2 Golf, but also that the pounds had piled on from the days when the newly launched Mk3 ran into a brick wall of criticism concerning its alleged middle-aged spread.

Breaking the mould, the Mk4 was the first Golf, and only the second Volkswagen, to benefit from the use of galvanized body parts, an advance introduced by Audi in the 1980s, based on experience gained building the Porsche 924 at its factory at Neckarsulum. As a result of this improvement, the Golf Mk4 was offered with what at the time was an unrivalled twelve-year anti-corrosion warranty, which, providing any accident damage was repaired quickly and to a similar standard as that set by Volkswagen in the course of manufacture, ensured that many a fourth-generation Golf would be on the road for many, many years to come.

Visually, and intentionally, there was no mistaking that the Mk4 was the successor to three previous generations of Golf. The C-pillars were characteristically wide, appearing to be even more substantial than previously, although as the tailgate glass area had also been increased, rearward visibility was as good, if not better, than previously. The car's appearance from the back was notable for its near-vertical tailgate, the lower parts of which were more or less encased by a big bumper assembly. This, in turn, was at least partially protected by hardened black plastic protection strips in the case of the lower specification models and by similarly robust colour-coded inserts for the costlier, higher-powered cars. At the front, the bonnet sloped more sharply than that of its predecessor, but the most distinctive features of the whole car were its headlamp assemblies, units that for the first time incorporated all functions behind a single plastic lens. Indeed, so individual were the new style of lamps that Volkswagen's marketing department chose to

adopt the most unusual of covers for its well-presented, carefully designed and exquisitely produced literature, featuring a headlight, part of the bonnet and a modest amount of the two-bar mock radiator grille, and little else. Each headlight assembly contained the reflectors for main and dip beams, DE fog lamps (if part of the model's specification) and amber indicators. The headlamp beams were shaped solely by the reflectors and were initially praised for their effectiveness on a variety of roads.

Externally, one model of Golf looked very much like another, black bumper strips and steel wheels initially being one of the few giveaways that the car parked opposite was not a GTI. Later in the Mk4's production run even the wheel means of detection wasn't infallible, as around the time of the introduction of the high specification, low-cost Golf Match alloys filtered down to all but the most basic of offerings. For the GTI enthusiast, sadly here was a further generation of their favourite car that lacked the once all-important red-line branding, while additionally the traditional extended plastic wheel-arch trims last seen in muted form on the Mk3 were also a thing of the past. Contrasting side stripes had withered away to nothing, separate housings for the twin headlamps had died the death with the demise of the Mk2 and now gone too was the prominent, or at least large-lettered, GTI badge on the car's front. Undeniably to the contempt of the proud stylists of the original GTI, the only real clue to the identity of the two models of

With the Mk4 finished in Reflex Silver and closer to the camera a section of the Mk5 in Tornado Red, again it's easy to notice the similarity between two generations. The Mk4 is a V6 4MOTION, as evidenced by the badge on its rear.

Mk4 GTIs lay in three diminutive chromed letters on the cars' respective hatches. Small and undoubtedly overlooked by all but the enthusiast, plain shiny letters referred to one model in the form of a capital 'G', a 'T' and an 'I', while two chrome letters, a 'G' and a 'T', plus an 'I' infilled with red, the other car.

The inevitable proliferation of press releases at the time of a new model launch helps to ascertain the general policy strategy and direction of the company at the time. The example following illustrates why the Golf Mk4's legacy was intended to be one of both quality and good taste: 'Priced alongside its popular UK rivals, its strength, rigidity and quality of construction help provide the comfort, safety and refinement of a much larger car. High production volumes and economies of scale within the Volkswagen Group enable these standards to be combined with high equipment levels.'

An undoubted highlight of the new car's specification was its interior, the visual quality of the fittings and the cleverly modern yet reassuringly conservative nature of the layout raising the stakes towards the executive car class, even at base model, or 'E' specification, level. One magazine even went so far as to refer to the interior trappings as being similar in nature to those of a BMW, no doubt to Volkswagen's secret delight and to ever superior BMW's eternal dismay. As will become apparent later, Mk4 Golfs of either a sporting, or simply a powerful, nature were further enhanced with the trappings of luxury, including black wooden or the even more lavish walnut trim inserts. Worthy of further note too was the sophisticatedly luxurious dominantly blue, yet red highlighted, illumination of the dashboard instruments and other controls at night.

From the model's inception, the message of interior quality and luxury was told in Volkswagen's literature. 'The interior of the new Golf exudes quality' was how one paragraph started, while an image of the interior was captioned with the words: 'The true colours of the new Golf. Distinctive, stylish and ergonomic combined with unsurpassed attention to detail.'

For the lower specification models, the luxury message was encapsulated with words such as 'for your convenience' before reference to 'twin cupholders in the front and a third sun visor situated above the rear-view mirror'. Move up a step and the first words about the SE model pertained to luxury: 'The SE model is equipped with an even more luxurious specification, further adding to the new Golf's reputation as a mid-range hatchback with an "executive" feel.' Comprising a carefully balanced blend between interior and exterior luxury, the text skilfully wove a web to entangle those drawn into its spell:

> Take, for example, a remote control alarm system, electric door mirrors, one-touch electric front windows, a glass electric sunroof, rear centre armrest with built-in compartment box, rear cupholders and a multifunction computer, all fitted as standard equipment. For added security, the central locking also incorporates anti-hijack locks. This feature allows all doors to be locked by one button conveniently located on the driver's door ...

Finally, authorization of the bid confirming the opulent nature of the latest Golf, even when positioned against names that were once more prestigious, was apparent when simply trawling through the inviting list of optional extras, particularly as during the latter years of the Mk4's run, some of the must-have goodies once reserved for aristocrats of the range became a standard part of the specification for even the plebeian runner-up models:

> The high level of standard equipment on the new Golf is just one of the reasons why it represents such outstanding value for money. But for those who desire something different an extensive range of optional equipment is also available. You'll find luxurious features such as manual air conditioning or the more accurate Climatronic air control that will maintain the temperature at a pre-programmed level. And on SE models and above, air conditioning is available at a reduced rate if fitted in lieu of a sunroof. Or you may desire the options

Golf or Beetle: The World's Most Produced Car

A useful, but disputed, record – Volkswagen claimed the V5 pictured to be the car that overtook the Beetle's legendary status as the most produced car in the world. Air-cooled fans thought not, while Toyota also had comments to make. (Photograph Courtesy of Volkswagen UK Press Office)

It was during the lifespan of the Mk4 Golf that total production of the three previous generations, added to the number so far built of the latest car to bear the same name, finally came to more than the cumulative sum for single-model Beetle manufacture. Undoubtedly an achievement, 21,517,415 Volkswagen Golfs in twenty-eight years could not be sniffed at. The example to claim the honour on 25 June 2002 was a V5, finished in Reflex Silver and fitted with extras such as electronic climate control and parking sensors. Confirmation that the ceremony was little more than a means to spin a development success story, the car in question wasn't intended for Wolfsburg's museum, but instead was destined to enter daily service for a customer in Hamburg.

packs? The Weather pack, for example, includes heated front seats, retractable headlight cleaning system, heated windscreen washer jets and a visual warning light to remind you when the washer fluid needs refilling. There is also a selection of innovative options you'd normally associate with a larger executive class car. These include cruise control, an automatic dimming rear-view mirror and the ingenious rain sensitive windscreen wipers.

Model to Model

Production of right-hand-drive cars destined for the UK market began in February 1998, allowing stocks to build and orders to be taken for the official launch in May. Initially, the range consisted of a petrol-fuelled 1.4-litre, 75ps engine offered with base model trim (E-level, in the then current parlance). The three- and five-door 1.4 was also available with the enhanced S level of trim, which was also an option for owners specifying the larger 1.6 100ps engine, although the number of doors was restricted to the single option of a family-friendly five. The most luxurious offering with a 1.6 engine was the SE, which was available as either a manual or an automatic five-door. Next came the Golf 1.8 GTI 125ps, which was available as both a three- and five-door model. Above this model there was reference to the 2.3-litre, 150ps Golf V5, again promised as a five-door hatch only, but in both manual and automatic guise. At this point the debate rages. Volkswagen's releases were amazingly contradictory. One minute the

V5 was the flagship model, the next it was a second option on the GTI theme. For the moment at least, it's best to go with the notion that the true top of the range model was a GTI, the GTI 1.8T, which, like the V5, generated 150ps.

With the emphasis so far being on petrol engines, the range also included a base model diesel, the 1.9 E SDI with 68ps at its disposal, a 1.9 S TDI offering 90ps and either three or five doors, plus an SE trim version, this preference only coming with five doors, but also available as an automatic. Top of the diesel listings was the three- and five-door 110ps GT TDI model, again available as both a three- and five-door car. Volkswagen was at pains to point out that all but two of the engines offered were new to the Golf, while 'every engine derivative' was 'either quicker and more fuel efficient, and in many cases both, than its equivalent in the previous range'.

Of particular interest here was 'the outgoing 2.0-litre 115ps engine which powered the GTI 8V', as this was 'replaced by a 1.8-litre 20-valve 125ps engine' that ensured the new Golf GTI was 'swifter, knocking half a second off the 0–62mph acceleration time of the previous model'. Meanwhile, the perpetuators of the two-model GTI story advised that the old GTI 16V was 'replaced by the new GTI 1.8T powered by a 150ps 20-valve engine with light-pressure turbocharger'. German, or perhaps more correctly, continental press releases told a rather different story, with all the emphasis being placed on the 1.8T.

Listed but unavailable at the very beginning of Mk4 production, another player, the V5, was suggested as a possible contender for the GTI's crown: 'The GTI 1.8T retains the Golf performance crown until a successor to the widely acclaimed VR6 is introduced in early 1999.'

Although the best part of a year away from ready availability, sufficient space was allocated in press releases to hint at the model's market: 'Derived from Volkswagen's famous VR6 engine, the new 2.3-litre V5 150ps unit will be offered alongside the 1.8T. Performance is similar for both yet their characters are very

different, the V5's distinctive engine sound being particularly noteworthy.'

Quickly stepping back to the Mk4's launch, the diesel story was suddenly of interest on a set devised for the glorification of the performance Golf. Whereas diesels had previously been glorified for their fuel economy, with little emphasis being placed on performance, it was all-change for the new top of the range oil-burning engine:

> The new Golf GT TDI 110 promises to redefine the performance hatchback class – it combines a 0–62mph acceleration time of 10.6sec with a tremendous 57.6mpg figure. A torque figure of 173lb ft, equal to the VR6 engine's but accessible at lower engine revs, gives sparkling in-gear acceleration.

In summary form, the revolution had gathered pace. If the Mk3 VR6 had posed a threat to its sibling GTI's crown, during the lifetime of the Mk4 many more such vehicles were to emerge, while the non-turbocharged car cast as a GTI in the UK did the car's reputation no great favours. Reference to the UK line-up of Golfs at the end of the Mk4 era serves to demonstrate just how far forward the performance agenda had moved in a few short years, eclipsing once and for all the GTI's shining rays as the only hot model in the Golf range. Pitch a diesel, for example, against the original Mk1 GTI and there's enough to make an owner of the petrol offering shake in his shoes – 150ps and a quoted 0–100km/h time of just 8.6sec, linked to a top speed of 216km/h (134mph) was a far cry from the days when diesel performance was synonymous with a farming inheritance.

Discounting the shopping or family holiday Golfs, the hot Mk4 run-out line covered five options listed by Volkswagen UK as: the 2.0-litre, 115ps GTI; the GTI 1.8T – with 20 valves and both 150 and 180ps at its disposal; the 2.3-litre V5 that notched up 170ps; and the 204ps V6 4MOTION; plus the crème de la crème R32 'sports car', with 240ps available and a 0–100km/h time of only 6.6sec.

However, the GT TDI PD, with its 130ps engine, top speed of 204km/h (127mph) and 0–100km/h time of 9.6sec, plus the even more powerful 150ps model already alluded to, guaranteed a line-up of seven cars, each of which is more than worthy of more detailed description and evaluation in a volume intended to glorify not just the GTI but all members of the Volkswagen Golf hot-hatch story.

The Golf GTI

Perhaps Volkswagen's copy in its UK market Mk4 brochures goes some way towards adding weight to the theory that the once magical GTI letters on a Golf had become little more than a sporting trim:

> The new GTI is a statement of quality and exclusivity. From the height adjustable sports seats with firm lateral support to the use of the finest materials

such as the leather-trimmed three-spoke steering wheel, sport gear shift and handbrake lever. The luxurious equipment level continues with remote central locking and alarm, electric windows, front and rear centre armrest with compartment box, electrically adjustable and heated door mirrors and stylish 15in Avus alloy wheels.

Early UK market material sought to associate three cars with the GTI brand, all of which, it can be argued, were nothing of the sort. The best, and in reality, the only genuine GTI was left to last, so much so that it was allocated its own pages in the brochures:

> Whichever engine you choose, the performance is sure to impress. You can opt for either a 1.8-litre, 125ps engine or 2.3-litre V5, 150ps unit ... Or perhaps the first GTI class diesel engine? ... And for additional safety, all petrol GTIs benefit from the new EDS traction control that helps improve grip on poor road surfaces.

Elegant, refined and attractive, but how do you know it's a Mk4 GTI? No red-line identity, no grille badge.
(Photograph Courtesy of Volkswagen AG)

Golf GTI Mk4 1.8 1998

Engine

Type	Front in-line 4-cylinder transversely mounted Belt-driven single overhead camshaft. 5 valves per cylinder
Bore and stroke	81.0mm × 88.4mm
Capacity	1781cc
Compression ratio	10.3:1
Fuel injection	Multipoint injection
Max. power	125ps at 6,000rpm
Max. torque	125lb ft at 4,200rpm
Fuel capacity	55ltr (12.1gal)

Transmission

Gearbox	Five-speed all indirect with synchromesh
Mph per 1,000rpm in top gear	20.2

Suspension and Steering

Front	MacPherson struts, coil springs and lower wishbones, 20.7mm anti-roll bar
Rear	Torsion beam, trailing arms, coil springs, 18mm (0.7in) anti-roll bar, toe-correcting mountings
Steering	Power-assisted, maintenance-free self-adjusting rack and pinion
Tyres	195/65R 15Y
Wheels	6J × 15 Avus alloys

Brakes

Type	Diagonally split circuits. Servo-assisted. Load sensitive brake pressure regulator ABS with EBD (Electronic Brake-pressure Distribution) Traction control system (EDL)
Size	Front 288mm (11.3in) diameter discs, internally ventilated – single piston sliding caliper Rear 232mm (9.1in) solid disc and single piston sliding caliper

Dimensions

Track	
Front	1,513mm (59.6in)
Rear	1,494mm (58.8in)
Wheelbase	2,511mm (98.9in)
Overall length	4,149mm (163.3in)
Overall width	1,735mm (68.3in)
Overall height	1,439mm (56.7in)
Unladen weight	1,270kg (2,800lb) two-door; 1,306kg (2,880lb) four-door Unladen weights include the driver

Performance

Top speed	200km/h (125mph) 0–100km/h (0–62mph) 9.9sec

The GTI with the 1781cc 20-valve non-turbocharged engine had a bore and stroke of 81.0 × 88.4mm, a compression ratio of 10.3:1 and developed 125ps at 6,000rpm. The car's top speed was 200km/h (125mph) and it covered 0–100km/h in 9.9sec. Like many of Volkswagen's engines, the 1.8 was an Audi-derived unit with three inlet and two exhaust valves per cylinder. The engine needed revving hard, as there was little in the way of torque at low speeds, resulting in a relatively dead feel. While winding an engine up might be deemed appropriate for a GTI driver, the 1.8 lacked the bite of a truly sporting car. The truth of the matter was that it had been deliberately designed with other objectives in mind, one being low emissions, in which respect it was a great success, the other relating to better fuel consumption: a goal that wasn't achieved in full. Volkswagen claimed an overall gas-guzzling figure of 8.3ltr/100km (34mpg) in its literature, which for a genuine GTI wouldn't have appeared thirsty, but most test driving or owning the car found they achieved little more than 10.1ltr/100km (28mpg) overall, taking economy well into the hot-hatch stakes without the consolation of performance to match.

To the surprise of many, it was all change in the early months of 1999 when the Mk4 GTI was bestowed with the 1984cc engine reserved for the New Beetle, a power plant that had previously been in use in the Mk3 Golf, albeit with a different cylinder head. All the skills of the Press, PR and Marketing departments were required to reverse the storyline they had been actively promoting over the last year and more. Talk of the 1.8-litre 20-valve unit being an 'uprated' engine offering 125ps compared to the 115ps of the Mk3 model had to be quickly brushed under the carpet. Under a banner heading of 'The Golf GTI takes its heart from the New Beetle', the UK Press Office quickly spun a convincing web: 'The Volkswagen Golf GTI is to receive the 2.0-litre engine from the New Beetle, replacing the existing 1.8-litre unit, to bring extra refinement, more torque at low engine speeds and even better fuel consumption to the model'.

In greater detail, the writer obviously expected the average journalist to forget what had been written so recently:

Torque, or pulling power, and the engine speed at which it is developed, is more important to everyday driving than the engine's horsepower output. High torque at low engine speeds makes for flexible performance and better fuel economy – this is

---

Golf GTI Mk4 2.0 2000

Engine			
Type	Front in-line 4-cylinder transversely mounted Belt-driven single overhead camshaft. 2 valves per cylinder	Wheels	6J × 15 Avus 11 alloys
Bore and stroke	82.5mm × 92.8mm	**Brakes**	
Capacity	1984cc	Type	Diagonally split circuits. Servo-assisted. Load-sensitive brake pressure regulator ABS with EBD Traction control system (EDL)
Compression ratio	10.5:1		
Fuel injection	Multipoint injection		
Max. power	115ps at 5,200rpm		
Max. torque	125lb ft at 2,400rpm	Size	Front 288mm (11.3in) diameter discs, internally ventilated – single piston sliding caliper Rear 232mm (9.1in) solid disc and single piston sliding caliper
Fuel capacity	55ltr (12.1gal)		
Transmission			
Gearbox	Five-speed all indirect with synchromesh	**Dimensions**	
		Track	
Mph per 1,000rpm in top gear	22.0	Front	1,513mm (59.6in)
		Rear	1,494mm (58.8in)
		Wheelbase	2,511mm (98.9in)
Suspension and Steering		Overall length	4,149mm (163.3in)
Front	MacPherson struts, coil springs and lower wishbones, 20.7mm anti-roll bar	Overall width	1,735mm (68.3in)
		Overall height	1,439mm (56.7in)
		Unladen weight	1,153kg (2,542lb) two-door; 1,194kg (2,632lb) four-door Unladen weights include the driver.
Rear	Torsion beam, trailing arms, coil springs, 18mm (0.7in) anti-roll bar, toe-correcting mountings		
Steering	Power-assisted, maintenance-free self-adjusting rack and pinion	**Performance**	
		Top speed	195km/h (121mph)
Tyres	195/65R 15V		0–100km/h (0–62mph) 10.5sec

just what the 2.0-litre supplies. The maximum torque figure of 125lb ft is unchanged but in the 2.0-litre unit, it is developed at just 2,400rpm instead of the outgoing 1.8-litre's 4,200rpm. Fuel consumption is another area of improvement, with the combined fuel consumption figure increasing to 35.8mpg from 34.0.

In reality, while maximum torque was achieved at lower rpm, power levels had wilted too, down from 200km/h (125mph) with the 1.8 to 195km/h (121mph) with the new car, the most notable feature of the 2.0-litre engine being its reluctance to perform much above 5,000rpm. Presumably to Volkswagen's eternal embarrassment, the 0–100km/h figure had gone in the wrong direction too, with 10.5sec being recorded for the sprint with the 2.0-litre model, making it a full half second slower than the 1.8. Worse still, as the 1.6 engine allocated to the Golf bounced up from 100ps to 105ps in the summer of 2000, so did its 0–100km/h figure drop from 10.9 to 10.8sec, while the old top speed of 188km/h (117mph) crept encouragingly upwards to just 1.6km/h (1mph) short of 193km/h (120mph). If the gap hadn't closed completely, it was certainly narrowing.

The 2.0-litre engine remained the mainstay of the Golf GTI in non-turbocharged form to the end of Mk4 production, which occurred in the final months of 2003. Bore and stroke stood at 82.5 and 92.8mm respectively; the compression ratio was 10.5:1. From 2000 it was possible to specify the Mk4 Golf GTI with a combination of sports suspension and wider, larger 6.5 × 16 Montreal alloys; the cost, at £530, wasn't earth-shattering. However, having said that, as the Mk4 GTI undoubtedly offered comfort through a good combination of ride and handling, rather than the all-out sporting nature of the Golf GTI 1.8T, the car's performance was such that any expense was hardly warranted. Later, sports suspension alone became available, but even at the snip price of £150, the same question arose.

Whether it was the Mk4 GTI's engine that didn't quite live up to the expectations of GTI

ownership, the lack of a need to add genuine sports equipment, or even something simple like the perfectly adequate nature of the sporty seats that lacked the support of a Recaro, realization quickly dawned amongst potential owners that purchase of the Mk4 GTI didn't imply an all-out desire to own and run the fastest car in the street. Closer examination of those 6 × 15 Avus alloys gave the game away. Fitted with 195/65R 15 tyres, this could never be considered as a high-performance offering, the tall sidewalls allowing excess lateral movement and creating a banshee of squeals and squeaks under hard cornering. This GTI was a branding exercise to increase sales of the Golf here in the UK, nothing more, nothing less, for across Europe the car was simply promoted as a 1.8- or 2.0-litre; a car with a high specification of trim, certainly above the already generous SE package, perhaps most readily associated with tags such as a Highline. Once properly identified for what it was, a Golf with a performance level and handling attributes more than adequate for everyday family motoring, the car was ideal, but it did not qualify as a worthy holder of the coveted GTI badge. At least at the outset, that honour remained the sole preserve of another GTI, the GTI 1.8T.

'A Born Leader – The Golf GTI 1.8T'

> The old GTI 16V is replaced by the new GTI 1.8T powered by a 150bhp 1.8-litre 20-valve engine with light pressure turbocharger. ... The GTI 1.8T has its own specification. Latest design Recaro seats and black-stained wood trim make the 1.8T's interior a special driving environment. Externally, the model is differentiated by 16in BBS split-rim design alloy wheels and a red 'I' on the rear 'GTI' badge.

Written in March 1998, a good two months ahead of the UK launch of the Mk4 Golf, those few brief words indicate that the GTI 1.8T was clearly going to be something a little special. For dedicated GTI spotters put off their stride by the lack of red-line branding since the days of the Mk2, the new model had a tiny but significant identification mark. While anybody could and frequently did upgrade their set of steel or even alloy wheels to create a GTI lookalike, few owners of the 1.8- or 2.0-litre cars would bother to 'ink in' the 'I' on the hatch badge with red paint!

Early Mk4 Golf brochures sold the GTI 1.8T in the following way:

> The Golf GTI 1.8T offers the perfect combination of style, performance and comfort. Its distinctive interior is elegantly finished with black wood inserts to the centre console, ashtray lid, gear lever and inside door handles. And is complemented by the leather-trimmed Sport steering wheel, gear lever surround and handbrake. The Recaro sports seats confirm the 1.8T's lively image and include lumbar adjustment and telescopic under thigh support for maximum comfort. External aesthetics are enhanced with 16in Montreal alloy wheels and 205/55 low profile tyres, colour co-ordinated bumper strip and a grey tinted sun strip on the laminated front windscreen. But the heart of this new GTI is its 1.8-litre, 20V 150bhp engine boosted by the latest turbocharging technology. The effect is dramatic. It accelerates the 1.8T from 0–60mph in a mere 8.5sec and reaches a top speed of 134mph where the law permits. To accommodate such impressive performance, the suspension is lowered and this plays a significant role in the 1.8T's adept handling and superb roadholding. On the open road, squeeze the throttle and you'll soon discover why the 1.8T has just redefined the GTI class.

Key to the numerous accolades heaped on the GTI 1.8T immediately upon its launch was the vehicle's startling performance. Its engine, although ideally suited to the hottest Golf, had not been designed for it and had indeed already been thoroughly tried, tested and written about, for the 1.8T was a product of the Audi development team. The best part of fifteen years earlier, in 1985, Audi had taken the first tentative steps down the road of 5-valve technology. The experimental monster thus created, a 5-cylinder, 5 valves per cylinder, turbocharged engine developed an unbelievable 650ps. Initially perceived as a means of producing raw power, as calculated development progressed the real aim of generating better and entirely usable torque became apparent. By the time the 1.8T had found its way into the fourth-generation of Golf, it had already seen service in both the Audi A4 and the A3, and in the context of the relatively lightweight latter car produced a pocket-rocket 0–60mph time of just 7.3sec. Owners of the latest Passat could also benefit from 1.8T technology and almost contemporaneously to the launch of the Mk4 Golf GTI 1.8T the engine found its way into the Sport version of the Sharan MPV.

The 150ps, 1781cc engine had a bore and stroke of 81.0 and 86.4mm respectively. The compression ratio stood at 10.9:1 and maximum power was achieved at 5,700rpm. Perhaps somewhat surprisingly, the total power output of the GTI 1.8T was no more than that of its predecessor, the Mk3 GTI 2.0-litre 16-valve. Considering the new car's larger size, for which read additional weight, those who were shocked to discover that it was fractionally slower in an all-out sprint to the magical 100km/h shouldn't have been. Certainly, it was inevitable that the Golf endowed with the 1.8T engine would be slower than its equivalent in the Audi family due to the obesity factor. However, where the Mk4 Golf GTI 1.8T, and for that matter the Audi, scored over the Mk3 GTI 16-valve was in relation to torque. With the addition of a low-pressure KO3 turbocharger maximum torque hit the 155lb ft mark, compared to the Mk3's 133lb ft. Of even more significance still was the very wide range over which the maximum was achieved; all the way from 1,750 to 4,600rpm, compared to the Mk3's somewhat limited 4,000 to 5,600rpm. Head on with the Mk3 GTI 16-valve, this translated into considerable advances over the older car between 48–80km/h (30–50mph) and 80–113km/h (50–70mph), one such example being an 11sec time for the Mk3 to move from 50–70mph in fifth, compared with

While the main image might be of a V5 as evidenced by the badge on its front, its external appearance is virtually the same as that of the 1.8T. The best key to the identity of the hot GTI, the 1.8T, is its red infilled 'T' on the hatch badge.

just 8.6sec for the newer car. The net result for Volkswagen was that the Mk4 GTI 1.8T offered an outstanding response at just about any engine speed, was fully capable of speeds in excess of 209km/h (130mph), and presented a dynamic 0–100km/h time without costing a fortune at the pumps. (Volkswagen claimed a combined fuel consumption of 7.8ltr/100km (36.2mpg), while even the most spirited or heavy footed of drivers found it difficult to drop much below 9.4ltr/100km (30mpg).)

Driver satisfaction inevitably increased by leaps and bounds; it was far easier to leave others trailing, while fast driving was achieved with less effort.

To complement the Mk4 GTI 1.8T's performance the car's suspension was lowered slightly, by some 10mm (0.4in) at the front and 15mm (0.6in) at the rear. Wheels and tyres were similarly meatier with 6.5 × 16in Montreal alloy wheels running on 205/55 tyres, although, as has already been mentioned, in later years owners of 'ordinary' GTIs could add both options, at a price. Never an exclusive, but still important to mention on a car of this calibre, were the 1.8T's highly capable brakes. Up front 288 × 25mm (11.3 × 1in) ventilated discs brought the car to both a quick and positive halt, while at the rear 232 × 9mm (9 × 0.4in) solid discs common to all Mk4 Golfs at

---

Golf GTI Mk4 1.8T 1998

Engine		Tyres	205/55R 16W
Type	Front in-line 4-cylinder transversely mounted Belt-driven single overhead camshaft. 5 valves per cylinder Turbocharged	Wheels	6.5 × 16in Montreal alloys
		Brakes	
		Type	Diagonally split circuits. Servo-assisted. Load-sensitive brake pressure regulator ABS with EBD Traction control system (EDL)
Bore and stroke	81.0mm × 86.4mm		
Capacity	1781cc		
Compression ratio	10.9:1		
Fuel injection	Multipoint injection	Size	Front 288mm (11.3in) diameter discs, internally ventilated – single piston sliding caliper Rear 232mm (9in) solid disc and single piston sliding caliper
Max. power	150ps at 5,700rpm		
Max. torque	155lb ft at 1,750–4,600rpm		
Fuel capacity	55ltr (12.1gal)		
Transmission		**Dimensions**	
Gearbox	Five-speed all indirect with synchromesh	Track	
		Front	1,513mm (59.6in)
MPH per 1,000rpm in top gear	23.6	Rear	1,494mm (58.8in)
		Wheelbase	2,511mm (98.9in)
Suspension and Steering		Overall length	4,149mm (163.3in)
Front	MacPherson struts, coil springs and lower wishbones, 20.7mm (0.8in) anti-roll bar	Overall width	1,735mm (68.3in)
		Overall height	1,439mm (56.7in)
		Unladen weight	1,270kg (2,800lb) four-door Unladen weights include the driver.
Rear	Torsion beam, trailing arms, coil springs, 18mm (0.7in) anti-roll bar, toe-correcting mountings		
Steering	Power-assisted, maintenance-free self-adjusting rack and pinion	**Performance**	
		Top speed	216km/h (134mph) 0–100km/h (0–62mph) 8.5sec

If the opportunity arises, compare the GTI pictured with the example illustrated in a Mk4 brochure of later years. It could be the same car – even the number of doors is alike and, perhaps illustrating the quiet external nature of the Mk4, are four in number, equating to a family friendly saloon!

Mk4 GTI Paintwork Options 1998 and 2001

Instantly noticeable was Volkswagen's intention that it was no longer necessary for the Golf GTI to stand out from its lesser brethren. Theoretically at least, the lowliest of models could be delivered to a customer in the shades – all fourteen of them – allocated to the GTI and other top of the range options.

There was also a more noticeable empathy with the spirit of the times, a combination of health and safety mania and the green, green saving of the planet. There follows a short extract from the paintwork colours page of the first-year brochure: 'Volkswagen only uses environmentally friendly, water soluble paints in the manufacturing process. For German TUV approval, all textile and leather materials have the toxproof and SG signs to indicate that no harmful substances have been used.'

In what was described as Non Metallic Paint, there were four options. These were long-enduring Black, endemically bright Flash Red, sugary and sweet Candy White, and academically staid Ink Blue. The metallic selection also totalled four in number and apart from the now familiar Satin Silver included Tropic Orange, Cosmic Green and Futura Yellow, this last-mentioned option appearing much more like a tarnished gold than a true yellow. Pearl Effects were the most prolific, totalling six options. Diamond Black remained firmly in place, while the one-time Colour Concept option of Jazz Blue was joined by Grey Anthracite, Canyon Red, Atlantic Blue and Bright Green. This last colour was in reality far more restrained than metallic Cosmic Green, being a rich darker shade of green definitely suited to the luxuries of the V5 as well as the GTI.

For the 2001 model there were one or two surprises in store, while the basic pattern for the remaining years of Mk4 production was now firmly established. Non-metallic options by this time had increased to five in number, the extra offering simply being branded as Yellow, where perhaps Canary Yellow, or even Bright Yellow, might have been appropriate. Linked to a revival in the fortunes of the Colour Concept ideal, this shade was fairly short-lived. The big surprise was that Flash Red had been replaced by Tornado Red, and whether or not this colour was an exact match of the shade of the same name in Mk2 days is of little relevance. Bright and bold was out in the red story – class and luxury had made a return. Metallic options were down to two in number, with neither having been on offer at the start of Mk4 production. Saturn Silver had been dismissed to be replaced by Reflex Silver, a tone of silver more than reminiscent of the long-lived shade of Diamond Silver. The other option was inappropriately named as Desert Beige. Sandy tones it might have had, but here was a classy light gold worthy of a name with royal connections.

Pearl Effects were multitudinous in number, with eight options on offer at extra cost to the buyer. These were: Grey Anthracite; Bright Green; Diamond Black; Jazz Blue; Green Collection; Indigo Blue, Oceanic Green; and Berry Red.

Volkswagen UK's example of a GTI is a 1.8T, as indicated by the red infill to its badge. The car has been fitted with 7J × 17 Santa Monica alloys and was built during 2003 at the end of the Mk4 production run.

the time, supported the process more than adequately. Darkened tail lenses, a typical device employed by sporting stylists, were shared with a selection of other Golf Mk4 owners, as were built-in front fog lights. Far less noticeable, a grey windscreen top tint started life as a GTI 1.8T exclusive, but had been dropped by the 2001 model year.

Inside, the most notable feature was the inclusion of Recaro seats. The firm bolsters tucked the driver and front seat passenger in equally tightly, ensuring that however much the car was thrown around corners, its occupants would be held in place, while for extra comfort a second side wheel allowed for the useful adjustment of lumbar support. If there was a disadvantage to be found with Recaro seats it came in the form of their larger than average size, resulting in more restricted legroom for rear seat passengers. Most, of course, would argue that the Mk4 GTI 1.8T looked its sleekest and meanest in two-door guise, opening the gate for the old adage of a sporty car really only being for two people, while rear seats were intended strictly for occasional, or emergency, use. But this was not what Volkswagen had in mind, for any Mk4 GTI 1.8T built after June 1998, which is to say more or less all such models, were endowed with three full rear seat belts and headrests to match.

Although bodily the 1.8T, like other members of the original Mk4 Golf family, didn't change during the car's lifespan, subtle improvements occurred over the years in which it was produced. From the early days of a Gamma Radio Cassette and a glass electric slide and tilt sunroof, neither of which were exclusive to the 1.8T, modifications to the specification occurred that were hardly ground-breaking. The MFA display was altered in 1999 to allow a separate and permanent display of the time, while in 2000 manual air-conditioning became standard, replacing the sunroof. In came a front-loading single CD player and later still the option of a six-CD auto-changer. Late models benefited from such goodies as ESP, Volkswagen's Electronic Stabilization Programme, a system that could control both disproportionate understeer and oversteer by selectively braking the car. However, the really big change to the 1.8T package came as the by-product of a promotional model, the Golf Anniversary.

The Golf GTI: Twenty-Fifth Anniversary Edition

Although clearly starting life as a marketing ploy like its carefully trimmed predecessor dating from 1996, nevertheless the Twenty-Fifth Anniversary Edition holds a vital place in the development of the GTI concept. For this was the first model to feature an uprated version of the dynamic 1.8T engine, coupled to a newly introduced six-speed gearbox at least as far as petrol engine cars were concerned. Possibly even more momentous was the breaking news that there was to be a second derivative of the Anniversary model, a diesel option no less, and one that was to be openly branded as a GTI.

In a press release dated 11 September 2001, exactly twenty-six years to the month and even

the day that the original GTI was seen at the Frankfurt Show in Germany, Volkswagen launched the Twenty-Fifth Anniversary Edition, which, apart from featuring the innovations already referred to, included a whole host of attractive add-ons. In so doing, the combined forces of VW's skilled engineers and the equally gifted stylists created one of the most desirable Golfs of any generation to date. If there was a downside, it came in the form of two large doors, something always more appropriately sporty looking on a hot hatch, but a curse to the family man eager to keep in touch with real power under the accelerator, for, unlike the Mk3 Anniversary model, the Mk4 was only ever available with two doors.

For British enthusiasts the big question had to be if and when the Anniversary model would be available in the UK. Eight months later and

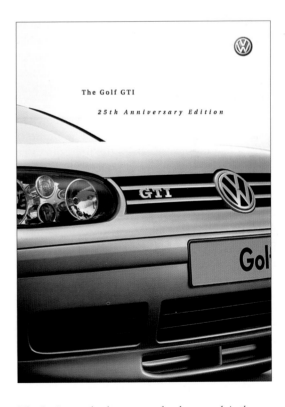

The Anniversary brochure was produced very much in the house style of the Mk4 range in general, with less than the whole car being depicted.

to coincide with the date of the first GTI to be registered in Britain, a UK version was reality. From 13 May 2002, petrol Anniversary models could be ordered from Volkswagen dealers across the country, although those opting for a diesel had to wait just a little longer.

Of unequalled interest to would-be owners was the upgraded petrol engine. The figure of 150ps had never really been the full story as far as the 1.8T went; Volkswagen could have squeezed a great deal more out of its best GTI to date. A brisk trade had grown up in remapping the engine management system to figures of 180, or even 190ps, and that was without changing the turbo! Audi's experience both with the TT and the S3 demonstrated that with a different turbo, in such instances the larger KO4 offering, 225ps was entirely possible in a standard state of tune. To give the Anniversary model that extra bit of sparkle, Volkswagen's engineers modified the Engine Control Unit (ECU), raising top-notch power from 150 to 180ps, whilst achieving this leap forward at the slightly lower engine speed of 5,500 revs compared to 5,700rpm. Even more significantly still, maximum torque was increased to 173lb ft over an extended 1,950–5,000rpm range,

With more power at its disposal than the already stunning
GTI 1.8T and a trim package that stood out from the Mk4
crowd, the limited 25th Anniversary Edition will undoubtedly
become a sought-after item by collectors and enthusiasts. Note
especially the special valances and sills – distinctive, sporty, but
certainly not brash.

resulting in an already flexible power unit developing even more beef.

If 0–100km/h (0–62mph) had looked good at 8.5sec with the 150ps engine, it looked better still at 7.9sec with the Anniversary. This was the pattern as the going got even faster too, with 0–129km/h (0–80mph) achievable in 13.5sec behind the wheel of the 150, but in just 10.7sec with the raw meat of an extra 30ps pumping away. Those determined to test maximum speed out to the full where the law permitted and sometimes perhaps where it didn't, would have seen their exuberance peak at 216km/h (134mph) with the 150, but bounce the needle onwards and upwards to 222km/h (138mph) with the Anniversary.

The addition of a sixth gear in the box of the 180ps Anniversary was like the proverbial royal icing on the already heavily brandy-soaked Christmas cake. The new gearbox's closer ratios throughout and its higher top gear generated a more instant response in the lower gears, coupled to easier cruising in sixth, which in turn led directly to less fuel usage, an accomplishment particularly noticeable on a long run. As a result, despite the extra power available, overall fuel consumption was more or less identical with that of the 150ps model.

Golf GTI Mk4 Anniversary 2002

Engine

Type: Front in-line 4-cylinder transversely mounted. Belt-driven double overhead camshaft. 5 valves per cylinder

Bore and stroke: 81.0mm × 86.4mm
Capacity: 1781cc
Compression ratio: 9.5:1
Fuel injection: Multipoint injection
Max. power: 180ps at 5,500rpm
Max. torque: 173lb ft at 1,950–5,000rpm
Fuel capacity: 55ltr (12.1gal)

Transmission

Gearbox: Six-speed all indirect with synchromesh

Ratios:
1st 3.36
2nd 2.09
3rd 1.47
4th 1.15
5th 0.93
6th 0.76

Suspension and Steering

Front: MacPherson struts, coil springs and lower wishbones, anti-roll bar, track stabilizing steering geometry

Rear: Torsion beam, trailing arms, coil springs, track correcting bearings, anti-roll bar

Steering: Power-assisted, maintenance-free self-adjusting rack and pinion
Tyres: 225/40Z R18
Wheels: 7.5J × 18in BBS alloys

Brakes

Type: Diagonally split circuits. Servo-assisted. Load-sensitive brake pressure regulator. ABS with EBD and ESP

Size: Front 312mm (12.3in) diameter discs, internally ventilated – single piston sliding caliper. Rear 288mm (11.3in) diameter discs, internally ventilated – single piston sliding caliper

Dimensions

Track
Front: 1,513mm (59.6in)
Rear: 1,494mm (58.8in)
Wheelbase: 2,511mm (98.9in)
Overall length: 4,149mm (163.3in)
Overall width: 1,735mm (68.3in)
Overall height: 1,439mm (56.7in)
Unladen weight: 1,279kg (2,820lb) Unladen weights include the driver.

Performance

Top speed: 222km/h (138mph)
0–100km/h (0–62mph) 7.9sec

Volkswagen claimed a combined total figure of 8.5ltr/100km (33.2mpg) for the 180 and 8ltr/100km (35.3mpg) for the 150ps engine.

As might be expected of such a power house, sports springs and dampers were fitted, while anti-roll bars were firmer than on the average Golf. Key to the specification, though, and contrary to the details presented in the special Golf GTI Twenty-Fifth Anniversary Edition brochure, the rear discs were ventilated, an addition to the standard 312mm (12.3in) ventilated front discs of any Golf GTI 1.8T.

The Twenty-Fifth Anniversary GTI was available in three colours, recalling the launch of the Mk1 GTI a quarter of a century earlier. Apart from the highly appropriate jubilee shade of Reflex Silver, which followed closely in the footsteps of Diamond Silver, Tornado Red echoed the Mars Red gloss of a quarter of a century ago, while Diamond Black Pearl Effect was a modern-day interpretation of the straightforward Black GTI of years gone by. All three shades were standard to the Golf range of the day and it was therefore left to a host of other external features to distinguish the Anniversary model from the rest of the pack.

At the back of the car a top-mounted tailgate spoiler and a slightly different than standard colour-coded lower valance differentiated the Anniversary, while the car also sported darkened rear-light clusters, as per other members of the hotter Golf family. At the Anniversary's front a similarly body-coloured, rather than standard black, lower valance of a unique and more purposeful design distinguished the car, as did specially darkened, near black, headlamp bowls. A chromed GTI badge of the original style with serif letters adorned both the grille at the car's front and the tailgate, the former being a welcome addition to the lamentable lack of distinguishing marks apparent on a Mk4 GTI of any description. Widened sills were instantly apparent along the car's side, although only a true model expert would have been aware that the door mirrors were slightly smaller than was the norm.

Particularly attractive, but incredibly difficult to keep clean, 7.5J × 18in BBS RC alloys shod with 7.5 × 18in Michelin Pilot Sport tyres were probably the most noticeable aspect of the car, but sadly these wheels were not the most robust item ever offered on a Volkswagen, with many deteriorating so rapidly that warranty issues were quickly upheld. Their clever alternate Y- and U-shaped sixteen-spoke formation made many an owner cling on to them, however, even when corrosion had taken its toll. For the true enthusiast, the much beefier size of tyre, compared to those bonded to a standard GTI wheel, and the sharper more precise steering this undoubtedly contributed to, was worth the slightly unsightly appearance of some of the BBS wheels. Following in the footsteps of the Mk3 Anniversary, the brake calipers were painted red and, thanks to the design of the alloys, were clearly visible between the spokes.

Interior-wise, the Anniversary model not only offered a very high level of specification, considerably over and above that of the normal GTI, but also sported a series of desirable exclusives, virtually guaranteed to make it a collector's classic in years to come. Most noticeable, and definitely desirable to all, were the Recaro sports seats, which were trimmed in Le Mans cloth, a distinctive black with thin red stripe pattern, stitched together with bright red thread. The finishing touch came in the form of a woven-in GTI logo, once again prepared in striking red. Brushed aluminium trim panels tended to replace the GTI's norm of darkened wood and were particularly noticeable on the centre console, around the gear lever and door handle surrounds, not to mention the driver's window and door-locking control panel, which formed part of the armrest. Attractive aluminium sill protectors sported the initials 'GTI' in red and were balanced by two meticulously spaced and detailed series of black circles 'printed' onto the metal. Race-inspired drilled aluminium pedals added one finishing touch, while grey-faced instrument gauges with chromed rims proved to be another. The welcome return of the quirky golf-ball

Darkened headlights.

The return of the GTI letters to the front grille.

7.5 × 18in BBS RC alloys.

Distinctive red calipers.

gear knob was doubly enhanced by the magic initials 'GTI' embedded in the descriptive disc on its top and the use of red stitching on the leather gaiter. This eye-catching stitching was extended to the perforated leather-covered steering wheel and handbrake lever, while the black carpet mats were also edged in red. Equally stylish were the red-edged seat belts at both front and rear. A true limited edition, all cars should have been supplied with a chromed plaque attached to the return panel work by the side of the driver's door and only visible when the door was open. This plaque bore the immortal initials 'GTI' in red, together with a number between one and 1800, also in red. The message 'Twenty-Fifth Anniversary Edition' etched out in black completed this desirable memento of ownership.

Scrolling down the lengthy list of standard equipment detailed in the special brochure and comparing it with the standard GTI specification of the day, it became clear why the car would carry a premium price even if the engine hadn't been special. Most noticeable on the luxury front was the six-disc CD front-loading auto-changer (compared to the 1.8T's single CD player), and full Climatronic air-conditioning rather than the manual air-conditioning normally offered. Factory-fitted options listed were short and sweet, being restricted to satellite navigation and cruise control. Curiously, the Anniversary model lacked provision for headlamp washers and hence as a result wasn't endowed with the popular but optional full winter pack. Again on the downside, the brochure suggested inclusion of the latest GTI specification of three rear-seat headrests, but this was not the case. Additionally, such goodies as parking sensors and a centre armrest weren't part of the Anniversary package, but considering that many regarded these as the province of the middle-aged or elderly driver concerned with luxury rather than all-out power, perhaps this was understandable.

180ps Plus Six as Standard

As Twenty-Fifth Anniversary GTI sales grew towards their expected target figure of 1,800 UK cars, with near non-existent pizzazz Volkswagen launched a regular 1.8T with both 180ps and a six-speed gearbox. Although this car cost in the region of £1,000 more than the 150ps model, it was similarly cheaper than the Anniversary GTI, a more than adequate reason for the softly, softly approach.

Outwardly virtually indistinguishable from the 150ps model, which remained an essential part of the line-up, under the bonnet the 180ps model's chrome 1.8T logo on the engine cover had a red infill on the T, unlike that of the 150ps car. Almost invisible to the naked eye, the ventilated discs on the rear wheels, first witnessed on the Anniversary model, had been carried over to the standard issue 180ps model, while those really keen to know which type of GTI they were looking at had only really to check out the six-speed diagram inset on the gear lever, as the 150ps car retained its five-speed box. Some would-be purchasers thought that they should be getting a little more for the additional money, citing a rear spoiler and an all-red GTI badge on the tailgate as the kind of status upgrade they had come to expect elsewhere.

The petrol engine Anniversary model's performance we know about, but it came at a price, appreciation of the 180ps's premium already having been gained and the cost being significantly more than the lower-powered, but equally genuine, 150ps GTI. Further, such was the movement in Volkswagen's parade of models that a Bora with the same engine and box

came out at well over £1,000 cheaper than the four-door version of the 180ps Golf, while the most powerful diesel-aspirated Golf cost only £50 more but delivered near-equal performance and offered great gains in the way of fuel economy. It was possible to spend more, considerably more, on a hotter Golf, as will become apparent when the V6 4MOTION comes under the magnifying glass, not to mention the awe-inspiring R32. Truth to tell, though, by the middle years of Mk4 production, the GTI no longer held such a unique place in Volkswagen's performance model story. Instead, it took a limited-edition model to lift even the best engine out of the jostling crowd of would-be contenders for the car's crown.

Diesel Anniversary GTI

All that remains now is take a look at the diesel version of the Anniversary edition. Short of opening the filler cap and peering at the sticker, or lifting the bonnet and even then overlooking the GTI badge, the only clear way to identify a diesel Anniversary model from its petrol counterpart was at the rear of the car, for the diesel's exhaust system was hidden out of sight, resulting in a smoother look to the design of the already modified rear bumper. Volkswagen's undoubted wish would have been to display a meaty and preferably chromed tailpipe or two. However, to fall in with such a notion on a diesel and its inevitably sooty exhaust particles would have been to make the rear bumper look industrially unsightly on each occasion the car was taken for even the shortest of blasts.

The 150ps TDI PD engine that powered the diesel version of the Anniversary model had been launched in December 2001 as far as the UK market was concerned, its purpose being to head a new generation of hot diesels bristling with powerful intent. As will be revealed shortly, it was perceived as a great triumph to all followers of diesel power that at last, at long last, a car so aspirated could be openly badged as a GTI. That it was considered not just appropriate but essential to extend this achievement to the limited-edition model created to celebrate twenty-five years of GTI history was indeed ground-breaking.

North American Twentieth Anniversary GTI

US GTI fans must have been confused. While Volkswagen could legitimately celebrate a twenty-fifth anniversary in Britain and even more so in Germany and other European countries, the only option in America, with its late starter date for GTI sales of 1983, was for the marketing professionals to link into such events by promoting the Anniversary model as the GTI 337, the code name afforded to the

original GTI project. Unquestionably tenuous, the car had to sell on its undeniable merits rather than on the back of a silver jubilee. As a result, the GTI 337 was available just in Reflex Silver, with a target of 1,500 sales overall being set for the dealers.

However, hot on the heels of this engineered sales campaign, a genuine US milestone appeared on the calendar. Available in Pearl Effect Jazz Blue, Imola Yellow and Black Magic Pearl, all of which were new colours to the American market, the Twentieth Anniversary GTI made its debut at the Chicago Auto Show in February 2003. Conveniently, the Twenty-Fifth Anniversary GTI for European markets was still hot news and the US limited-

---

A Potted Diesel History Lesson

The Golf and a diesel engine go back many years; all the way to the car's infancy and 1976, in fact. In those almost primeval days the 1.5-litre churned out a leisurely 50ps, ensuring no more performance than the 1.1-litre petrol engine; a car of little interest to anyone looking for power and performance. Chugging slowly forward, Volkswagen added a turbocharger in 1982 and by so doing boosted ratings to 70ps and the car's output to something roughly equivalent to that of the 1457cc petrol engine. As such, the diesel could top 96.5km/h (60mph) in roughly 12.5sec and, given sufficient wind-up time, was capable of 164km/h (102mph). Although not available in the UK, it was this engine that first became associated with the GTI, when Volkswagen produced the Golf GTD, a hybrid with a diesel power plant and the trim of the hot hatch.

The first turbo-diesel to find its way to the UK was a Mk2, although for the majority of its life it was only available in relatively lowly CL trim, and throughout as a four-door model. This was no hot hatch in disguise, for its meagre maximum power of 70ps was coupled to a peak torque figure of 98lb ft produced at 2,600rpm. Purchasers were looking for fuel economy and engine longevity pure and simple, as further evidenced by a five-speed box with a high fifth gear, labelled at the time as 4+E, the 'E' being for economy. In 1990 the engine was upgraded to 80ps through the addition of an intercooler. What extra power there was showed itself in mid-range acceleration, while 0–60mph remained stubbornly slow at over 12.0sec.

With the passing of the Mk2 Golf, Volkswagen in the UK tried to educate the population into an understanding of 'technologically advanced turbocharging', even persuading legendary rally driver Paddy Hopkirk to say that the TDI was 'deceptively quick'. By then pumping out 90ps and offering maximum torque of 149lb ft at 1,900rpm, the TDI still didn't look good when up against the traditional benchmark of 0–60mph performance. Perhaps in Wolfsburg such a criteria for diesel production was irrelevant, but in the UK Paddy Hopkirk went on to state that, despite a 0–60mph time of 12.8sec, 'the TDI is easier and more forgiving to drive' than a GTI. Careful spin ensured that the diesel story had a happy sales-engendering conclusion: 'The TDI is almost the GTI's equal in usable performance, and I can imagine its softer ride and easier handling suiting plenty of people. The GTI would still be my choice as a driver's car, but it's staggering that a diesel can come so close.'

Towards the end of the life of the Mk3, Volkswagen's Twentieth Anniversary GTI was also to be found with a diesel engine. This was the 110ps version of the 1.9TDI that would first be used in Britain under the bonnet of the Mk4. Diesel technology might have moved on in leap and bounds; it must have, to be even loosely linked with the 115ps and 150ps Mk3 GTI petrol engines. However, as far as being truly a hot hatch, there was still more of the mountain to climb.

edition model was based on this car and the related GTI 337. Pumping out 180ps and offered with a six-speed box just as the GTI 337 had been, apart from the colour options, the main differences came in the wheels, which were the 7.5 × 18in Aristo alloys borrowed from the R32, silver and grey upholstery instead of the normal red and black, plus red GTI initials both front and rear, rather than the standard chrome affairs. An exclusive came in the form of a reproduction of the old Rabbit badge, while each car sported a special individually numbered plaque mounted on the dashboard in place of the cupholders. An electric sunroof was standard, as was cruise control, side airbags and a Monsoon sound system that included a CD player. The edition extended to 4,200 cars, only 200 of which were allocated to Canada, the rest being quickly snapped up by American buyers.

Mk4 Diesel: Shattering the 'Diesels are Dull, Slow and Dirty' Myth

Who would have thought it, just a couple of years before the demise of the Mk3 Golf GTI and probably even when the new Mk4 Golf GTI was launched, that one day soon the top of the range GTI, the new 1.8T, would share a page with a diesel! Not any old diesel of course, but nevertheless an oil burner. For the 2002 model year UK brochure, there it was, two cars vying for pole position in the hot-hatch stakes:

The GTI 1.8T and GTI 1.9PD offer the perfect combination of style, performance and comfort ... The heart of the GTI is its engine – either a 1.8-litre, 20V turbocharged petrol unit or one of the most powerful diesels produced by Volkswagen – the 1.9-litre TDI PD developing 150ps. The two units share a top speed of 134mph, where the law permits, and a 0–100km/h acceleration time of just 8.5sec in the 1.8T and 8.6sec for the 1.9-litre TDI PD. To accommodate such impressive performance, lowered suspension and ESP (including

EDL and ASR) are standard. These two features play a significant role in the GTI's adept handling and superb road-holding.

However, perhaps the tell-tale signs of the way at least one diesel engine was going were apparent in the press release announcing the UK launch of the Mk4:

The entry-level Golf diesel is now powered by a direct injection, naturally aspirated 1.9-litre unit with 68ps. The SDI is new to the Golf in the UK and gives a combined fuel consumption figure of 55.4mpg, up to 9.1mpg on the previous model. The new TDI 90ps is more fuel efficient again with a combined cycle of 56.5mpg. The new Golf GT TDI 110 promises to redefine the performance hatchback class – it combines a 0–100km/h acceleration time of 10.6sec with a tremendous 57.6 combined mpg figure. A torque figure of 173lb ft, equal to the VR6 engine's but accessible at lower engine revs, gives sparkling in-gear acceleration.

Brochures produced to promote the 1998 Mk4 Golf indexed the most important models, or even trim levels, as the SE, the GTI and the GTI 1.8T, and this remained the case until the 2002 model year, when suddenly the 2.0-litre petrol engine GTI was bracketed to the GT TDI, while the GTI 1.8T was partnered with the GT TDI PD 150ps. How this came about was to be explained through the revolution known as PD (*Pumpe-Düse*) technology – the creation of diesels easily worthy of a place in the line-up of hotter hatches.

In 1998, the official message relating to the 110ps engine was one of 'good performance, easy maintenance and fuel efficiency'. For performance, re-read that message of 0–100km/h in a little over 10.5sec, while adding a top speed of 193km/h (120mph). Better still, some journalists found that the 110ps TDI Golf could outperform its own official figures, with claims of a 0–60mph romp of just 9.4sec and, even more interestingly, a big bang of just 7.3sec between 80–113km/h (50–70mph), making the diesel only a tad slower than the acknowledged petrol leader, the 1.8T, at least in that respect.

Pumpe-Düse technology made its debut in the dying months of 1999. PD, the literal translation of which is 'unit injector', could operate at pressures of up to 2,050bar or 30,000psi, figures considerably in excess of the common rail systems of under 2.0-litres which had reached in the region of 1,350bar or 20,000psi. Higher injection pressures led to better mixing of fuel and air, allowing more to be burnt cleanly in each cylinder, thus creating for Volkswagen not only a benchmark for others to follow, but also an engine that comfortably outperformed new stringent EU 111-D exhaust emission regulations.

Unlike an older TDI engine, where fuel was pressurized by a distributor injector pump and fed into the individual injectors, PD technology combined the injector and pump into one unit for each cylinder and was operated by the engine crankshaft. Hence, a finer adjustment of the fuel-injection process with a much higher pressure was possible with unit-injector

expertise. The crucial result was more torque; Volkswagen's press releases emphasized 20 per cent more torque, but not at the expense of fuel consumption or CO_2 emissions. The flexibility of a six-speed gearbox and Anti-Slip Regulation (ASR) traction control raised the stakes even further for Volkswagen's competition.

Comparative performance figures between the TDI 110ps and the TDI PD 115ps engine

Yes, the alloys have been swapped, but other than that, is this a GTI or a dirty diesel? The answer is that it is neither. This is the GT TDI, a new fighting force to be reckoned with.

made interesting reading. Maximum output was achieved at 4,150rpm in the case of the older engine and at 4,000rpm with the 115ps unit. Top speeds differed little, with 193km/h (120mph) recorded for the 110ps and (195km/h) 121mph for the PD. Fuel consumption erred in favour of the 110ps, although once again only marginally. Volkswagen recorded a combined measure of 4.9ltr/100km (57.6mpg) for the 110ps and 5.1ltr/100km (55.4mpg) for the 115ps PD engine. Where one key difference came was in 0–100km/h acceleration, with 10.6sec being recorded for the 110ps TDI, as noted previously, compared to 10.3sec for the 115ps PD. Even more important was the disparity in torque. The older engine developed 173lb ft compared to the new unit's 210lb ft, each being achieved at 1,900rpm.

Those with a vivid interest in badge status would have been delighted to discover Volkswagen's latest strategy, particularly bearing in mind that what was being offered apparently suggested a rating above that of the petrol engine 1.8T, with its single 'I' etched out in red: 'To signify the engine upgrade, the boot lid TDI badge now contains a red "D" in addition to the red "I" which distinguished the TDI 110 from the 90ps model'.

Although well on the way to meeting the criteria for a hot-hatch badge, there was still a little way to go, for not only would the 115ps engine be replaced by a more powerful unit, but also a new top of the range diesel, worthy of a position alongside the 180ps petrol engine in the Golf GTI Twenty-Fifth Anniversary Edition, had yet to be developed. One obstacle to global PD ascendancy came in the form of intrinsic resistance to diesels as a breed, with more than a few diehards demanding to know why the 115ps PD engine should be endowed with the hallowed letters GT, as in GT TDI PD! Sadly, at such a ground-breaking time, another obstacle was of Volkswagen's own making, for in June 2000 the company had no option but to reintroduce the 110ps engine, due to an inability to cope with the demand for the new 115ps PD unit. Although the 115PD engine

was still shown on the price list in the late spring of 2001, it was also marked as 'not available to factory order'.

Launched in the Passat in January 2001, the 130 TDI PD engine ousted the 115PD in the Golf in late June of the same year. To accommodate the extra 15ps, the injectors were modified to increase the speed with which fuel entered the combustion chamber, while the geometry of the injector openings was also amended. Of all the changes brought into effect, one of the most far-reaching was to the pistons, which now featured an aluminium alloy with increased heat-resistance and a strengthened gudgeon pin. The net result of this and a great deal more detailed activity was an increase in power over that of the 115ps engine of some 13 per cent, coupled to a boost in torque of 9 per cent, or from 210 to 228lb ft, all of which was still achieved at an impressively low 1,900rpm. This afforded the Golf GT TDI PD a top speed of 204km/h (127mph), an official 0–100km/h figure of 9.6sec, plus better acceleration throughout the range, while retaining excellent fuel economy with a combined figure of over 5.4ltr/100km (52mpg). Gearing was high, so high that at 113km/h (70mph), the engine was turning over nothing more than 2,000rpm in sixth gear. Crucially, as one motoring magazine pronounced, 'the TDI trounces the 1.8T in terms of in-gear times, over 1.5sec ahead in some increments'.

More or less irrelevant to the hot-hatch story, the 100 TDI PD replaced the 90ps TDI unit and for the UK market was launched simultaneously with the 'long-awaited' 150ps engine. At last, the diesel had made GTI status. Volkswagen's UK press office couldn't have been more specific, even outlining the difference between a Golf and a Bora endowed with the 150ps engine: 'Badging for the new models is simple and the result of research with drivers and insurers. The Golf will be badged GTI with a red 'I' (the same as the petrol GTI 1.8T) and the Bora simply TDI, with all letters in red.'

Although the index of the 2003 model year brochure, launched in June 2002, appeared to muddy the previously crystal-clear waters, with reference to 'The Golf GTI and GT TDI PD', meaning the 2.0-litre petrol engine model and the 130 TDI PD, followed by a single allusion to 'The Golf GTI 150ps' and nothing more, all became clear within the pages. Covering the subject of the 130 TDI PD with the words, 'If a GTI class diesel is more your style, there's the *"Pumpe-Düse"* 1.9-litre GT TDI 130bhp', the following pages moved on with the heading 'The Golf GTI 150ps', before launching into the text used to introduce the notion of a hot diesel Golf.

Born on the back of the 130ps TDI PD engine, the 150ps model sported: modified injector nozzles, facilitating a further reduction of 25 per cent in particulate emissions; modified pistons, thicker connecting rods; lighter yet stiffer piston gudgeon pins; a larger, more efficient (at least 86 per cent efficient) and better positioned intake air intercooler; and a larger turbocharger with higher maximum boost pressure (2.1bar, up from 1.9bar). The UK press office was proud to announce that, 'for its capacity, the new 1.9-litre TDI PD 150 engine is the most powerful diesel unit available in a passenger car; it also boasts the best maximum thermal efficiency at 43 per cent of any liquid-fuelled production car'.

Translated into black and white figures, the most powerful diesel had a top speed of 216km/h (134mph), while the 0–100km/h benchmark was achieved in just 8.6sec. Maximum torque of 236lb ft at 1,900rpm was up on that of the 130ps model but not significantly. Fuel consumption was inevitably heavier than that of the 130ps model, but the engine's main claim to fame was its ability not only to outperform the 150ps petrol engine as housed in the Golf GTI 1.8T in terms of both 48–80km/h (30–50mph) and 80–113km/h (50–70mph) in the gears, but also to leave it standing to the tune of half-a-second in that all-important 0–100km/h scramble.

One magazine summed up what the real message of the 150ps diesel GTI was. While other TDIs might be described as economical cars with good performance, here was a car with real performance that happened to be reasonably economical.

Clearly the 'traditional' GTI had something to contend with if it was to remain supreme. Diesel popularity had grown in leaps and bounds, to the extent that it was anticipated that more than half the Golfs sold in the UK would be so aspirated, while 3,000 of those would be of the 150ps ilk. The petrol engine 1.8T, and particularly so in 150ps guise, had a pack of wolves baying at both its three- and five-door body. Whether 150ps TDI technology would take over completely had yet to be seen, but most imagined, as had been the case when contenders for the petrol-head's crown had first appeared in the shape of the V5 and then the V6 4MOTION, that at least in the future there would be far more opportunities to indulge in hot-hatch technology and in this instance at least, through a medium offering a sensible return when it came to miles per increasingly costly gallon.

'A New Type of Luxury Car from Volkswagen – The Golf V5'

The initial message behind the V5 was one of slight confusion. Was the Mk4 Golf V5 a direct rival to the GTI 1.8T, or was it a straight successor to the Mk3 VR6, a car that had, as has already been discovered, created a near-exclusive niche of executive comfort with potent power and an ability to travel faster than the Mk3 GTI in 16-valve guise?

> The outgoing 2.0-litre 115ps engine which powered the GTI 8V is replaced by a 1.8-litre 20-valve 125ps engine ... [in the] new GTI ... The old GTI 16V is replaced by the new GTI 1.8T ... Derived from Volkswagen's famous VR6 engine, the new 2.3-litre V5 150ps unit will be offered alongside the 1.8T. Performance is similar for both yet their characters are very different, the V5's distinctive engine sound being particularly noteworthy.

So wrote Volkswagen's UK Press Office in

March 1998 at a time when the UK launch of the Mk4 Golf was fast approaching.

As the GTI 1.8T's reputation flourished, the answer to any queries relating to the V5's purpose in the range became increasingly obvious. The model wasn't destined to be the acknowledged top of the range Golf. It wasn't a direct successor to the Mk3 VR6, but it shared some of that car's characteristics. Even the first-year brochures for the Mk4 went some way to make this point, omitting the V5 as a talking point in itself, merely including its engine as the one with the largest cubic capacity available at the time.

In creating the V5 engine, Volkswagen simply removed one cylinder from the old VR6 unit, in the process reducing displacement from 2.8 litres to 2.3 litres, or 2,324cc to be pedantic. The precedent had already been set for an odd number of cylinders thanks to, amongst others, Audi's Ur-Quattro, one of a series of developments on the by then famous in-line 5-cylinder engine developed some years earlier. Audi had already proved that a 5-cylinder engine would run more smoothly than a 4-cylinder one, while, as it was both lighter and shorter than a 6-cylinder engine could ever be, it was eminently capable of revving more freely.

Golf TDI PD 150ps 2002

Engine

Type	Front in-line 4-cylinder transversely mounted Belt-driven single overhead camshaft. 2 valves per cylinder
Bore and stroke	79.5mm × 95.5mm
Capacity	1896cc
Compression ratio	18.5:1
Fuel injection	*Pumpe Düse* – combining the injector and pump into one unit for each cylinder. Turbocharged with intercooler – maximum boost pressure 2.1bar
Max. power	150ps at 4,000rpm
Max. torque	236lb ft at 1,900rpm
Fuel capacity	55ltr (12.1gal)

Transmission

Gearbox	Six-speed all indirect with synchromesh

Suspension and Steering

Front	MacPherson struts, coil springs, anti-roll bar. Track stabilizing steering geometry
Rear	Torsion beam trailing arms, with track connecting bearings and anti-roll bar
Steering	Power-assisted, maintenance-free self-adjusting rack and pinion

Tyres	205/55 R16W
Wheels	6.5J × 16 Montreal 11 alloys

Brakes

Type	Diagonally split circuits. Servo-assisted. ABS with EBD Front: Ventilated discs Rear: Discs

Dimensions

Track	
Front	1,513mm (59.6in)
Rear	1,494mm (58.8in)
Wheelbase	2,511mm (98.9in)
Overall length	4,149mm (163.3in)
Overall width	1,735mm (68.3in)
Overall height	1,439mm (56.7in)
Unladen weight	1,270kg (2,800lb) four-door Unladen weights include the driver

Performance

Top speed	216km/h (134mph)
	0–100km/h (0–62mph) 8.6sec

Fuel Economy

Urban	7.2ltr/100km (39.2mpg)
Extra-Urban	4.4ltr/100km (64.2mpg)
Combined	5.4ltr/100km (52.3mpg)

The V5's single block with a one-piece head was designed to accommodate five cylinders in a staggered line, equating to one bank of two and one bank of three set at a narrow angle of 15 degrees. With two valves per cylinder, a camshaft serving each was driven by a chain.

Complex two-stage inlet manifold geometry led to a high, flat torque curve which offered a maximum of 151lb ft at 3,200rpm, but with 90 per cent available from 2,300 to 5,300rpm, on the one hand, and a maximum power of 150ps, which was delivered at 6,000rpm, on the other.

The 'new' V5 had more torque and more power as might be expected from a 170ps engine. However, it could only be distinguished from its earlier incarnation by the chrome 'V' and red '5' badges and 16in Montreal 11 alloys. (Photograph Courtesy of Volkswagen UK Press Office)

Acceleration from 0–100km/h was achievable, according to Volkswagen's figures, in 8.5sec, exactly in line with the Golf GTI 1.8T. Its top speed in the early days was again the same as that of the 1.8T at 216km/h (134mph), while note was taken of its smooth and refined performance in achieving this. Combined fuel consumption was perhaps the car's weakest point, with Volkswagen recording a figure of 7.8ltr/100km (36.2mpg) for the GTI 1.8T, but only 9.3ltr/100km (30.4mpg) for the V5.

UK press releases described the Golf V5 as 'a unique new luxury car ... which provides an unusual blend of refinement, quality and comfort', before launching into a lengthy list of attributes 'in keeping with its positioning as a small luxury car'. In the light of what was to follow during the lifespan of even some of the more mundane members of the Mk4 Golf family, some today may wonder what all the fuss was about. However, at the time the V5's specification was excellent, even though it erred away from the attributes normally associated with a fast and powerful car. Luxuries therefore included: full Climatronic air conditioning; leather-covered steering wheel; sports seats; front fog lights and darkened rear light lenses; 6.5J × 16 Montreal alloy wheels; three rear head restraints as opposed to lower-specification two; and, in the same vein, colour-coded bumpers, side strips and door handles.

Golf Mk4 V5 1999

Engine		**Tyres**	195/65 R15Y
Type	Front in-line 5-cylinder transversely mounted 2 valves per cylinder – camshaft for each bank of cylinders, chain-driven	**Wheels**	6J × 16 Montreal alloys
		Brakes	
		Type	Diagonally split circuits. Servo-assisted. Load-sensitive brake pressure regulator
Bore and stroke	81.0mm × 90.2mm		ABS with EBD
Capacity	2324cc		Front: Discs, internally ventilated – single piston sliding caliper
Compression ratio	10.0:1		
Fuel injection	Bosch Motronic		Rear: Discs – single piston sliding caliper
Max. power	150ps at 6,000rpm		
Max. torque	151lb ft at 3,200rpm		
Fuel capacity	55ltr (12.1gal)		
		Dimensions	
Transmission		Track	
Gearbox	Five-speed all indirect with synchromesh	Front	1,513mm (59.6in)
		Rear	1,494mm (58.8in)
Mph per 1,000rpm in top gear	22.0	Wheelbase	2,511mm (98.9in)
		Overall length	4,149mm (163.3in)
Suspension and Steering		Overall width	1,735mm (68.3in)
Front	MacPherson struts, coil springs and lower wishbones, anti-roll bar	Overall height	1,439mm (56.7in)
		Unladen weight	1,353kg (2,893lb) five-door Unladen weights include the driver
Rear	Torsion beam, trailing arms, coil springs, toe-correcting mountings, anti-roll bar		
		Performance	
Steering	Power-assisted, maintenance-free self-adjusting rack and pinion	Top speed	216km/h (134mph) 0–100km/h (0–62mph) 8.5sec

Omitting to note that the car lacked both Recaros and sports suspension, that leather was an optional extra, as were heated seats, headlamp washers, an automatic dimming mirror and rain-sensing wipers to mention but a few out of a long list, Volkswagen was anxious to point out that options previously reserved for larger luxury cars were available. Top of the list undoubtedly was 'a factory-fit satellite navigation screen' featuring a 5in LCD screen. This state-of-the-art luxury fitted entirely with the message Volkswagen was trying to convey: 'The interior of the new V5 Golf has been designed to give its occupants the sensation of travelling in a far more expensive car. Volkswagen calls this "democratizing luxury".'

The only problem with such a message was that in many, if not all, instances other members of the Mk4 Golf family were similarly endowed, destroying the illusion of exclusivity at a stroke. Following on immediately from the 'democratizing luxury' statement, the release proceeded to refer to nothing that a base model wouldn't have included: 'Attention to detail beyond any other medium car shows itself in design details such as soothing blue backlighting for the instruments, the precise action of the switchgear operation and even a glovebox lid that glides open due to a damper unit filled with silicone fluid.'

During 2000, the V5's specification was reassessed, adding more previously extra-cost options into the standard specification. Key to this package was a six-CD auto-changer, but conveniences such as an auto-dimming mirror and rain-sensing wipers were likewise appended.

Come the winter of 2000 a more significant 'improvement' had been announced. An extra 20ps and a 10 per cent increase in torque were achieved by the introduction of multivalve technology, affording 4 valves per cylinder, making a total of twenty in all. According to Volkswagen initially, and most who tested the car subsequently, the upgrade meant that the engine revved both more freely and smoothly, while the increased power improved performance at the top end of the car's rev range. Although hardly earth-shattering, Volkswagen was delighted to note an improvement in fuel consumption too, with the older engine being attributed a slightly worse combined total of 9.4ltr/100km (30.1mpg) than when it was launched, compared to the 170ps's 8.7ltr/100km (32.5mpg).

With top speed having increased from 216km/h (134mph) to 224km/h (139mph), and 0–100km/h performance having likewise been clipped from 8.8 to 8.2sec, making it faster than the Golf GTI 1.8T, perhaps Volkswagen's goalposts for its executive Golf had been moved. As if to emphasize the V5's extra sporting prowess afforded by the increase in power, for the first time it became available with the choice of two instead of four doors, while as an optional extra, costing close on £1,000, a sports pack was on offer. This consisted of sports suspension, which lowered the car by 15mm (0.6in), gave stiffer springs and dampers for a firmer, sportier ride, while including 17in five-spoke Santa Monica alloy wheels. Externally, and very much in the spirit of the time, both the V5 badge on the hatch and its counterpart on the grille featured a chrome 'V' as before, but were distinguished with a red '5'.

By the time of the V5's upgrade a further model had joined the Mk4 Golf line-up, apparently another contender in the king of the power stakes. Volkswagen recognized that the V5 held a special place in the model range, but that it had not been and would not be its best-seller. For the calendar year 2001, the prediction was that 1,200 V5s would be sold in the UK. However, that compared less favourably to the envisaged 1,700 V6 4MOTIONs and somewhat dismally against the anticipated 6,500 bonanza of GTI 1.8Ts.

The final clue to the V5's role also came when the V5 was endowed with even more power. An automatic option, a recognized preference of the middle-aged and executive car class buyer, had always been available. Now this was upgraded to the new and more sophisticated five-speed automatic Tiptronic box.

V6 4MOTION – Performance Prototype or Supreme Tow Car?

'Eagerly awaited' was how the UK press office chose to describe the arrival of the nearest replacement in Mk4 terms to the Mk3 VR6. Time had certainly ticked by, for it was more than two and a half years since the last of the VR6s had rolled off the assembly line before the V6 4MOTION made its debut in the UK in the spring of 2000.

Volkswagen's intention with the V6 4MOTION was blatantly obvious; the V5 had never quite matched the opulence of the Mk3 VR6 in its trim level, nor had it been designed to match the performance attributes of the older car. How could it when the GTI 1.8T had been singled out as the Mk4 with the distinctly unique interior specification? How could it when a cylinder had been unceremoniously lopped off? The new V6 4MOTION, however, was more or less engineered and trimmed to pick up the story from where the Mk3 car had left off. The 2001 model year brochure introduced the V6 4MOTION thus: 'When a car is powered by a V6 engine and employs four-wheel drive, you can expect outstanding performance and road-holding. The Golf V6 4MOTION is such a car and it will satisfy your highest expectations'.

Power came from further development of the VR6 engine, which now had 4 valves per cylinder. The 24-valve, 2.8-litre (2,792cc) engine developed 204ps at 6,200rpm. With a bore and stroke of 81.0mm × 90.2mm, compression stood at 10.5:1. Variable valve timing not only gave greater torque at low and mid-range engine speeds, but also developed more power at higher revs. Peak torque of 199lb ft was reached at 3,200rpm, which was lower and more accessible than previously. Compared to the VR6 of old, the V6 4MOTION achieved greatly enhanced performance through the gears, particularly between 48–80km/h (30–50mph) and 80–113km/h (50–70mph), partly due to the differing gear ratios between the old and new, but primarily owing to the newer engine's greater

torque. As the press office was keen to point out, 'not surprisingly' the Golf V6 4MOTION was the fastest-accelerating hatchback so far sold. The car was capable of 0–100km/h in just 7.1sec and could achieve a top speed of 235km/h (146mph) with ease. This left the benchmark GTI 1.8T 150ps struggling by 1.4sec in the zoom up to 100km/h stakes, before it became little more than a spec on the horizon through the Golf V6 4MOTION's rear window, thanks to its foot-on-the-floorboards top speed of 216km/h (134mph), 19 vital km per hour (12mph) behind the maximum achievable by the new player on the street.

However, all was not perfectly plain sailing for the Volkswagen boffins responsible for the new, most powerful Golf, for with this kind of acceleration the V6 4MOTION could easily have run into difficulties if restricted to front-wheel drive. The Mk3 VR6 had depended very much on traction control systems to alleviate more than the worst of the wheel-spin problems associated with front-wheel drive, but this car, with an extra 30ps under its belt, needed something more. The answer for the Mk4 came in the form of 4MOTION, Volkswagen's new permanent four-wheel-drive system that employed a Haldex coupling. Old-timer models with syncro had involved a differential that had driven two output shafts; the new set-up applicable to the V6 4MOTION only drove one. Thus the coupling was incapable of influencing the drive to the front wheels, but also couldn't push the rear ones faster than those at the front. The added advantage of the coupling arrangement was that the torque it sent to the rear wheels could be adjusted, through electronically controlled hydraulic actuation of its clutch plates, dependent on both the accelerator position and driving conditions, such as braking and cornering, plus both engine torque and wheel speed.

Positioned at the back end of the propshaft and by the side of the rear differential, when associated with the slightly larger fuel tank of 63ltr (13.8gal) capacity attributed to the V6 4MOTION compared to the norm of 55ltr

(12.1gal), the Haldex coupling was intrusive, the result being a reduced luggage-carrying capacity, caused by a higher boot floor. With the back seats in place, the Golf V6 4MOTION offered only 2.5cu m (8.7cu ft) of luggage space, compared to the rest of the ranges' 3.3cu m (11.7cu ft). Pushing the rear-seat backrest down predictably improved matters, but even then the load floor suffered from an obtrusive step in levels.

Clad with 6.5J × 16in seven-spoke Brands Hatch alloys and shod with 205/55 R16 W tyres, while sporting the same three-spoke steering wheel as the GTI 1.8T and packing the punches with its six-speed gearbox, some might have thought the V6 4MOTION to be the most sporty Golf of the extended Mk4 range. Corroborative evidence came in the form of twin chrome exhaust pipes, which demanded a unique cut-out in the rear valance, the archetypal red '6' as an integral part of the V6 grille badge, plus a slightly revised front valance incorporating important brake cooling ducts. Despite this accumulation of proof in support of such a theory, sporting prowess was not Volkswagen's primary intention. The Golf V6 4MOTION didn't come with sports suspension as standard and it lacked Recaro seats, relying instead for bolster support on Volkswagen's own brand of sports seats. Both missing ingredients were essential features of a truly sporty hatchback; instead, the V6 4MOTION wallowed under the spell of the machinations of pure luxury.

Walnut inserts were to be found on the centre console, the ashtray cover, the edge of the driver's door control panel and wood even formed the basis of the unique 4MOTION gear-stick knob. The driver luxuriated in every conceivable extra of the day save satellite navigation and a full leather interior. This thrust towards luxury was strongly promoted within both the brochure images and the press releases distributed to convince journalists that here was something worthy of more than passing mention. The latter even concentrated valuable space on Volkswagen's Digital Sound Processor, designed to bring a listener 'right in the heart of the music', while also taking pains to mention optional gas discharge headlights.

This press image issued at the time of the launch of the Mk4 V6 4MOTION indicates once again why spotting the model identity of a Mk4 is so difficult. Here the clue comes in the alloys, the design of which was known as Le Mans, and of course the V6 badge on the grille. (Photograph Courtesy of Volkswagen UK Press Office)

Three V6 4MOTIONs caught on camera in Yorkshire, Cornwall and Worcestershire respectively, hopefully indicating that despite its high cost for what might be a glorified tow car, people across the nation made their purchases. In gas-guzzling terms, a deep back pocket was definitely required.

Of undoubted significance to the relatively brief story of the Golf V6 4MOTION was that it was awarded the title 'Tow Car of the Year' by the Caravan Club in the autumn of 2000, shortly after its launch. Ask if any truly sporting option would really be offered such an accolade and the answer is fairly obvious. However, with a cost price of some £4,000 more than the V5 and £4,500 in excess of that required to purchase a GTI 1.8T, the V6 4MOTION was hardly the vehicle that those practised in the art of numerous but economical holidays might indulge in. Nor did combined fuel consumption of just 11ltr/100km (25.7mpg) make for tempting reading, particularly when a V5 could achieve considerably more and the 1.8T appeared positively thrifty at 8ltr/100km (35.3mpg).

R32 – Keeping the Best Till Last

Throughout much of the life of the Mk4 Golf there was a distinct feeling emanating from Wolfsburg that the GTI should not, indeed would not, be even partially eclipsed by more powerful models. Just as the more potent VR6 of Mk3 days had not been openly allowed to lead the field, so it was with first the V5, then the V6 4MOTION and latterly the authoritative challenge of tempting *Pumpe Düse* technology, although at least in 150ps guise this was sanctioned to adopt a sliver of the GTI's rounded heritage. In many ways, Volkswagen was its own worst enemy when it came to both the Mk3 and Mk4 GTI. What was there, particularly in the case of the genuine Mk4 GTI, the 1.8T, to make the car stand out? Red-line assertiveness had gone; wide wheel arches had been banished; only reference to a tiny badge tagged onto the hatch with the 'I' etched out in red distinguished the car from its compatriots. Only a limited-edition Anniversary model had been allowed to break the rules, and then not by a great deal!

Then suddenly it was all change; a concept car was to become reality, deposing the GTI on all counts, on genuinely beefy looks, on

hitherto unbelievable power, on unprecedented torque, on infinitely superior handling, on incredible four-wheel traction, on a genuinely sporty interior and, above all, on an image that set the coldest heart pounding.

The R32 made its debut on the racing stand at the Essen Motor Show in November 2001. Officially still nothing more than a concept car at the time, it was clear to all that production beckoned; deposition of the GTI had finally been sanctioned. The R32 was aired before the masses once more at the Madrid show in May 2002, while British enthusiasts were given their own preview at the Birmingham Motor Show held in October of the same year.

Initially planned to be available in strictly limited numbers, in three-door guise only and

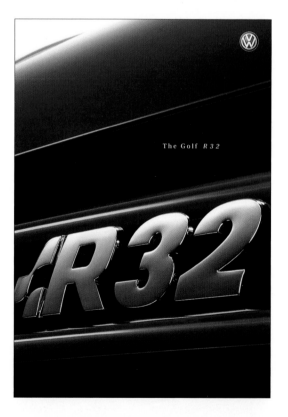

More than one R32 brochure was produced. This early version was by far the most dramatic with its reproduction of the R32 badge – stylized segments of a chequered flag bonded to the letter 'R', the international symbol of Volkswagen racing.

painted in the single shade of Deep Blue Pearl Effect, even by the time the first UK brochures were released such notions had gone to the wall. From one to three colours and later to seven, from three-only to five doors as an option, and from just 750 cars to 1,700 examples in the first year, the R32 was a resounding triumph for Volkswagen in the UK, only finally halted when the life of the Mk4 Golf itself expired in August 2003.

For the first time in many years, a Golf looked the part, so much so that Volkswagen acceded to customer demands and went on to produce an R-line body kit for lesser breeds, which sadly had to include the GTI. As one of Volkswagen's UK press releases acknowledged, 'the newcomer's appearance leaves onlookers in no doubt about its dynamic potential'. A unique and overtly deep front spoiler-cum-bumper featured three massively hostile, mesh-fronted air intakes. Hefty sill extensions beefed up the car's sideways appearance to Aberdeen Angus proportions, while an aggressively re-designed rear bumper and valance, with widely spaced and massively proportioned cut-outs for two pulsing chrome tailpipes, transformed the Golf's rearward aspect, aided by the addition of both a smallish spoiler bonded to the top of the tailgate and near-obligatory darkened rear lenses. To complete its big and bad looks, the R32 sported four 7.5J × 18in Aristo multi-spoke

alloys shod with uncompromisingly low profile 225/40 ZR 18 tyres, which carefully revealed the car's dynamically unique and eye-catching blue-painted brake calipers. Distinctive stylized segments of chequered flag alongside a bold and italicized letter 'R', the international symbol of

Deep Blue Pearl Effect.

Volkswagen racing, bonded together with the magical digits '3' and '2' to form a unique chromed badge which adorned both the front grille and rear hatch, in the former instance restoring Volkswagen's hot-hatch message to where it should be and in the latter case replacing an unnecessary endorsement of the Golf brand.

As might be expected of a real sporting spectacular, the R32 was lowered – by 20mm (0.78in) compared to the standard Golf and by 10mm (0.4in) even when matched against the ground-hugging GTI 1.8T. Although this inevitably meant restricted ground clearance in certain circumstances, the car looked both forcefully meaner and sportily desirable.

With the added advantages of tinted rear and side windows, gas discharge (Xenon) dipped beam, visible headlight washers and five exciting pearl effect paint colours – Moonlight Blue, Grey Anthracite, Diamond Black, Indigo Pearl and the much vaunted Deep Blue original – plus trusty Reflex Silver metallic and sporty Tornado Red, the R32 not only stood out from the crowd, but begged even the less than remotely interested to come a little closer.

Opening the door, there to behold was an interior worthy of any Porsche, from the R32 logo etched onto the sill thresholds to ergonomically crafted König sports seats, specifically designed with pronounced side bolsters and integral headrests for premium support when the R32's power was in use to the full. Their look was almost 'race style', but the Königs incorporated opulence, from adjustable heating in cold weather driving conditions to both lumbar and height adjustments. The seats, available in Monte Carlo Anthracite or Flannel Grey upholstery as standard, or trimmed with black leather at extra cost, were duly emblazoned with the R-flag logo, as were many other aspects of the car's unique interior, most noticeable being the brushed aluminium racing pedals, the three-spoke leather-rimmed steering wheel with a column adjustable for both reach and height, and the chunky gear

Initially offered in Reflex Silver Metallic, Diamond Black Pearl Effect and, exclusively to the R32, Deep Blue Pearl Effect, other colours soon followed. These included Indigo Pearl Effect, which is also shown here. Undoubtedly meatier in its appearance, no doubt to match its exhilarating performance, the R32 is already a sought-after classic with exceptionally strong second-hand values.

Diamond Black.

Indigo Pearl Effect.

Reflex Silver and the R32 badge on the rear of the car.

stick, which moreover reminded driver and passengers alike that the car's specification included 4MOTION. A logo also appeared at the centre of the rev counter and was further woven into each of the black floor mats. The brushed aluminium theme was extended to the centre console, the gear-lever surround and the interior door handles, while the chrome-ringed instruments blended perfectly with the intended look.

The higher echelons of standard equipment included climate control, MFA trip computer, six-CD auto-changer, rain-sensing wipers and an automatic dimming rear-view mirror. Optional extras fitted by the factory centred around satellite navigation, cruise control and an electric sunroof.

While the R32 certainly looked the part, it wouldn't have been the first car in the world, albeit not from the Volkswagen stable, to have presented a snarling wolf appearance only to hide sheep-like performance. Of course, this was far from the case, as hordes of followers discovered immediately upon its launch.

Golf Mk4 R32 2003

Engine

Type	Front in-line 6-cylinder Otto transversely mounted
	Narrow angle V6 with 24 valves, variable timing, variable length inlet manifold
Bore and stroke	84.0mm × 95.9mm
Capacity	3189cc
Compression ratio	11.3:1
Fuel injection	Bosch Motronic
Max. power	240ps at 6,250rpm
Max. torque	236lb ft at 2,800rpm
Fuel capacity	63ltr (13.8gal)

Transmission

	Four-wheel drive with Haldex coupling
Gearbox	Six-speed all indirect with synchromesh
Mph per 1,000rpm in top gear	23.7/1,000rpm

Suspension and Steering

Front	MacPherson struts, coil springs and lower wishbones, anti-roll bar
Rear	Multi-link, fully independent, coil springs, anti-roll bar
Steering	Power-assisted, maintenance-free self-adjusting rack and pinion, suspension 20mm (0.78in) lower than standard Golf
Tyres	225/40 ZR18
Wheels	7.5J × 18 Aristo alloys

Brakes

Type	Diagonally split circuits. Servo-assisted
	ABS with EBD and ESP, including ASR and EDL
Size	Front: Discs, internally ventilated, 334mm (13.6in) diameter
	Rear: Discs, internally ventilated, 256mm (10.1in) diameter

Dimensions

Track	
Front	1,513mm (59.6in)
Rear	1,487mm (58.5in)
Wheelbase	2,518mm (99.1in)
Overall length	4,149mm (163.3in)
Overall width	1,735mm (68.3in)
Overall height	1,444mm (56.9in)
Unladen weight	1,512kg (3,334lb)
	Unladen weights include the driver

Performance

Top speed	245km/h (152mph)
	0–100km/h(0–62mph) 6.6sec
Autocar	
0–60mph	6.5sec
0–100mph	15.6sec
evo	
0–60mph	6.4sec
0–100mph	16.4sec

Performance was nothing short of electric, even more so than might be expected from an enlargement of the 2.8-litre V6 as used in the 4MOTION to a cubic capacity of 3189cc, or 3.2-litres, as the R32's designation implied. Both bore and stroke were increased to 84.0 × 95.9, respectively. The narrow-angled V6 sported 24 valves, continuously variable inlet valve timing, a variable geometry intake manifold and a knock sensing system, causing the UK press office to write of the engine's 'deep growl' being accompanied by impressively strong performance. Maximum power of 240ps standing was achieved at 6,250rpm, while 236lb ft of torque was available in the range between 2,800 and 3,200rpm. Volkswagen declared a 0–100km/h acceleration time of 6.6sec, although the original UK press release had clipped that back to 6.4sec, a stunning time confirmed by *evo* magazine, which also went on to decree a 0–100mph time of just 16.4sec; 30–50mph in fourth cost 4.6sec and 50–70 in the same gear just two points of a second more. A top speed of 244.5km/h (152mph) set the R32 well apart from any other model in the Mk4 range. One magazine wrote of the R32 combining 'the mid range response of a powerful diesel with the high-revving ability of a multi-valve petrol and the silky smoothness of six cylinders'.

Key to the R32's unendingly urgent performance was the certainty that the car's front wheels weren't going to spin hopelessly when the accelerator was floored, that the suspension was geared to the most exhilarating of rides and the sure-footed awareness that whatever the conditions the brakes would bring the driver and occupants swiftly and efficiently to a safe standstill.

The Haldex coupling, central to the car's permanent four-wheel-drive performance, in turn supplemented by ESP, which included EDL and ASR, ensured that the R32 could be effortlessly and safely powered along the twistiest of slippery roads that would leave the rest of the pack hopelessly struggling. Wheel spin at take-off, however aggressive the right foot became, was unheard of.

The R32's suspension was designed for race tracks – stiffer springs, stiffer dampers and stiffer anti-roll bars, coupled with that combination of wheels and tyres already referred to, and steering that required fewer turns from lock to lock, guaranteed little if any roll. Cornering at high speed might have been successfully accomplished by the most inexperienced of drivers.

Vented discs – 334mm (13in) diameter at the front and 256mm (10in) at the rear – with twin pot calipers at the front, supported by Brake Assist, a device capable of detecting excessively rapid pedal movement under hard braking conditions and consequently boosting the braking force, and further supplemented by both ABS and EBD, ensured that the R32 came to a safe stop with the minimum of fuss and in the shortest of times, whatever the conditions.

'With the R32 it's not just about raw power, it's about blending engineering, high technology and performance data into a genuine driving experience.' So wrote Volkswagen's copywriter charged with the simple task of selling in print a phenomenon that had taken the legendary Volkswagen hot hatch to new heights.

The Bora: Engines and Trim for the Rising Executive

Having failed to convince all but the American market of the merits of the third-generation Golf with a boot, the Vento, Volkswagen decided that a further name change in Europe was essential. Named after an Adriatic wind, the Bora was intended to mirror prestige German compact executive sports saloons and as such particular emphasis was placed upon luxury and quality in UK launch press releases. 'Materials used throughout the cabin will shame cars costing thousands more, let alone those of direct rivals', was typical of the style employed. Although still recognizably from the Golf stable, the Bora's prominent, angled grille with a large VW roundel and square headlights if anything gave it a more aggressive and sporty look than its sibling. However,

The Bora – the most elegant of the booted Golfs, seen here in V5 guise as evidenced by the grille badge. (Photograph Courtesy of Volkswagen AG)

despite both these features and a combination of a steeply sloping rear window plus short, notch-back tail, the GTI designation, even in 2.0-litre guise, was absent from the model's line up.

Top of the range was the Bora V5, while the most powerful diesel engine of the day, the 110ps, and the 2.0-litre petrol engine were offered with a 'Sport package'. The name was somewhat confusing, in that the specification amounted to nothing more than 6.5J × 16in Le Castellet alloy wheels shod with 205/55 R16 tyres, front fog lights, sports seats of the same style as those fitted to the 2.0-litre GTI, plus a walnut gear knob and walnut trim inserts on

the dashboard and door pulls. That the V5 carried the same package of equipment, save that it also benefited from what Volkswagen now called 'set-and-forget' Climatronic air conditioning, only confirmed an emphasis on luxury rather than blatant power. The ultimate in leather upholstery was an optional extra on both models.

However, May 2001 seemed to bear witness to something approaching a change of heart. Having extended the line of vehicles privy to the Golf GTI's 1.8 150ps engine to include the New Beetle and lowlier trimmed models of the Passat, the Bora too was so endowed. Sadly, the specification for the new engine did not

This is a Bora Sport TDI 130PS, although if the badge on the car's rear wasn't checked identification wouldn't be that easy. Such a car epitomized the crossover between sporty performance and saloon opulence. Finished in Blue Graphite Pearl Effect, the Sport featured amongst its attributes 6.5J × 16 Le Castellet alloys, walnut wood inserts throughout the interior, leather sport seats, six-CD interchanger and full electronic climate control.

extend to typical GTI hallmarks such as Recaro seats and black wood trim.

> This engine [the 1.8T] has ... been extended to the Bora compact saloon range in Sport trim. Offering a highly specified package, with air conditioning, CD auto-changer, front fog lights, sports seats and 16in Le Castellet alloy wheels ... this is a superb choice for company car drivers looking for something different and sporty at a competitive price ...

Although the company car angle remained a priority in the marketing of the Bora, it was offered in just about every powerful guise afforded to the Golf. Press releases announcing the evolution of *Pumpe Düse* technology from 115, to 130 and 150ps blocked the Golf and Bora together in one message, while with petrol engines the saloon had received the upgraded V5 170ps engine at the same time as the hatch, as it did with the launch of the V6 4MOTION option.

A press release dated August 2002 confirmed the power with luxury strategy once more:

> Volkswagen has added even more sporting flavour to the Bora range, with the introduction of a 180ps version of the 1.8T engine. This powerful petrol unit, which was first seen earlier this year in the Golf GTI Anniversary, is available in DT and Sport models. ... The new unit joins a host of high-performance engines available to Bora customers, including the 150ps 1.8T, the 130 and 150ps TDI PD turbo-diesels, the 170ps V5 and the range-topping 204ps V6 4MOTION.

Still no GTI, though, and this was to remain the case to the end of Bora production during 2005. With the Mk4 Golf having given way to the Mk5 in the summer of 2003, the Bora's specification became even higher, as Volkswagen attempted to buoy up sales of a by now obviously soon to be replaced car. Although the V5 and V6 4MOTION had been deleted from the line-up, both the upmarket Highline and Sport trims led to the creation of truly executive saloons. In addition to the goodies

of old, it was not uncommon to see Boras with leather upholstery, cruise control, multifunction steering wheels, parking sensors, headlight washers, satellite navigation and much more.

The Mk4 Golf in the United States, 1999–2005

Thanks to the launch of the New Beetle in 1998, Volkswagen sales in the USA generally appeared healthier than they had been for many a year. The fourth-generation Golf debuted there in 1999. It was offered with just

Keen observers at GTI International 2007 would have seen two US-market cars parked in close proximity to one another. Speaking to the owner of the Mk4 Jetta – the name Bora wasn't used in America – the curious would have discovered that only the alloys were non-standard to the specification. The other car was an Imola Yellow US market Twentieth Anniversary GTI – a Golf based on the German market Twenty-fifth Anniversary model and the related limited edition US market GTI 337.

This 2.0-litre Cabriolet, which in saloon form would have badged as a GTI for the UK market, illustrates several points. First, despite its Mk4 front end, the side profile clearly indicates a Mk3 heritage, as does the interior shot with the Mk3 dashboard. Second, this a Colour Concept Cabriolet, as evidenced by the yellow leather trim, which extended from the seats to the door cards and minor items like the handbrake cover. Finally, without a top, the Golf's status as a smaller vehicle rather than a medium one is more obvious.

three engines. These were the 115ps 2.0-litre, branded as the GL and therefore more or less in line with the strategy in most European countries other than Britain, and the 90ps TDI, which was exported for its fuel economy. Top of the range, however, was the Golf GTI GLX, which from launch to the end of 2000 was powered by an updated version of the VR6 engine from the third generation.

Offering 174ps, this was supplemented in 2001 by the 1.8T engine, which had the somewhat dubious honour of becoming the base offering in the GTI, the overall package being branded as the GTI GLS. The R32 made its way to America in 2004, while the fifth-generation Golf didn't debut in the USA until 2006, being preceded, as might be expected, by the fifth-generation Jetta.

The pictures say it all! Another new Cabriolet? Well no, not really, for here was the Golf Mk4's front welded onto the platform, back end and even the dashboard of the Mk3. The tactic worked, even though there were a few cynics who insisted on calling the vehicle the Golf Cabriolet Mk3.5. (Photograph Courtesy of Volkswagen AG)

The 'Final Edition' of the Golf Cabrio and apparently no prospect of a further model in the foreseeable future. Many would argue that the New Beetle Cabrio was destined to carry Volkswagen's open-top heritage forward, while others would suggest that, despite its size, the Eos was the true successor to the soft-top Golf and with appropriate engines to match. Note that the Final Edition Golf Cabriolet was endowed with the 2.0-litre engine, which in Britain in saloon form only was branded as a GTI. (Photograph Courtesy of Volkswagen AG)

6 Five: A Modern Way of Staying the Pace

Starting Posts

Although claimed to be the 'biggest step forward so far in the evolution of the model', there were serious omissions in the all-new line-up heralding the arrival of the Golf Mk5, a car that made its international debut at the 2003 Frankfurt Motor Show on Press Day, 9 September. Pizzazz and unmitigated hype ruled as the new model was ceremoniously unveiled amidst the eagerly anticipated deluge of paper proclaiming the Mk5 Golf's obvious merits, but a dark shadow was cast over the proceedings as there was no red-hot GTI to be seen and not even a glimmer of a scintillating R32.

With a wheelbase 67mm (2.6in) longer than that of the Mk4, the overall length of the car increased by 57mm (2.2in) to 4,204mm (165.5in), while an extra width of 24mm (0.9in) made for a chunky overall measurement

After two generations of faceless GTIs the original hot hatch was back in a big way with the Mk5. The fact that it wasn't available at the general launch of the model was only of concern until it did make its debut! Not only had red-edge grille technology returned, although that isn't overly noticeable on the example pictured here, but also thanks to a clever reworking of the front valance and grille the car stood out from the crowd. Even those three famous initials 'GTI' took pride of place up front once more. Cutting-edge wheels, raucously apt sporting interior … the list is seemingly endless.

of 1,729mm (68in); even the height of the vehicle was greater than previously at a sterling 1,483mm (58.4in), an increase of 39mm (1.5in). And to what purpose? With the rear wheels positioned as far back as possible, this still incredibly compact car offered more interior space and particularly so for rear seat passengers whose available legroom increased by 65mm, while with 24mm more headroom there was no longer an excuse for slouching. Predictably, increased size heralded a further increase in weight, something not alluded to in the numerous press releases issued to promote Volkswagen's traditionally best-selling model. Shrouded in the complexities of unladen weights including or excluding a driver, the base model Mk4 with occupant tipped the scales at 1,163kg (2,564lb), while the equivalent empty Mk5 pounded the road at 1,319kg (2,908lb). Somehow, on this occasion, nobody really seemed to mind!

Significantly new was the rear suspension, although it had been thoroughly road-tested in the Touran before being included in the specification of a mainstay model like the Golf. Aided by an increase in track for improved stability, press releases referred to a new 'multi-link rear suspension layout', the settings of which were intended to 'give a ride that is both sporty and comfortable'. Against a backdrop of technical diagrams and under a general heading indicating that 'For challenging road surfaces, there's an easy solution', Volkswagen's brochure copywriter advised that the Mk5 Golf delivered 'through a four-link rear axle. A highly effective arrangement allows the length and cross dynamics to be tuned separately with great results'.

Emphasis was also placed on the 35 per cent increase in the torsional stiffness and 45 per cent more dynamic stiffness of the new bodyshell when compared to that of the Mk4. The extension of six-speed gearbox technology to all but the most basic of Golf models in the new line-up was deemed newsworthy, but perhaps predictably stylistic developments were given pride of place in most circles:

The front end is completely new and designed to reduce further aerodynamic drag, while distinctive twin circular headlights with the glass tapering towards the centre of the car give a dynamic look. At the rear, the Golf Mk5 has a strong visual presence with twin circular tail lights, which have become an immediately recognizable feature of current Volkswagen design.

Of particular importance in the hot-hatch story that would eventually emerge was the decision to offer greater visual distinction between the profiles of the two- and four-door models. Acknowledged already as lending itself most to sporty applications, the two-door Mk5 featured what Volkswagen's stylists chose to describe as 'a "kicked-up" rear side window', which was 'intended to convey a more sporty and dynamic message'.

With something akin to the frontal appearance of the less extreme members of the sadistically crass Peugeot family, and thanks to an interior that was stainless steel, anthracite plastic, state-of-the-art modern but somehow lacked the timelessly classic look of the Mk4, not everyone took the new car to their hearts immediately. Indeed, some of the more obdurate swore a solemn oath that they would not desert the Mk4 and amazingly an increasingly small number of diehards stuck to that pledge throughout the lifetime of the Mk5. In the early days, Volkswagen would naturally hear none of that and while almost admitting the gaffe committed by not launching a Mk5 car bearing the magical letters GTI from day one, the company boasted that the buying public had committed to orders 20 per cent in excess of target. 'This is all the more remarkable when it is noted that the most famous Golf of all – the GTI – is not due to arrive until the end of this year', someone confessed in March 2004.

Opening Lukewarm Gambit
To counteract the effects of not offering a Mk5 GTI when the new model was launched, Volkswagen had its strategy carefully prepared. From the five engine options announced for

the UK market in December 2003, the figure had lifted to seven by the following March. Two of these, the 140ps 2.0-litre TDI, available to order from the start, and the 150ps 2.0-litre FSI, a spring 2004 addition, had been carefully groomed to carry the hotter attributes of Golf ownership forward into the latest generation.

As the Press Office judiciously announced in December 2003: 'these two models fall under the "GTI" family in the price list, and will be joined by a 2.0-litre FSI turbocharged GTI 200ps towards the end of next year.'

Already available in the Touran compact MPV, the 140ps six-speed diesel engine offered would-be Golf GT TDI owners a top speed of 203km/h (126mph) and 0–100km/h performance of 9.3sec. Maximum torque of 236lb ft was available between 1,750 and 2,500rpm. Bore and stroke stood at 81.0 × 95.5mm, while the compression ratio was 18.5:1. Fuel economy, if that mattered, according to Volkswagen came out at a healthy 5.7ltr/100km (49.6mpg) on the combined cycle. As for the petrol engine 2.0-litre FSI, the letters standing for Volkswagen's latest electronic direct-injection technology, the 1984cc unit offered a top speed of 206km/h (128mph) and 0–100km/h acceleration in 8.9sec. Bore and stroke stood at 82.5 × 92.8mm respectively, while the compression ratio of the 150ps engine was 11.5:1. Maximum torque of 148lb ft was achieved at 3,500rpm. Inevitably not as frugal with fuel as the diesel, the petrol engine achieved 8.5ltr/100km (33.2mpg) overall.

In keeping with the best practices of hotter models, suspension was duly lowered by 15mm (0.6in) and suitably stiffened, allowing cornering with less body roll, and the adoption of a driving style in keeping with the wishes of the former GTI owner.

To a Mk4 owner tempted by the status of possessing the new-generation Golf before the rest of the crowd, the visual appearance of the two GT models was entirely in keeping with the philosophy Volkswagen had propagated since the previous generation's introduction. Externally, the two cars could only be identified by a discreet badge on the hatch, a larger and distinctive breed of alloy reserved for the upper echelons shod with chunkier tyres than other models save those allocated the Sport level of trim, fog lights mounted in the grilles which were part of the front bumper, and the by now old-hat addition of fully colour-coded bumper mouldings and door handles. Inside, sports seats were standard, while Siempre cloth upholstery distinguished the model from the family hatches with S or SE trim levels. A leather-trimmed steering wheel, gear knob and gaiter and handbrake grip, were what GT owners would have come to expect.

Those who purchased either GT model in the belief that if they were going to be the owner of a car that might not have quite the dynamic power of the GTI when it arrived, but at least had something that would look the part, were in for a surprise – the biggest sensation in Volkswagen's history for the best part of the last fifteen years!

GTI – 'The Legend Returns'

> The badge says it all. As soon as you set eyes on the new Golf GTI, you'll find a stirring within. Could it be the wide track, lowered sports suspension and 17in Monza alloy wheels that have set your pulse racing? Maybe the rear roof spoiler and GTI styling with its deep front spoiler and unique honeycomb front air intake? Step back, take a deep breath, your journey is about to begin.
>
> *(UK launch brochure, October 2004)*

Long before purchasing a GT, the really astute hot-hatch follower could have worked out that Volkswagen was likely to break the mould of recent times with the fifth generation of GTI, when a design study made its appearance at the Frankfurt Motor Show in September 2003 and took the motoring scene by storm.

The UK Press Office packed its story with superlatives guaranteed to make even the most laid-back journalist take note. Starting with the obvious – 'the GTI not only sits at the heart of a complete class of vehicles, the hot hatchback sector – but is synonymous with the Volkswagen name itself' – red-hot headlines followed swiftly, for example: 'Though the design is modern and dynamic, it is instantly recognizable as a Golf GTI thanks to styling

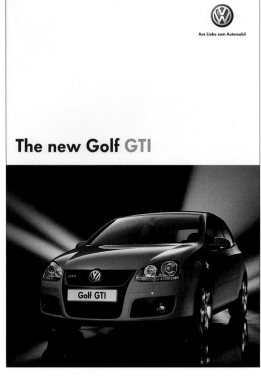

The hot-hatch brochure in Mk5 guise – certainly some story to tell!

themes inspired by the original 1976 model. These include a black grille with a red outline; distinctive GTI logos; black sills and bumper skirts; and a prominent roof spoiler.'

Back in Germany the marketing department had worked hard on its segment analysis. Yes, there was the crucial element of Mk1 GTI styling to encompass the older drivers wishing to recapture their youth, or who simply desired to remain young at heart. But also there was the 'young, self-confident male, aged 25–35', an official line disseminated to any journalist who cared to take note. The blatant look of the Mk5 GTI shouted 'must have' for those to whom money was not an issue. Yuppies may have been dead and buried, but here was a car designed for the breed's successors; even the sporty three-door styling of the Mk5 in general played right into the hands of this cash or credit rich market.

At a single stroke, the Mk4 GTI was decidedly old hat; even the new holder of the hottest-hot-hatch crown, the R32, apparently a one-marque model anyway, appeared somewhat tarnished. Every aspect of this impressive design study was destined to restore what had gradually been lost – red-line brutality was back in a big way. Better still, despite the concept GTI's 'evocative styling clues', it didn't merely replicate all the good things of the past, it added a new dimension to Volkswagen's 1.5-million-to-date performance powerhouse:

This press shot compares the original GTI with the Mk5 version – the model that saw the return to red-line technology and a whole host of identifying brand marks. (Photograph Courtesy of Volkswagen UK Press Office)

Around the time of the debut of the Mk5 GTI, press releases from Volkswagen UK inevitably reached near fever pitch. Here are two of the images issued for use by journalists and authors. (Photograph Courtesy of Volkswagen UK)

In addition, the GTI prototype features twin exhaust pipes; 18in alloy wheels; red brake calipers; and a striking arrow form that plunges from the bonnet, around the honeycomb grille and down into the deep front air dam. Inside, extensive use of aluminium in the pedals, trim, floor and steering wheel join sports seats and chrome-ringed instruments to create a bold, sporty ambience.

What did appear highly unusual was that the GTI's all-new engine was going to be linked to an automatic gearbox: 'A 2.0-litre turbocharged, direct-injection FSI engine, producing 200ps, provides the level of performance expected of a GTI, which is transferred to the road via Volkswagen's innovative DSG direct-shift gearbox. The already dynamic suspension, which utilizes a multi-link design at the rear, is designed to perform outstandingly on this new GTI.'

More or less exactly twelve months to the day since the design study appeared, on 23 September 2004, the confirmed package that was the fifth-generation GTI made its debut at the Paris Motor Show. In reality, little had changed from the design study's specification, including the option, but not an all-embracing one, of DSG, to all intents and purposes an automatic under a new name.

As Volkswagen bombarded journalists with deluges of releases, one theme more than any other emerged – the realization that the unintentional downgrading of the GTI's identity over the lifespan of the third, and particularly the Mk4 Golf's production run, had been a mistake. The storyline wasn't put quite like that, but that is what was meant. 'The GTI is now more clearly distinct from other models in the Golf range than ever before', announced one release, another making reference to both two- and four-door models with the message that 'the visual appeal of both versions has been enhanced, with more individual styling compared with other Golf models in the range'. Britain's first exclusively GTI brochure for the Mk5 model took the message one step further with the simple but carefully crafted heading: 'GTI. The legend is reborn.'

'Plunging' remained the in-word with reference to the deep-black honeycomb grille framed out with the welcome return of red, the finest distinguishing mark imaginable. A tip picked up from the Mk4 Anniversary model was the reinstatement of the serif-style GTI badging, both at the car's front and on the hatch, a location where its significance was enhanced

by the decision to drop the normal Golf badge in chrome; a laudable move to further set apart the GTI from the rest of the pack.

Many of the other features guaranteed to set fans' pulses racing were verbally beefed-up as the message gathered both pace and volume. The 'black, widened' sills, the 'high-gloss covered' B-pillar, the 'new' front and rear spoilers, or alternatively at least at the front, 'the deep air dam', and the 'double stainless steel exhaust pipes', to mention but a few, had all been there before, but were now gaining minute-by-minute significance. Features obvious to a sporting legend worth its salts added veracity to an already exhilarating story, and included 'blue heat-reflective windows and tinted headlight

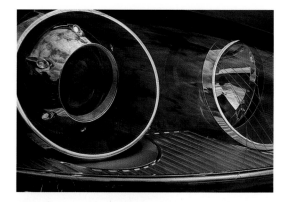

Passing a VW dealer, a Mk5 GTI always stood out. The black example pictured here more or less masks a Mk5 R32.

White might not have been the most popular colour in paint options for a potential GTI owner, but it does demonstrate the Mk5's sporty aspects to maximum effect. For the record, the exact shade is Candy White, apparently a favourite in America.

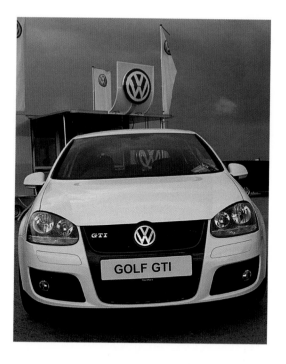

The 17in Monza alloys and a tailgate spoiler make all the difference.

housings', 'lowered sports suspension' and 'striking 17in alloy wheels', although in this last instance 'optional 18in versions' (Monza 11) were expected to be a popular choice.

To the inevitable delight of fans far and wide, all the classic GTI paint colours were offered from day one, as well as an exciting collection of typically classy alternatives. Non-metallic originals ranged from Black, via Candy White, to winning Tornado Red, with Ink Blue thrown in for those oblivious to nostalgia. Supplementing metallic Reflex Silver as a substitute for first-generation Diamond Silver were Steel Grey and Shadow Blue, while modern-day pearl effects allowed a second choice of black, with Diamond Black, as well as new tasteful options such as Blue Graphite and Laser Blue.

'Inside, the GTI theme is reinforced', proclaimed a pre-release bulletin, and so it was. The seats, commanding a remarkably sporty appearance, thanks in part to considerable extra side bolstering, were trimmed out in eminently contemporary Interlagos cloth – a chequered pattern involving red, silver, grey and anthracite, reminiscent of the Mk1 GTI's loud tartan upholstery, but with all the crudeness siphoned away. The steering wheel, sporty in its three-spoke appearance, the rim trimmed in leather,

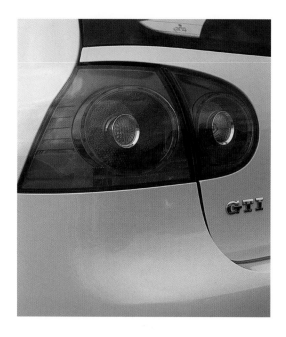

The honeycomb and red-edged grille, accompanied by three magic letters.

In the Volkswagen house style of the post Mk4 era, the rear light lenses suit themselves to the aggressive appearance of the GTI. Note the discreet GTI badge.

bore an aluminium GTI badge to confirm its nature. Both themes, leather and aluminium, were extended elsewhere. Leather was used for the gear-lever gaiter and handbrake grip, unless optional Vienna leather upholstery in beige, but more normally in anthracite, was specified to grace the interior with its opulence. The specially designed aluminium gear knob and the brushed aluminium instrument surrounds with GTI logo emphasized the dynamic and powerful nature of the beast, while the full gambit of pedals, which in the case of the manual GTI extended to clutch, brake, accelerator and footrests, were similarly decked out in aluminium in true racing style.

That the GTI was bequeathed the most powerful engine of any such car excluding the usurping fourth-generation R32, now apparently dead and buried, laid to rest any fears that stylists had succeeded where engineering had failed in the quest to create a new generation must-have hot hatch. Described variously as 'sophisticated', or as 'a true performance

hatchback', on this occasion there was no attempt to offer a badging exercise as well as the real thing, as the Mk5 GTI's single engine, a turbocharged version of the normally aspirated FSI unit, had a great deal going for it. The 1984cc 16-valve direct-injection engine with a compression ratio of 11.5:1 and a bore and stroke of 82.5 × 92.8mm respectively, as per the GT 2.0-litre FSI, swept that model away thanks to the aforementioned turbocharger. Acceleration to 100km/h from a standing start took just 7.2sec in the manual version of the GTI, before the car pushed the needle up to 235km/h (146mph) with consummate ease. But that wasn't the full story, far from it. Although maximum output was achieved at 5,100rpm, unlike many another

A little imagination made all the difference to the anonymous days of the Mk3 and Mk4.

engine it didn't suddenly drop away from that peak, but instead remained fairly steady until finally ebbing away at around 6,500rpm. Strong acceleration from the lowest of engine speeds, the result of a particularly flat torque curve, where the maximum of 207lb ft was achieved at just 1,800rpm but then remained absolutely level until around 5,000rpm, made the GTI powerful, but smooth at all speeds. The combination of red-line driving joys and the lack of town centre hesitation made the Mk5 GTI simply the best. The accolades poured in.

Temptation to avoid the invariably generous remarks of single-marque magazines such as *Volkswagen Driver* has on this occasion been resisted for reasons that it is hoped are obvious. Writing in the March 2005 edition, editor Neil Birkitt could hardly contain his enthusiasm for the new GTI:

This new turbocharged 2.0-litre FSI is quite simply the most satisfying 4-cylinder engine we've ever driven. Everything about it, from its soul-stirring sound to its smooth and muscular power

---

Golf Mk5 GTI 2.0 FSI Turbo 2005

Engine

Type	Front in-line 4-cylinder transversely mounted Belt-driven single overhead camshaft. 4 valves per cylinder
Bore and stroke	82.5mm × 92.8mm
Capacity	1984cc
Compression ratio	11.5:1
Fuel injection	Turbocharged fuel-stratified direct injection (FSI)
Max. power	200ps at 5,100rpm
Max. torque	207lb ft at 1,800–5,000rpm
Fuel capacity	55ltr (12.1gal)

Transmission

Gearbox	Six-speed manual or six-speed DSG (Direct Shift Gearbox)
Mph per 1,000rpm in top gear	25.1, or 25.8 DSG

Suspension and Steering

Front	Optimized MacPherson struts, coil springs with telescopic shock absorbers, all elements integrated in chassis legs
Rear	Multi-link with gas pressure shock absorbers and separate springs Lowered by 15mm (0.6in) compared to standard Golf and with 20 per cent stiffer anti-roll bars
Steering	Maintenance-free self-adjusting rack and pinion

Tyres	225/45 R17
Wheels	7.5 × 17 Monza alloys

Brakes

Type	Diagonal twin circuits. Electro-mechanical servo-assisted. Load-sensitive brake pressure regulator Traction control ASR, ESP supported by ABS and Hydraulic Brake Assist (HBA)
Size	Front 312mm (12.3in) diameter discs, internally ventilated Rear 286mm (11.3in) solid disc

Dimensions

Track	
Front	1,539mm (60.6in)
Rear	1,528mm (58.8in)
Wheelbase	2,578mm (101.5in)
Overall length	4,216mm (166in)
Overall width	1,759mm (69.3in)
Overall height	1,469mm (57.7in)
Unladen weight	1,336kg (2,945lb) six-speed manual, 1,355kg (2,988lb) DSG Unladen weights exclude the driver, but include 90 per cent tank capacity

Performance

Top speed	235km/h (146mph) manual, 233km/h (145mph) DSG 0–100km/h (0–62mph) 7.2sec manual, 6.9sec DSG

Even though the Mk5 GTI had near perfect looks, some owners couldn't resist a little personalization. Extending the dynamics of the GTI's frontal appearance by painting part of the bonnet black certainly doesn't distract from its beefy appeal.

delivery is so sublime as to be almost ridiculous. It is everything that a modern GTI engine should be: not only potent but also smooth and refined, it almost urges you to run it to the red line. But it is no way cammy or compromised ...

When the GTI won *Top Gear*'s 'Car of the Year' award for 2005, Jeremy Clarkson committed the words 'absolute sensation' to print, going on to say:

The 2.0-litre engine is probably the strongest link of what's a fairly unburstable chain. There's no lag at all and even if you can't be bothered to change gear, there's always a bagful of torque on hand. ... The simple fact of the matter then is that no matter how you cut it, the Golf is either brilliant or

excellent in every single area. It's fast, it handles well, it's easy to park, easy to run, socially acceptable anywhere, comfortable and well made to boot ...

What Car similarly named the GTI 'Best Hot Hatch' of 2005, putting it streets ahead of what it referred to as '*stiff competition*'. The summary reason for choosing the GTI was even better!

What sets the Volkswagen apart from more frenzied rivals is the way it develops strong, usable power right across the rev range. With 197bhp [sic] to call upon from its turbocharged 2.0-litre engine, there's little need for a heavy right foot or hectic gear-changing to unleash the car's potential. ... Frankly it's hard to think of a model more in tune with the needs of the 21st century hot-hatch driver.

Auto Express was so impressed with the GTI that instead of presenting one award to Volkswagen, it heaped two honours on the company in a single go. Apart from scooping the Hot Hatch Trophy, the GTI triumphed over a wide-ranging collection of performance cars, some of which cost significantly more, to take the Sporting Car category too. 'Put simply', wrote *Auto Express*, 'the Golf GTI is a driver's delight. … How highly do we rate the Golf GTI? Well, since the German hot hatch is picking up its second award, it's safe to say that since its arrival, everyone on out test team who's driven it has loved it.'

As a final sting in the tail to any unwitting owners of pre-GTI launch petrol-fuelled GTs, even economy wasn't the flag to fly. Nobody would argue the GTI was the most frugal of vehicles and with a suitably booted heavy right foot it was quite easy to record wallet-denuding figures. But checking out Volkswagen's official ratings, the GTI had the upper hand over the GT on every single occasion, providing DSG technology was a part of the hot hatch's make-up, while straightforward manual-geared comparisons left the smaller-engined car only a short gasp ahead. With DSG then in both instances, urban driving clocked up 10.8ltr/100km (26.2mpg) for the GTI and only 11.9ltr/100km (23.7mpg) for the GT. Extra-urban results were similar, with 6.3ltr/100km

(44.8mpg) being recorded in the GTI's favour against the 6.6ltr/100km (42.8mpg) for the GT. Overall, the DSG GTI recorded 8.0ltr/100km (35.3mpg) against the GT's 8.5ltr/100km (33.2mpg). Manual guns at the ready, the situation was reversed, but considering neither car was bought for its economical qualities, the figures are revealed without comment. Urban 11.1ltr/100km (25.4mpg) for the GTI, 10.8ltr/100km (26.2mpg) with the GT; extra-urban 6.3ltr/100km (44.8mpg) for the former and 6.1ltr/100km (46.3mpg) for the latter, all of which leaves the overall consumption for the GTI at 8.1ltr/100km (34.9mpg) and slightly more for the GT, at 7.8ltr/100km (36.2mpg).

Story Without End

With the reverberations of such rave reviews still only too apparent, the Mk5 GTI chapter could legitimately be cast as the shortest in the book. What more can be said? The GTI of 2005 was still pounding the roads as the last echoes of the Mk5 sounded in Wolfsburg's cavernous halls. But in its infinite wisdom Volkswagen still had plenty up its proverbial sleeve once the GTI had taken the world by storm. Ruling out the need to write about the Mk5 version of the 4MOTION concept, on the grounds that it was linked to the also-ran 2.0-litre FSI and TDI engines, it is also worth pointing out that the once-innovatory V5 had died the death with the passing of the Mk4.

Of the goodies in reserve then, DSG – Direct Shift Gearbox – was already known of; it had christened the Mk5 GTI concept and although so far overlooked went on to play a valuable part in its victorious story. The spectre of the R32 rose once more, not necessarily to unbridled praise, but nevertheless cannot be disregarded, while thirty years of GTI history unveiled an even more powerful GTI. Most important of all, though, was a unique embracing of turbocharger and supercharger, a combination that opened up a far more serious threat to GTI supremacy than could ever have been thought possible.

Mk5 GTI Paintwork Options 2005

Just as the Mk5 GTI saw a return to red-line design technology, so too was there a regrouping on paint policy. The days of proliferate pearl-effect options were over, as now it was a case of four non-metallic choices, three metallic paints to select between and another three pearl-effect alternatives. Black, Candy White, Ink Blue and Tornado Red heralded no change in non-metallic paints. Shadow Blue, Steel Grey and Reflex Silver made up the metallic options, while Blue Graphite and Laser Blue were new to the choice of pearl-effect paints, Diamond Black being the only ongoing shade.

DSG: The Automatic That Wasn't and the Clutchless System That Is

The revolutionary new DSG gearbox provides the best of both worlds, super smooth and extremely fast gear changes with performance and economy figures comparable to the manual.

(UK New Golf GTI brochure, 1 October 2004)

News that the new-generation GTI was to be coupled with clutchless driving outraged some of the more vociferous critics of the automatic box. However much Volkswagen argued the cause for the advanced technology behind DSG, epitomized in its name of direct-shift gearbox, some had already made up their minds. Never before had a genuine GTI been pushed along by anything other than a fully manual box; providing that the brief appearance of DSG in conjunction with the Mk4 R32 for the European market only was conveniently overlooked, such a thought now was inconceivable. Undoubtedly the province of the older driver and his or her more leisurely approach to life, in Mk4 days it had been acceptable to offer auto-Tiptronic with the V5, for this car's credentials had been analysed sufficiently for all to know that it wasn't a serious contender in the all-out sporting hatch stakes. As for the V6 4MOTION, another power-house but not in the GTI stakes, that hadn't been specced up with an auto-box and, of course, neither had the R32. What an outrage to even think of it! All of which left the big, bad diesels; the 130ps and particularly the 150ps TDI. Check out any latter day UK listing of the full Golf Mk4 range and there wasn't a sniff of an auto-box to be seen over and above the gently, gently 100ps offering. Add a boot, another preserve of the older driver, and tag on the Bora name and matters changed, for the 130ps engine could be specified with auto-Tiptronic, but even then that's as far as it went. The notion of a genuine GTI in automatic form was unprecedented.

DSG first saw light in the Audi TT, and not just an also-ran TT, but the most powerful, the TT 3.2 Quattro. Not that DSG was developed purely for such a breed; far from it. For the Volkswagen-branded goods at least, DSG was going to be offered across a wide range of models and in conjunction with engines of varying power. Here some day would be a genuine successor or rather a replacement for the leisurely automatics of old. Wherever mated, DSG would add to, rather than detract from, the package.

Put at its simplest, with a manual gearbox there is one gear wheel for each ratio. Matching wheels on the output shaft slide along when the driver changes gear either up or down until such point that the two gears link together. At the crux of DSG are two input shafts instead of the normal one, the first carrying the odd-numbered gears from first through to fifth, the second the evens of second, fourth and sixth, plus reverse. Each shaft has its own wet clutch allowing it to bond with the drive shaft from the engine. Control mechanisms prevent more than one input shaft being mated at any one time. Setting off with first gear automatically selected, the input shaft allocated to that gear is engaged with the engine. However, as second is demanded, the first shaft disengages as the other shaft takes over, the original preparing to engage third gear, and so on. The pre-selection of the next gear is carried out by an electronic control unit, the speed of the change therefore depending solely on the rate at which the automatic clutches can operate. With the might of technical wizardry behind them, the hydraulic shifters can inevitably move the gears both in and out of engagement faster than even the slickest of drivers can operate with a conventional gearbox.

Volkswagen's own official 0–100km/h times confirm the DSG system's lightning ability when linked to an appropriate engine such as the GTI's, with two-input shaft expertise clipping the manual boxes sprint time of 7.2sec down to 6.9sec. For those sufficiently at ease with DSG to let it work at its own incredibly slick pace, all that is required is to ease the stubby lever from 'P' for park, to 'D' for drive, the traditional mode of an automatic. For the rest, Volkswagen added 'S' for sport, whereby when selected the DSG gear system hangs on a little longer to each of the lower gears, thus creating an even greater response from pressure on the accelerator. Then again, for those wishing to be more involved, the manual sequential mode offers the opportunity to change gear by prodding the shifter forward to go up a gear, or backwards to go down.

Once everyone had calmed down, one genuine blip in the DSG system was highlighted. To the intense disappointment of the adventurous driver wishing to take a corner on full throttle, the system changed up at 6,800rpm, inconveniently short of the 7,100rpm limiter. As for the greatest benefit, well, once the novelty had worn off, most GTI owners came to realize that in a world of ever more crowded urban roads, the advantages of not having to worry about frequent gear changes was well worth the relatively small premium on the price of a manual model.

Another R32!

Safe in the assumed knowledge that the Mk4 R32 was strictly a one-off – a sort of reborn Mk2 Rallye Golf without the need to build it for homologation purposes – a few with money to burn holes in their pockets bought their Mk4 'exclusive' strictly for investment purposes. Hardly driven, if at all, such cars found their way into carefully cocooned environments, no doubt with the plan that they should resurface in five, ten or even fifteen years time to be sold at vastly inflated prices – a certain solid investment if ever there was one. But the bubble burst with a particularly loud pop when in August 2005 Volkswagen announced that a second-generation model would make its international debut at the IAA Frankfurt Motor Show the following month.

Thanks to *VW Driver* magazine, the reason for a second R32 is fully known. Editor Neil Birkitt was fortunate enough to speak with Dirk Jünger, the Wolfsburg executive charged with bringing the whole project to fruition. No doubt to the frustration of those who had squirrelled away a Mk4 in a centrally heated corner, Jünger went a good way to confirming that the original R32 had been conceived as a limited edition; a project making use of diverse elements of up-to-the-minute technology:

> You must remember that the original R32 was developed because we had some outstanding technology available and we wanted to produce the ultimate production Golf. We had the powerful 3.2-litre engine, the Haldex four-wheel-drive system and the DSG gearbox and we felt it would be worthwhile to marry these together in a special model ...

Justification for repeating the model came essentially in the form of meeting the demands of customers wishing to be the owners of a super-Golf. Cynics reading a UK press release heralding the Mk5 R32's unveiling might just have had a different opinion, a slightly more jaundiced reason for Volkswagen's eagerness! 'The original Golf R32, based on the Mk4

Golf, outperformed all sales expectations, with over 2,300 sold in the UK alone'.

Whether there was any legitimacy in such thoughts is neither here nor there, for at least Herr Jünger went more than a little way to explain Volkswagen's philosophy regarding the Golf in the first decade of the 21st century. Gone was the Mk3 era notion of a top-of-the-range Golf that had as much, if not more, power than the GTI, but which was deliberately diverted in the direction of opulent luxury. Swept away too was the Mk4 story of creating bigger and more powerful GTI engines to ensure that the 1.8T held onto its title as the best of the sporting bunch across a range of motoring manufacturers. At last came the realization that the GTI was an important, even vital component of the Volkswagen's performance story, but no longer was it necessary for it

To more than a few the impact of the Mk5 R32 was not quite what it should have been. Compare the cover of the R32 brochure with that of the GTI and possibly the R32 detractors did have a point.

to wear the sporting crown if confidence was to be maintained in the brand. Indeed, and though not apparently strictly relevant to the R32 story but in reality a vital ingredient to the hot-hatch legend in Mk5 days, both cars were to be joined by a third vehicle, a reborn, genuinely upgraded car, fully worthy of both its GT badge and its equal footing place in the trio:

> Now ... we have to make a clear separation between three performance Golf models. We already have the very successful GTI, we will soon have the GT with the supercharged TSI engine, and we are now launching the R32. It is much more expensive than the GTI and, as well as the 3.2-litre and four-wheel, it is better equipped and will appeal to those who are prepared to pay for the ultimate Golf in the range.

Fortunately for those rather too easily deluded owners of pristine, non-existent mileage Mk4 R32 cars, there was a little ray of hope. Not everyone was enamoured with the appearance of the new R32, others were disappointed with its all-out performance, while in price terms for the UK market it had leapt up from £22,608 to £23,745 for a like-for-like two-door manual version. Prices held really well for the Mk4, certainly for a sufficient length of time for an older version to be offloaded; a demand was there.

Place a Mk5 R32 against a GTI and which looked the sportier of the two? The GTI without a doubt and particularly so from the front, for not only did the R32 possibly excusably lack the GTI's instantly sporty red-line hallmark, but also the significant presence of mean and moody black, the somehow aggressive honeycomb grille and even such apparent trivialities as lower grille mounted fog lamps. Instead, the R32's predominant feature was a grille that bore more than a passing resemblance to that of the latest version of the booted pipe and slippers Volkswagen, the Bora, or in Mk5 guise, the Jetta. Too glossy, too shiny, or, as one person simply said, it was just too 'over the top' and that was before mentioning a set of incredibly impractical alloys that didn't even have the

punch of the GTI's; the new R32's visual impairments appeared plentiful.

The people at Volkswagen predictably didn't see the model quite as its detractors did. For them, the 'unique' styling pack featured 'a bold aluminium full-length grille, centrally positioned twin exhaust pipes, darkened rear lenses, new front spoiler with imposing air scoops, plus a full depth painted rear bumper (with black middle section) and signature blue brake calipers.'

For those using the available press packs as a basis for their reports, subtleties like '*polished aluminium*' for the grille to distinguish it from the Jetta's chromed version, not to mention 'shield shaped', something the saloon's certainly wasn't, and reference to 'two pairs of aluminium cross struts in the radiator intake area', to set it apart from the lower-specification Golfs, certainly helped. Photography of a Reflex Silver car where the R32's trappings melded into the general look of the car were equally beneficial, at least until buyers had become fully acquainted with and more receptive to Volkswagen's latest family look. One external feature, however, remained somewhat difficult. While Volkswagen considered the 7.5 × 18in Zolder alloy wheels, so-named after the race track and shod with 225 × 40 R18 tyres, to be 'inspired', most commentators regarded them as simply unnecessarily complex in their design. 'Twenty spokes on each wheel' might 'still' have allowed 'a glimpse behind of the blue brake calipers' but for most this was just too much. Even the most restrained let their opinions slip when they noted that the bolt pattern of a Mk5 Golf was different than that of the Mk4 and, as a result, it was impossible to swap one design to another.

Colour-wise, some Mk4 shades made it through to the Mk5 R32, including the shade the car had made its own, Deep Blue Pearl Effect. Both Steel Grey and Shadow Blue had been added to the straightforward metallic offerings, although Moonlight Blue, Grey Anthracite and Indigo Blue had all disappeared from the pearl effects, with plain Black added as an extra shade to supplement the pearl-effect Diamond Black option.

While a polished shiny look might not have instantly shouted power, grunt or beef, like the stark black and red image of the Mk5 GTI, nevertheless the new R32 set in isolation from other hot Golfs looked the part. The example photographed, a hotter looking two-door, is finished in Deep Blue Pearl Effect, the iconic colour for an R32.

R32 emblem on the front grille …

… and on the rear.

18in Zolder alloy – not easy to keep clean!

The Mk5 R32 with a GTI in the background.

Overall, thank goodness that somebody, somewhere took the decision to retain the single R32 badge on the hatch: no need of a plain old Golf logo here. Inside the Mk5 R32, it was obvious that the stylists had been happy with the results produced for the previous generation, as a quick recall of the Mk4 specification read in conjunction with what the UK press office had to say on the matter confirms: 'The interior of the new R32 offers distinctive instruments, sports seats, aluminium pedals and leather with aluminium-trimmed gear knob and steering wheel.' Nevertheless, some spotted an excessive use of sparkly trim both around the dash and on the door panels, likening it to the worst of fairground extravaganzas. However, well and truly on the plus side, this time around it was also possible to specify 'dramatic racing-style Recaro bucket seats', an option which was available from £945. As for leather, the Vienna trim option added £1,645 to the price, and of course that was on 'ordinary' sports seats.

Simply referring to the Mk5 R32's engine as a 'development' of the proven 3.2-litre narrow-angle V6 petrol engine, the aim appeared to be concentrate on the car's performance rather than its attributes compared to those of the Mk4. Previously developing 240ps, the R32 now offered 250ps. The 0–100km/h sprint was achieved, according to Volkswagen's official figures, in just 6.5sec with the manual R32, making it one second faster than the older R32 despite the increase in weight, and in 6.2sec with the advantages of DSG technology. The car's top speed was recorded as 249km/h (155mph), although the appendage of 'limited' in brackets was intended to convey that the R32 had more, much more in reserve. Torque figures remained unchanged, the new car's 236lb ft at 2,800rpm being identical to those circulated for the Mk4 R32.

Surprisingly, the somewhat academic issue of fuel consumption was afforded both importance and space. The brochure produced to launch the R32 in the UK revealed the story

When launched, the Mk5 R32 was available in seven colours with two or four doors and as a car with a manual gearbox, or DSG. This example is finished in Steel Grey Metallic.

Golf Mk5 R32 2005

Engine

Type	Front in-line 6-cylinder transversely mounted Narrow angle V6 FSI technology, with 24 valves, variable timing, variable length inlet manifold
Bore and stroke	84.0mm × 95.9mm
Capacity	3189cc
Compression ratio	10.9:1
Fuel injection	Turbocharged homogenous direct injection
Max. power	250ps at 6,300rpm
Max. torque	236lb ft at 2,800rpm
Fuel capacity	55ltr (12.1gal)

Transmission

Four wheel	4MOTION drive with Haldex coupling
Gearbox	Six-speed manual
Mph per 1,000rpm in top gear	24.0

Suspension and Steering

Front	Optimized MacPherson struts, coil springs with telescopic shock absorbers, all elements integrated in chassis legs
Rear	Multi-link with gas pressure shock absorbers and separate springs Lowered by 20mm (0.78in) compared to standard Golf and with 20 per cent stiffer anti-roll bars

Steering	Maintenance-free self-adjusting rack and pinion
Tyres	225/40 R18
Wheels	7.5 × 18 'Ronal Zolder' alloys

Brakes

Type	Diagonal twin circuits. Electro-mechanical servo-assisted. Load-sensitive brake pressure regulator ESP supported by ABS and HBA
Size	Front 345mm (13.6in) diameter discs, internally ventilated Rear 310mm (12.2in) diameter discs, internally ventilated

Dimensions

Track	
Front	1,533mm (60.4in)
Rear	1,515mm (59.6in)
Wheelbase	2,578mm (101.5in)
Overall length	4,246mm (167.2in)
Overall width	1,759mm (69.3in)
Overall height	1,465mm (57.7in)
Unladen weight	1,590kg (3,506lb) six-speed manual Unladen weights exclude the driver, but include 90 per cent tank capacity

Performance

Top speed	249km/h (155mph) 0–100km/h (0–62mph) 6.5sec

in even more blatant terms than any of the numerous press releases by then issued:

> The R32 is powered by an exceptional 3.2-litre V6 petrol engine, capable of generating a phenomenal 250ps ... This is only half the story, however. Thanks to innovative FSI technology, only the exact amount of fuel required is burnt, achieving new levels of efficiency and delivering a double-edged advantage – power and economy.

For someone buying an R32, if it really mattered that the engine was now more economical than it had been with the Mk4 model, was an extra-urban figure of 8.7ltr/100km (32.5mpg) with the Mk4 compared to one of 8.4ltr/100km (33.6mpg) with the Mk5, and overall figures of 11.5ltr/100km (24.6mpg) against 10.8ltr/100km (26.2mpg), of such significance?

While the Mk5 R32's engine was unquestionably upgraded compared to the Mk4's specification, there were distinct rumblings to be heard that the increase wasn't enough, particularly as the Mk5 in whatever form was always heavier than its Mk4 equivalent; size if nothing else ensured that. What R32 fans wanted was the 3.6-litre V6 with an output of 280ps and 265lb ft of torque at its disposal; the exclusive prerogative of American Passat owners at the time of the R32's launch.

And if that wasn't enough, there was a small matter of suspension. Yes, it was lowered by 20mm (0.78in), but as part of the revised multi-link suspension common to the Mk5 Golf chassis, rather than the Audi TT or S3 based arrangement of the Mk4 R32. Despite Volkswagen's claims that the new car would have firmer suspension than that of the GTI, another wail of protest arose. In fact, both cars featured stiffer springs and dampers plus thicker anti-roll bars, while at the same time there was a suggestion that the Mk4 set-up was too hard for all but straight track conditions and as a result the new car's would be somewhat less harsh. The argument immediately arose that Volkswagen was surreptitiously trying to reinvent the powerful executive car most successful

in the era of the Mk3. Damned by some, whatever it did, Volkswagen had no intention of changing course and once the initial shock was over, few, if any, persistent noises of discontent continued to be heard off centre stage.

At least nobody could raise wails of protest about the brakes, one key item to be upgraded. As indicated earlier, the twin-pot calipers were still painted blue, the difference being that the Mk5 sported discs with a 345mm (13.5in) diameter at the front, compared to the Mk4's 334mm (13in) versions, and 310mm (12in) ventilated discs at the rear, up by some 50mm (2in) on those of the older car.

TSI – The Petrol Revolution

A quiet revolution in engine technology provided Volkswagen with a third genuinely hot

Cleverly tuned photography, as used on the cover of the brochure produced when the GT was launched, made the car appear more sporting than it was.

The Golf GT photographed at the UK Press Launch. Although it didn't look particularly sporty, all those gathered together were duly impressed with the 1.4 170ps engine's performance.

hatch and this one came with both a diesel and a petrol engine, the former correctly overshadowed by the latter as it was there that a really sparkling advance had been made. Dirk Jünger had prophesied the new GT's existence; now Wolfgang Hüttner, Head of Product Marketing for Model Range A Passenger Cars, could confirm its position in the Golf line-up. The time was late summer 2005 and a few weeks ahead of the car's official launch at the Frankfurt Motor Show, where it shared the podium with the R32. Omnipresent Neil Birkitt was one of only two British journalists privileged to attend a top-secret rendezvous intended to disseminate advance information about the new breed of GT, and it's to his magazine, *VW Driver*, that all are indebted for the permanent record of Herr Hüttner's masterly 'take' on affairs. To him, the R32 was a 'top athlete in a three-piece suit', the GTI 'sportiness at its purest', which granted the GT 'the sports label' of the brand! Unquestionably both 'emotional and fun to drive', its TSI power plant would be 'a petrol engine which feels like a TDI – offering more performance, but less fuel consumption'.

At least initially, the TSI and its TDI counterpart bearing the new GT brand were little to look at. All that distinguished the model from the most basic members of the Golf range were the discreet chromed GT badges that shied away from public view on the front grille and the rear hatch, not particularly impressive front fog lights, exposed twin tailpipes, the double bars on the front grille, as favoured by the family Jetta and the neatly suited 'top athlete' R32, plus a bit of the usual colour coding. Volkswagen was later to market this most curiously as a 'GTI styling pack – including uniquely shaped front bumper'! Admittedly, the 7J × 17 ClassiXs alloys, shod with 225 × 45 R17 tyres, looked a little over-the-top for a base model, but few would even have noticed that the suspension was lowered by some 15mm (0.6in) and that hidden by the front wheels were 312mm (12.3in) diameter discs.

Inside, the story was little different. Yes, the GT had sports seats, a leather-trimmed steering wheel complete with GT logo, plus black Onyx decorative trim panels on both the dash and the door trim panels and, best of all, for its amusement and interest value if nothing else, a boost pressure gauge. But that was it!

Would the car sell on the back of such a package? You bet it would and soon it became a serious threat to the GTI. Priced at more than £2,000 less than a like-for-like GTI, the petrol GT had another ace up its sleeve – its economy. Such was the impact of TSI that over the coming months and years a whole series of Volkswagen models were endowed with partial or full TSI technology, giving more power but at considerably less cost at the pumps.

TSI, or Twincharged Stratified Injection technology, involved taking as a base unit the FSI engine from the EA111 series, in this instance the 1390cc, 1.4-litre FSI 4-valve, 4-cylinder unit, with a cylinder spacing of 82mm, plus a bore and stroke of 76.5 × 75.6mm, and dual-charging it. At its simplest, a belt, or engine,

17in ClassiXs alloys.

Twinset!

After a false start, the Mk5 GT 170ps TSI in Sport guise had the looks to qualify it for membership of the hot-hatch gang. If there was a snag, it came in the form of the 140ps TSI, which was also trimmed in this manner. (Photograph Courtesy of Volkswagen UK Press Office)

driven Eaton M24 supercharger operated at lower speeds, while an exhaust gas turbocharger arranged in series came in as the engine gathered pace. Vital to the twin-charger engine was the development of a highly resilient grey cast-iron cylinder block, which was capable of withstanding cylinder pressures of up to 21.7bar over sustained periods. The injection technology also had to be modified, leading to the creation of a multiple-hole high-pressure injector with six fuel outlet nozzles, while the maximum injection pressure was increased to 150bar in order to achieve the necessary wide range of flow rates. Volkswagen's engineers selected a compressor with a mechanical drive belt in order to increase torque at low engine speeds.

The overall objective of squeezing output in excess of 122ps per litre swept volume out of a 1.4-litre engine would never have been achieved if reliant solely upon single-stage supercharging. However, the impact of the compressor enabled the boost pressure build-up of the exhaust turbocharger to be increased by a significant amount. Essentially, the compressor was only required to generate the required boost pressure in the engine speed range up to 2,400rpm, as the exhaust turbocharger, designed for optimum efficiency in the upper power range, provided more than adequate boost pressure even in the medium speed range. However, under circumstances of hard acceleration in the lower speed range the

compressor was engaged to allow a very rapid boost pressure build-up. The complementary nature of the two systems ensured that there was never any turbo-lag.

Volkswagen was delighted to confirm the 1.4-litre TSI's performance as being equivalent to that of a 2.3-litre naturally aspirated engine. The 0–100km/h sprint was achievable in 7.9sec, while swift in-gear acceleration, for example 80–121.5km/h (50–75.5mph) in fifth took just 8sec, ensured sporty performance right up to a maximum speed of 220km/h (137mph). While laudable torque of 147lb ft was available from 1,250rpm right through to 6,000rpm, a maximum of 177lb ft was on hand between 1,750–4,500rpm. As the potentially fuel-guzzling compressor was only generally required at engine speeds below 2,400rpm, the 170ps TSI could be expected to return a combined fuel consumption figure of 7.4ltr/100km (38.2mpg), some 20 per cent less than the average engine with similar power and torque characteristics. Even better, on the average urban cycle, Volkswagen was able to announce a figure of 6.1.ltr/100km (46.3mpg).

As for the new but overlooked diesel engine, rumour had it that production capacity rather than any unmentionable technical difficulties delayed its appearance not only in the Golf GT but in other Volkswagens too. The 2.0-litre, 1968cc, 16-valve engine with a bore and stroke of 81.0 × 95.5mm and a compression ratio of

Golf Mk5 GT 170ps 2006

Engine

Type	Front in-line 4-cylinder transversely mounted Belt-driven single overhead camshaft. 4 valves, two inlet, two outlet per cylinder
Bore and stroke	76.5mm × 75.6mm
Capacity	1390cc
Compression ratio	10.0:1
Fuel injection	Fuel-stratified direct injection (FSI) at low throttle openings – modified multi-hole high-pressure pump injection valves with six fuel outlet elements Supercharger – Eaton M24 – positive displacement – maximum speed of 20,000rpm, producing 1.8bar 26ps – automatically disengaged at 3,500rpm Exhaust-driven turbocharger
Max. power	170ps at 6,000rpm
Max. torque	177lb ft at 1,750–4,500rpm
Fuel capacity	55ltr (12.1gal)

Transmission

Gearbox	Six-speed manual
Mph per 1,000rpm in top gear	19.0

Suspension and Steering

Front	Optimized MacPherson struts, coil springs with telescopic shock absorbers, all elements integrated in chassis legs
Rear	Multi-link with gas pressure shock absorbers and separate springs
	Lowered by 15mm (0.6in) compared to standard Golf and with 20 per cent stiffer anti-roll bars
Steering	Maintenance-free self-adjusting rack and pinion
Tyres	225/45 R17
Wheels	7J × 17 ClassiXs alloys

Brakes

Type	Diagonal twin circuits. Electro-mechanical servo-assisted. Load-sensitive brake pressure regulator Traction Control ASR, ESP supported by ABS and HBA Winter program
Size	Front 312mm (12.3in) diameter discs, internally ventilated Rear 286mm (11.3in) solid disc

Dimensions

Track	
Front	1,540mm (60.6in)
Rear	1,518mm (59.8in)
Wheelbase	2,578mm (101.5in)
Overall length	4,204mm (165.5in)
Overall width	1,759mm (69.3in)
Overall height	1,479mm (58.2in)
Unladen weight	1,429kg (3,151lb) six-speed manual Unladen weights exclude the driver, but include 90 per cent tank capacity

Performance

Top speed	220km/h (137mph) 0–100km/h (0–62mph) 7.9sec

18.5:1 was already well-known as the flagship diesel, offering a 0–100km/h time of 9.3sec and a top speed of 204km/h (127mph) when coupled to a manual box. The new unit had two advantages – it had been tuned to develop 170ps, making it the most powerful diesel engine in the passenger car line-up, while with the addition of a DPF (Diesel Particulate Filter) to strain away sooty materials, it was also one of the cleanest across the board of varying manufacturers' products.

Performance-wise, it was reminiscent of its petrol-powered twin in the GT and didn't really come across as having the GTI-like qualities of the old 150ps TDI engine of Golf Mk4 days. However, it did have one big advantage over the petrol engine and something that shouldn't come as a surprise to anyone conversant with diesel driving. Even though the TSI had been in part created for its fuel economy, the diesel engine was more thrifty getting about 4km more for every litre of fuel (10mpg). Acceleration from 0–100km/h took 8.2sec, making it slightly slower than the TSI on the all-important sprint, but as maximum speed was identical with both cars at 220km/h (137mph), the key to diesel power came in the machine's torque with 258lb ft at 2,000rpm.

Come the summer of 2007, Volkswagen heeded those voices critical of the GT's appearance, by claiming to meld the attributes of the Golf Sport trim level with the advanced engineering qualities of the GT. Whatever the legitimacy of such claims, the new, more pronouncedly sporting appearance made the GT visually a more fitting member of the GTI family trio. From the all-new darkened grille section, certainly a moodier looking affair than that of the R32, to the pair of darkened headlights, which had the effect of appearing to

separate the lenses into four individual units, and the dark tints of the rear windows, the GT looked altogether more aggressive. Even the ClassiXs alloys suddenly appeared genuinely sporty, while the twin chrome exhaust plus front and rear 'GT Sports' badges served to enhance the GT's image. However, there was a sting in the tail for the unwary, in that both the diesel and petrol 170ps models were joined by lesser GTs wearing the same attire, although perhaps a mere 140ps stood as adequate qualification for such armour.

Only the GT allocated a badge with the additional word 'Sport' looked the part of a fully fledged hot hatch. (Photograph Courtesy of Volkswagen AG)

The addition of the Sports package to the GT gave the car with superb performance the additional credentials to make it the third member of the hot-hatch trio. (Photograph Courtesy of Volkswagen AG)

The Golf GTI Edition 30

First shown as a design study at the Golf Record Day at the Veltins-Arena in Schalke, Gelsenkirchen, on 21 May 2006, sufficient interest was expressed in the car designed to celebrate thirty years of the GTI that Volkswagen pressed ahead to produce the Golf GTI Edition 30 for a public debut at the Essen Show in November of the same year. Somewhat unusually, UK enthusiasts hadn't that long to wait to get their hands on the new model, as the car made its debut in the UK in January 2007. Perhaps official recognition, as revealed in a UK press release, that the UK had the largest market for the GTI, greater even than that of Germany, had a bearing on this! Unlike the Mk4 GTI Anniversary, during the time the vehicle was offered in the showrooms the Golf GTI Edition 30 didn't carry any form of uniquely numbered plaque, nor was there an attempt to create both a petrol and a diesel version, production being strictly limited to an uprated version of the 2.0-litre 4-cylinder TFI petrol engine as fitted to the standard GTI. Openly promoted as a limited production run totalling just 1,500 examples, alarm bells started to ring amongst owners when the car was still readily available at the end of the first quarter of 2008. The delayed arrival of the Mk6 Golf, originally targeted for the summer, had resulted in what was to have been a particularly sought after run-out model continuing in production. The exclusivity badge was in danger of being devalued! When rumours of 2,300 examples of the GTI Edition began to gather pace, Volkswagen UK had little option but to backtrack on its original plan and produce a plaque proclaiming not only the car's limited edition status, but also its unique number in the total produced. Although instantly recognizable as a special type of GTI thanks to new body-coloured side skirts, plus a new chin spoiler for the front bumper and a body-coloured rear bumper, not to mention unique 18in fourteen-spoke Pescara alloys shod with 225/40 R18 tyres, tinted rear lights and an 'Edition 30' badge on the right-hand side of the hatch, it was for its engine that most examples were sold.

Although visibly identical to that of the standard GTI, which inevitably continued in production, the 2.0-litre FSI now produced an extra 30ps, up from 200ps at 5,100rpm to 230ps at 5,500rpm, or, as one wag put it, 1ps for every year the GTI had been in production. Torque increased correspondingly with maximums of 207lb ft between 1,800–5,000rpm as far as the standard GTI was concerned, compared with 221lb ft between 2,200–5,200rpm for the Edition 30. Slightly thirstier, the car with extra ps was capable of sprinting to 100km/h in 6.8sec with a manual box, or just 6.6sec with DSG, clipping 0.4 or 0.3 of a second off the standard GTI's figures respectively. For those wishing to risk their licences, the GTI Edition was capable

The Golf GTI Edition 30 as it was seen on UK roads when it was launched in right-hand-drive form in early 2007. The cars sat on 18in Pescara alloys. This example is finished in what the UK Press Office described as 'searing' Tornado Red.

Another Edition 30, this time finished in Reflex Silver, a colour that tones beautifully with the car's alloys.

Golf Mk5 GTI 2.0 T-FSI 230ps 2007

Engine

Type	Front in-line 4-cylinder transversely mounted Belt-driven single overhead camshaft. 4 valves per cylinder
Bore and stroke	82.5mm × 92.8mm
Capacity	1984cc
Compression ratio	10.3:1
Fuel injection	Turbo charged fuel-stratified direct injection (FSI)
Max. power	230ps at 5,500rpm
Max. torque	221lb ft at 2,200–5,200rpm
Fuel capacity	55ltr (12.1gal)

Transmission

Gearbox	Six-speed manual
Mph per 1,000rpm in top gear	18.7

Suspension and Steering

Front	Optimized MacPherson struts, coil springs with telescopic shock absorbers, all elements integrated in chassis legs
Rear	Multi-link with gas pressure shock absorbers and separate springs Lowered by 15mm (0.6in) compared to standard Golf and with 20 per cent stiffer anti-roll bars
Steering	Maintenance-free self-adjusting rack and pinion

Tyres	225/40 R18
Wheels	7.5 × 18 'Pescara' alloys

Brakes

Type	Diagonal twin circuits. Electro-mechanical servo-assisted. Load-sensitive brake pressure regulator Traction Control ASR, ESP supported by ABS and HBA
Size	Front 312mm (12.3in) diameter discs, internally ventilated Rear 286mm (11.3in) solid disc

Dimensions

Track	
Front	1,539mm (60.6in)
Rear	1,528mm (58.8in)
Wheelbase	2,578mm (101.5in)
Overall length	4,216mm (166in)
Overall width	1,759mm (69.3in)
Overall height	1,469mm (57.7in)
Unladen weight	1,357kg (2,992lb) six-speed manual Unladen weights exclude the driver, but include 90 per cent tank capacity.

Performance

Top speed	245km/h (152mph) 0–100km/h (0–62mph) 6.8sec

Candy White shows off the additional visual attributes of the Edition 30, which included new body-coloured side skirts, a chin spoiler up front and a colour-coded rear valance. Although somewhat unusual to UK eyes, the Monza alloys finished in flat black sit well against the body colour of the car.

of 245km/h (152mph) in manual guise and 243km/h (151mph) with DSG, a gain of 9.7km/h (6mph) in both instances over the 200ps engine. Although, as usual, some thought Volkswagen could have offered more, this was both an excellent package and one that took front-wheel-drive-only technology to its uppermost limit. Spinning at take-off proved only too easy.

Those demanding that the interior design should be similarly enhanced were not disappointed. Although the sports seats were shared with the standard GTI and both featured Anthracite Interlagos cloth, the side bolsters of the Edition 30 were trimmed with Vienna leather, as were the headrests. The distinctive golf-ball gear knob made yet another comeback, as it had done with the Mk4 Anniversary model, while references to the car's special identity could be found in as diverse places as on a decorative dashboard strip under the air vents and along the door sill strips, all etched out in red, the hallmark colour of both the early and latest GTIs.

Mk5 GTI Paintwork Options 2008

Although there was no basic change to the colours available by the time of the 2008 model year, a series of rules and regulations had been added, the net effect of which was to curb freedom of choice for Volkswagen's customers. There follow details of the restrictions exactly as they appeared in the 2008 model year brochure.

* Metallic and pearl-effect paints are optional at extra cost.
1 Candy White non-metallic paint is only available for the GTI and GTI Edition 30.
2 Please note that Candy White, Ink Blue non-metallic and Blue Graphite Pearl Effect paint are not available for the R32.
3 Please note that Ink Blue non-metallic, Shadow Blue metallic and Blue Graphite Pearl Effect are not available for the GTI Edition 30.
4 Deep Blue Pearl Effect paint is only available for the R32.

External paint colours were more restricted for the Edition 30 than for the standard GTI, but only the standard GTI and the Edition 30 could be specified in Candy White, a relatively early-day addition to Mk1 GTI shades and incidentally an all-time favourite in the USA.

The Mk5 in America

Having taken for granted that the fifth-generation Golf-based saloon, always known as the Jetta in America, would be the best-selling model in the USA, it won't come as a surprise that it was launched there first. Initially offered in 2005 with an engine unique to the American market, a 2.5-litre in-line 5-cylinder affair that produced 150bhp (SAE), it didn't really hit the sports market, taking 9.1sec to reach 60mph. Much later in the year, the Jetta GLi saw the light of day and, as the initials might imply, this sported the US version of the 200ps FSI engine designed for the Golf GTI. Although branded as a GLi, this Jetta featured full sports suspension, blue-tinted windows, the new hallmark GTI black honeycomb grille with red surround, alloy pedals and trim, sports seat fabric, as well as the European GTI's distinctive wheels and most other trappings of the hot hatch.

The fifth-generation GTI made its debut in the USA in December 2005 and for the first time was available there as either a two- or four-door hot hatch. Perhaps as a preamble to the return of the Rabbit brand at the New York Auto Show in the spring of 2006, the new car was simply known as the GTI 5, the word Golf having been discarded. Used to suffering watered-down versions of European or Far Eastern cars in general, Volkswagen fans were in for a pleasant surprise. The only major discrepancy was an increase in ride height of some 15mm (0.6in) in order that the GTI 5 would qualify on the scales of side-impact crash-test ratings, although sports seats only came trimmed in leather, much to the annoyance of fabric-preferring diehards.

Footnotes

As something of an afterthought following the undoubted razzle-dazzle success of the Edition 30 and a quick reading of the rather more dubious situation for Volkswagen with its American satellite, it's time for the Mk5 hot hatch to go out on a high note. Announced in the spring of 2007, DSG got a further boost with the addition of a seventh speed. Adopting a pair of dry, organic friction linings that didn't need cooling, unlike the clutches submerged in oil of old, the ultimate of the day was achieved by also making the drive train more efficient via an extra ratio and the fact that less power was required for gear selection and the clutch servo system. Measuring just 36.9mm in length and weighing no more than 79kg, the whole arrangement was remarkably compact. Through the adoption of a seventh gear, it was possible to lower the first gear, thereby improving acceleration from rest. Having also noted that UK drivers with a desire to have a booted Golf (once more carefully rebranded as the Jetta in deference to American sales), should have been able to get hold of the GTI's engine if not its trim and full sporting attributes, or could have settled for both top Golf GT engines (the 170ps TSI and the similarly endowed TDI PDF in plain Sport trim), it's worth taking a breath to glance at a last fling special edition and an out-of-bounds super GTI.

First up then, and originally only for the continental market, there was the GTI Pirelli, an adaptation of the Edition 30 and reminiscent of the Campaign GTI of 1983, commonly known as the Pirelli in Europe all those years ago. Recall that the Mk1 model was designed to boost sales with its extra goodies in anticipation of the soon-to-be launched Mk2 Golf and GTI. Despite the already referred to delays in getting the Mk6 Golf into the showrooms, in part caused by top-ranking internal politics at Wolfsburg – where did that nice Mr Director General Pischetsrieder suddenly disappear to? – the GTI Pirelli roots lay very much in the same kind of soil. Goodies over and above the Edition 30's engine included: specially designed 7.5 × 18 alloy wheels bearing, with a considerable stretch of the imagination, five elongated letter P spokes; a unique interior part-leather trim in black featuring a tyre tread pattern and yellow seam stitching; Pirelli logos on the tailgate, steering wheel and body strips: plus a full leather centre armrest in the rear and a front armrest holding either a CD changer or MP3 player. Available in a variety of colours, the Pirelli was also offered in Sunflower, a unique shade of bright yellow. By June 2008, when the Pirelli made its debut in Britain, the range of colours had been reduced to Reflex Silver, Diamond Black and Blue Graphite. Volkswagen's British Press Office wrote of the car's 'uprated dynamics and aesthetics' distinguishing it from a

The special edition Mk5 GTI Pirelli, 230ps finished in Sunflower. (Photograph Courtesy of Volkswagen AG)

The Pirelli special edition came with its own brand of 7.5 × 18in five-spoke alloys; the 'P' association is somewhat tenuous, however. Have you deciphered the far from obvious elongated 'P' design? (Photograph Courtesy of Volkswagen AG)

standard GTI and listed colour-coded side skirts and rear bumpers, smoked rear light lenses and tinted rear windows amongst the attributes denied to the ordinary GTI purchaser.

First shown at a GTI Festival held in Wörthersee, Austria, in May 2007, the Golf GTI W12-650 design study would have been beyond the pockets of all but the most highly paid football players had it gone into series production. At the heart of the fastest and most powerful Golf built to date was a bespoke mid-mounted W12 engine, linked to a pair of turbochargers. Volkswagen had no option but to create a unique aluminium subframe onto which the engine could be mounted, while the cooling systems were fed by a pair of side-mounted cooling vents placed in the airflow just ahead of the rear wheels.

Offering a 0–100km/h sprint in just 3.7sec and with a potential maximum speed of 324.7km/h (201.8mph), the 5,998cc W12 engine was an evolution of the 450ps version fitted to Volkswagen's ill-conceived and ill-fated all-luxury Phaeton. Made from aluminium to reduce weight, it featured 4 valves per cylinder and two overhead camshafts per head and was effectively made up of a pair of narrow-angle V6 engines laid alongside each other. Fitment of a pair of turbochargers ensured power rose to 650ps at 6,000rpm, while peak torque was capped at 553lb ft delivered at 4,500rpm. The engine was linked to a

The UK market was offered the GTI Pirelli in just three colours, including Blue Graphite as depicted here, but not the strident tones of Sunflower! (Photograph Courtesy of Volkswagen UK)

six-speed Tiptronic automatic transmission. Wider by 160mm (6.2in) than the standard GTI to accommodate the mid-mounted engine, bespoke drive train and side-mounted cooling systems, the W12 650's roof was constructed out of carbon fibre and featured an integrated cooling scoop designed to channel air into the rear-mounted radiators. The 19in wheels styled to mimic those fitted to the standard GTI were shod with 295-profile tyres to aid traction.

With its bespoke mid-mounted 5998cc, W12 650ps engine, the Golf GTI W12-650 design study could outpace the conventional GTI with a 0–62mph time of just 3.7sec compared to 6.9sec and with a top speed of 324.8km/h (201.8mph) against 233km/h (145mph). To accommodate the mid-mounted engine, unique drive-train and side-mounted cooling systems, the car was some 160mm wider than standard.

Index